Michigan Vacation Guide

Cottages, Chalets, Condos, B&B's

FIFTH EDITION

Editor/Writer: Kathleen R. Tedsen

Associate Editor: Clara M. Rydel

Writer/Photographer: Beverlee J. Rydel

Business Manager: Christian Tedsen

Cover Photographs:
Front Cover: Yelton Manor B&B, South Haven
Back Cover: Teal Wing (Vacation Home), Lake Gogebic

For information, contact:

TR Desktop Publishing
P.O. Box 180271
Utica, MI 48318-0271
(810) 228-8780

PRINTED IN THE UNITED STATES OF AMERICA

ISBN: 0-9635953-3-4

Michigan

Statehood: 1837   25th State of the Union

Let me take you to the land once called "Michigania" across flat planes to ever increasing slopes, hills and mountains; through virginal forests and crystal lakes, dotted by cottages resting on sugar white sand. Where falls are painted by an artist's brush and winters are blanketed in white. Here are the forests and wildlife, quaint cities and great cities, museums and shipwrecks, and so much more.

I am your dream maker ...
the great outdoors ...
the vacation land for all seasons.

by C. Rydel

HOW TO USE THIS BOOK

Welcome to the Fifth Edition of *The Michigan Vacation Guide to Cottages, Chalets, Condos, B&B's*. This simple to use publication, arranged by region and alphabetically by city, is designed to assist you with one of your first vacation priorities — WHERE TO STAY — and offers some interesting alternatives to the usual hotels/motels. We hope our Guide helps you find your perfect vacation lodging as quickly and effortlessly as possible.

Understanding Special Notes:

Editor's Note   Our staff has not had the opportunity to visit every listed property in this book. Many of the descriptions have been supplied by owners or chambers of commerce. When we have visited a lodging, we have made our personal comments at the bottom of the listing by using *Editor's Note*.

Editor's Choice   **EDITOR'S CHOICE** indicates places our staff have visited which, in our opinion, meet or exceed the basic requirements of comfort, cleanliness, location and value.

Reviews   This edition of the Michigan Vacation Guide features all new reviews never published in past edition of our guide. All comments are solely the opinion of our staff and do not necessarily reflect the opinions of others.

Whenever possible, prices have been included. One thing you should remember, **prices frequently change or fluctuate with the seasons.** We recommend you call to verify rates when making your reservations. If the owner requires an advance deposit, verify refund policies (if any). As a renter, be sure you understand the terms of the rental agreement.

CHECK OUT OUR WEB SITE!

WORLD WIDE WEB

For The Latest Information ... Contact Our Internet Affiliate:

THE MICHIGAN TRAVEL COMPANION

http://www.yesmichigan.com

SEE YOU ON ... THE WEB!

REGIONAL DIVISIONS

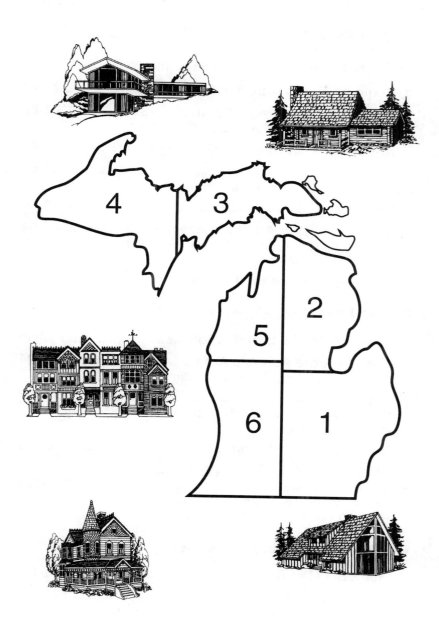

TABLE OF CONTENTS

REGION 6 (Southwest Lower Peninsula)

— IMPORTANT NOTICE —

Due to Michigan's on-going area code changes,
if you find an area code is not correct, call the
following toll-free number:

1-800-831-8989

or try the Internet at **www.codefinder.com**

SELECTING AN ACCOMMODATION

Staying at a cottage, condo or bed and breakfast is truly a unique and enjoyable experience. However, it is *different* than staying at a hotel or motel. We've provided some information to help you understand and appreciate the differences.

■ THE BASICS

Don't be afraid to ask the owner questions. Ask about the *House Rules*. If staying at a resort, private cottage, or condo, you may want to ask what you'll need to bring and what the owner's housekeeping policies are. Ask specific questions about amenities or location which are important to your comfort and enjoyment.

Always be sure you understand the terms of the rental agreement. Determine advance deposit and cancellation/refund policies prior to booking.

Clean up after yourself. Please be courteous and leave your lodging in the same condition in which it was found.

■ TERMINOLOGY

Fully Equipped Kitchens. Includes stove, refrigerator, pots, pans, dishes, eating utensils and sometimes (not always) microwaves, toasters and automatic coffeemakers.

A/C and CATV. A/C refers to air conditioning (may or may not be central air conditioning); CATV refers to color cable television.

Modern Cottage. Does not mean new. It refers to electricity and indoor plumbing (private bath, hot water, etc.). Most of today's cottages are considered modern.

On the Water. Refers to a lodging which fronts water. It does not necessarily mean the property has a swimming beach (see below) or a place to dock your boat.

Swimming Beach. A water area with gradual incline, no surprise drop offs, no strong currents. It may or may not be a smooth, sand beach.

Full Breakfast. Beverages, main course and, sometimes, dessert.

Continental Breakfast. Beverages with breads and/or pastries.

American Plan Resorts. All meals included in the price

9

MICHIGAN COTTAGES • CHALETS • CONDOS • B&B'S
What Are the Differences?

While it's impossible to give a single description for each type of accommodation, there are certain traits which make each distinctively different and appealing in their own way. Here's some guidelines:

Atmosphere: Most resorts were built during the 1950's and 1960's with some dating back even further. We've found that a great many of the guests come back year after year, even generations. They like the friendly environment and diverse amenities available.

While there are cottage resorts which provide "luxury" accommodations, most are simple in nature. You may find a ceiling fan but only a few have air conditioning. Floors are covered with linoleum, wood, or simple carpeting. Furniture is sometimes a collection of older, second-hand chairs, sofas, tables, dishes, pots, pans, etc. A cozy fireplace in your cabin is not uncommon and wood is usually provided. Resorts will clean the cottage prior to your arrival, but do not expect daily maid service.

Features: There are a broad range of features provided to guests which make resorts particularly appealing to families. For example, those by the water often have a safe swimming area with a canoe or rowboat as part of the rental price. You can usually bring your own boat (not all allow high speed motors). There may be a children's play area, badminton, basketball or tennis courts. Game rooms may include pinball, video arcades, pool tables and more. Many rent motors, paddle boats or pontoon boats, with others also providing sail boats, wave runners or kayaks. Nature and snowmobile trails, fish cleaning areas and chartered fishing trips along with planned daily activities, or American Plan programs are sometimes available.

Rates/Rental Policy: Resorts often provide the most economically priced lodging, especially those not located on the water. A few begin renting as low as $275 or $300 weekly with several exceeding $1,000.

During prime season, most require weekly rentals (Saturday to Saturday). Advance deposits are generally asked with refund policies varying.

What to Bring: You may need to bring towels, linens, cleaning and paper products.

> **Please remember, even the cleanliest cottage in the world will have an occasional spider or walking "thing" ... you're in a wooded area by the water ... it happens!**

Atmosphere: Guests choosing this type of accommodation will enjoy a very private vacation. Whether overlooking the water, woods or ski slopes, this place will seem like your own private retreat.

Since this type of cottage is used by the owner, interior decor will vary greatly depending on the comforts of the owner. Some are small and simply furnished while others are spacious, contemporary and luxurious in nature.

Please note, privately owned cottages or homes may or may not have a "cleaning service" and many have special "house rules". Be sure to ask about the cleaning arrangement and the house rules. Also very important, ask who your contact is should there be any problems once you arrive (i.e. a storm takes out the electricity, plumbing, etc.).

Features: You usually won't have all of the outdoor amenities found at resorts, such as basketball/ tennis courts or video game rooms. However, interiors tend be more comfortable and owners often supply a good selection of board games or lawn games. Private cottages may have fireplaces, but you'll probably have to supply your own wood. Other extra features may include ceiling fans, air conditioning, hot tubs, stereos, TVs, VCRs and kitchens with dishwashers.

Rates/Rental Policies: Owners frequently need to be contacted during evenings or weekends when they're not working. During prime season, most choose to rent weekly (Saturday to Saturday) some will agree to a 2-day minimum stay. Prices may be a little higher than resorts with average rates from $500 to $1,200. The larger vacation homes begin around $1,200 and some, with added luxuries, may rent for over $3,000. Most require up front deposits with varying refund policies.

What to Bring: See "Cottage Resorts".

Chalets are generally an A-frame lodging frequently found at or near ski or winter sport areas. They generally maintain full kitchen and bathroom facilities.

See Private Cottage for features, rental policies, what to bring, etc..

Atmosphere: For those who enjoy the anonymity and comfort a hotel/motel provides but also want the added convenience of a full kitchen, living room, etc., condominiums would be a good choice. While there are a few older condos, most were built in the last 5 to 20 years. You will generally find the interior furnishings newer with matching sofa, chairs, tables and decor.

12

Features: Air conditioning is often available. Rooms may have Jacuzzi tubs and wet bars. Condo "resorts" frequently feature championship golf courses, heated swimming pools, tennis and health clubs. Other amenities are in-house masseuses, nature and x-country ski trails or downhill ski slopes, boat and canoe rentals, swimming, sailing and more.

Rates/Rental Policies: Units are rented by private owners or by Associations with more flexible policies (not all require week long rentals). Weekly rentals prices are similar to private cottages from $500 to $2,000+. Advance deposits are generally requested with varying refund policies.

What to Bring: See "Cottage Resorts".

Atmosphere: B&B's and Inns provide a quiet, relaxing atmosphere and are equally enjoyed by business and vacation travelers alike. While some establishments welcome well behaved children, most cater to the adult traveler. A bed and breakfast is not the place for loud parties. However, with notice, many welcome small weddings or other memorable celebration gatherings.

Proprietors take great pride in decorating and maintaining their lodgings in a style which will welcome their guests and provide a comfortable, inviting setting. As a result, courtesy and respect of property is expected.

Features: These establishments can be very diverse in features and amenities. Some are traditional homes in quiet subdivisions with one or two guest rooms and a single shared bath. Others may be contemporary, large and opulent with multiple guest rooms, private baths, designer furnishings and decorations. Still others may be old and grand featuring significant historical background with Victorian, Greek Revival or other Old World styling. They are frequently decorated with antiques and/or authentic reproductions. Several feature in-room Jacuzzis and fireplaces. Air conditioning may or may not be available.

MICHIGAN COTTAGES • CHALETS • CONDOS • B&B'S

Price/Rental Policies: Prices vary greatly with averages between $60 to $90 daily and a few luxury suites exceed $200. Most bed and breakfasts rent daily and may offer special week or weekend package rates. Advanced deposits are generally requested and refund policies vary.

What to Bring: Just your clothes and a smile.

Breakfasts: Breakfasts are part of every B&B package (those categorized as inns may not include breakfast). Breakfasts vary from continental to full. Ask the owner about serving times. Some establishments encourage guests' mingling at a common table during breakfast. Others may provide private tables or will bring breakfast directly to your room. Many owners are happy to accommodate special dietary needs but will need to be told in advance.

Just remember, if you're not sure about something ... ASK THE OWNER.

We wish you a safe and most enjoyable Michigan vacation!

Reviews

Wilson Home

Lexington, Michigan
Reservations: 517-635-2911

Located in REGION 1 ❶

Proprietor:	Marlene Wilson
Accommodation:	Waterfront, 4-bedroom, private home
Extras:	Equipped kitchen; private baths; washer/dryer; CATV/VCR; linens; screened porch; fireplace (no heat - portable heaters available)
Rates/Payment:	Weekly $1,250-$1,500; check, cash
Miscellaneous:	No pets, security deposit $500 + full payment in advance
Open:	May to October

If you crave lots of room in your vacation accommodations, then the Wilsons' 3,000 sq. ft., two-story home might just be your choice. Sitting back from Lakeshore Road, this older, white frame home sits atop a bluff overlooking the lake and offers spacious rooms with great views.

Dating back 30 or more years, the home has been well maintained by the Wilsons. The east side has a wall of windows facing Lake Huron. It's pretty hard to miss the lake or spectacular sunrises from the sitting area, living room or bedrooms.

Spacious home on a Lake Huron bluff.

View of sitting room with living room entrance to the rear.

Inside, we found the living room to be our favorite with light, contemporary furniture, fireplace and beautiful hard wood floors. We thought it a nice place to chat with family and friends. Of course, it also includes that all important cable TV and VCR. Across from the living room is the sitting area which is highlighted by an expanse of windows overlooking the enclosed porch and grounds. The windows add a cheery brightness to this room which is offset with darker furniture and rug. A smaller side room is designated as the "Ping-Pong Room". Here you'll find the *official* ping-pong table and equipment ready for you to practice your tournament quality form. Also on the first floor, is a handy laundry room with washer, dryer and half bath with shower.

Other first floor rooms include the formal dining room with a large window that overlooks the front yard. The small kitchen, though simple in nature, is clean with new tile floors and is equipped with microwave, stove, refrigerator and all the basics.

The home's four bedrooms vary in size with the largest comfortably holding two beds and a private sitting area. There's also a second floor full bath for your convenience.

Moving outside you'll find the grounds to be spacious and accented with a scattering of mature trees. From the comfort of the fully enclosed porch, you'll be impressed by the view which overlooks the grounds and sparkling waters of

17

Largest bedroom — plenty of room with open sitting area.

Lake Huron. To get to water's edge, there's a handy stairway (42 steps) which leads directly to the beach. You may find the beach to be relatively rocky, but the water is still wonderfully cool and refreshing.

Located in Lexington and only 20 minutes from Port Huron, this private waterfront home provides the space you need in a prime location.

The Powell House B&B

Lexington, Michigan
Reservations: 810-359-5533

Located in ❶

Proprietor:	Nancy Powell
Accommodation:	4 Rooms; private/shared baths
Extras:	CATV; some ceiling fans; bicycles; full breakfast
Rates/Payment:	Daily $65-$75; check, cash
Miscellaneous:	No pets, smoke-free environment
Open:	Year around

Just off Lakeshore Road less than a mile from the cozy, lakeside community of Lexington is the gracious, white and rose trimmed Powell House. On four acres of well groomed grounds accented with bright annuals and perennials, it's a welcome site to visitors.

Originally built in 1852, the home has been lovingly restored in the Victorian spirit. Period furnishings combine with lace and floral highlights to create the engaging ambiance of an earlier time. Nancy Powell, the friendly proprietor, has a keen sense of the home's history as well as her own and proudly displays her families' photographs along with the original owners' on the wall ascending the stairs. If you're interested, she'll be happy to tell you about the home's background and the families that have become part of its history.

The 1852 Powell House sits on four acres of land.

19

Victorian styling highlights the charming Powell House.

The Powell House offers four guest rooms, one on the first floor and three on the second. Rooms are of moderate size, comfortable and pleasingly decorated with antiques, lace curtains and inviting colors. Ceiling fans in three rooms help to keep things cool during those warmer summer days.

In the morning, after one of Nancy's tasty full breakfasts served in the formal dining room, relax in the spacious yard and enjoy the lovely view of gardens. Perhaps you may want to stroll over to visit the two pet Angora goats or amiable

Cozy, antique-filled guest rooms are very comfortable.

cats kept on the grounds. Then take advantage of the bicycles Nancy makes available to guests and enjoy a leisurely tour of historical Lexington village. Visit the quaint shops, sandy beaches or marinas. The harbor, with its natural limestone seawall and promenade, is considered one of Michigan's most beautiful. It's a great place for a leisurely walk or a little fishing.

True bicycle enthusiasts will want to explore the four mile bike path to the historic town of Croswell. Or, if underwater adventure is more to your liking, charter a diving trip to 16 sunken vessels in the underwater preserve along the coast line. Chartered fishing boats are a popular activity with avid anglers. Golfers don't despair! Only one mile west of town is the 36-hole championship course at Lakeview Hills. On those cooler days, take your fun indoors and do a little shopping at the Harbor Bazaar, open year-round. On weekends, the Lexington Players present seasonal theatrical productions.

American Indian pow-wows, arts and craft shows and more ... guests will find plenty of area activities and events throughout the year ... and Nancy Powell will be your gracious and helpful hostess.

East Coast Shores Resort

Oscoda, Michigan

Reservations: 517-739-0123

Located in REGION 2

Proprietors:	Roy Wenner
Accommodations:	5 waterfront cottages
Extras:	Equipped kitchens with microwave; private baths; ceiling fans in some; linens and bedding included; CATV/HBO; playground; screened porches; BBQ grills; beach chairs; one cottage handicap accessible
Rates/Payment:	Weekly $525-$742 (daily rates available); major credit cards, check, cash
Open:	Year around

Down-to-earth hominess and simple joys await guests at Roy Wenner's cozy East Coast Shores Resort. Roy and his family have owned the resort for over five years and have done what many owners are doing on the east side of Michigan – renovation. This long-time popular vacation area was beginning to show its age awhile back, but there is change in the air and the Wenner family is definitely a part of the wonderful change.

Recent renovations and a great beach make East Coast Shores Resort a nice choice.

Since the Wenners bought the resort in the mid-1990's a great deal of time, effort and money has gone into totally refurbishing the cottages and land. Now guests will find East Coast Shores sitting on perfectly groomed and landscaped grounds with plenty of mature trees, grass and, of course, a beautiful 200 foot swimming beach.

Comfortably furnished interiors.

The property has everything you need to enjoy the outdoors. Besides the sunrises and natural beauty, there's a playground for young and young at heart, grills, lawn furniture and picnic tables. They have just about everything you would need for fun and relaxation by the water.

The traditional cottages are clean and comfortable, both inside and out. Knotty pine interiors are bright and kitchens are fully stocked. The living areas are furnished with newer, comfortable sofas, chairs, carpeting and tile. We were impressed with their very comfortable beds and sofa beds (an important feature for us). Four of the units face each other with approximately 20 to 30 feet of space separating them. Two additional cottages face the water and were our favorites. One had a new screened patio and the second a large pine deck.

If you're looking for a friendly, simple retreat with all the basic comforts, give East Coast Shore a try ... and enjoy spectacular Lake Huron sunrises.

El Cortez Beach Resort

Oscoda, Michigan

Reservations: 517-739-7884

Located in REGION 2

Proprietors:	Tim & Terry Richardson
Accommodations:	12 waterfront cottages/beach houses
Extras:	Equipped kitchens; private baths; linens; CATV; some with private decks and HBO; wave runners; beach ball; shuffleboard; BBQ grills; picnic tables; children's outdoor toys; fishing charters; indoor fish cleaning house; one unit with A/C, handicap accessible
Rates/Payment:	Weekly $445-$1,000 weekly (off-season rates available); Visa, Mastercard, check, cash
Open:	Year around

The El Cortez Resort ... a perfect example of why so many people like the east side of Michigan. The resort's spacious 160 feet of pure white sand beach slowly stretches into the blue waters of Lake Huron. It's a great place to relax, enjoy the sun and have some fun in the water. To take advantage of the beach, the Richardsons have a variety of amenities available for your outdoor pleasure including beach/water games and furniture.

A large, sandy shoreline ... terrific swimming at El Cortez.

24

The cozy white cottages are nicely spaced along the waterfront with many having a terrific views of Lake Huron.

Traveling through the cottages, we noted several significant renovations the young energetic couple have made in the past three or so years. Some of the most recent updates were new doors and windows, slate tile in some of the kitchens, new

View from second-story loft - one of two new beach houses available at El Cortez Resort.

carpeting, shower stalls and furniture in several units. The most recent additions to El Cortez are the very impressive beach homes which sit closest to the water. Tim and Terry told us they have plans for a lot more to come and, based on what we saw, we can hardly wait.

To describe the beach homes, they are spacious, two-story accommodations and very contemporary. Oak trim accents tall ceilings, large French doors and bright windows. Dark carpeting is offset with light, attractive furnishings. The great room combines living and dining area with a kitchen that is open and well equipped. These units are reminiscent of the condos often found at larger, luxury resorts. Priced at approximately $1,000 a week, they represent a very good value for what they offer.

The more traditional cottages have been around awhile. They feature dark paneled interiors and one or two bedrooms. Though not large, these units are comfortable

Standard cottage interiors are small but well maintained with some very nice renovations.

with good beds and furniture. All the kitchen/dining areas are well equipped with ample room to move around. Several appliances, refrigerators, and stoves were new and the others, though slightly older, were clean and in very good working order.

El Cortez has come a long way in a few years. Why not come out and enjoy the results of Tim's and Terry's hard work. The El Cortez, a very comfortable place to be with a fabulous beach.

Huron House B&B

Oscoda, Michigan
Reservations: 517-739-9255

Located in REGION 2

Proprietors:	Denny & Martie Lorenz
Accommodations:	Waterfront, 12 rooms/suites with private baths
Extras:	Continental breakfast brought to your room; some rooms with: fireplace, Jacuzzi, hot tub, refrigerator, microwave, wet bar, private sitting room, private deck, A/C, ceiling fan
Rates/Payment:	Daily $75-$145 (double occupancy); Visa, Mastercard, check, cash
Miscellaneous:	No pets, smoke-free environment
Open:	Year around

Just north of Tawas on US-23, along Lake Huron's waters, rests a lovely white home called the Huron House. Its attractive exterior, however, holds only a small clue to the true treasures which await guests inside. Elegantly styled rooms with fireplace, two-person jacuzzi, beautiful views of Michigan sunrises and

Beautiful garden and excellent Lake Huron views at the Huron House Bed and Breakfast ... a true romantic's haven.

27

MICHIGAN COTTAGES • CHALETS • CONDOS • B&B'S

moonrises create the mood for a wonderfully romantic experience to be shared with the one you love.

Danny and Martie are quintessential of innkeepers traditionally found in Vermont or Connecticut. Their warm and casual manner will welcome you while their attention to every little detail will keep you very comfortable.

This is a large bed and breakfast with 12 rooms on two floors. Almost all rooms have at least a partial view of Lake Huron. They are impeccably decorated, from the lace curtains to the tilt of the teddy bear found nestled in the mound of pillows on your bed. Deep rose, hunter green or textured carpeting accentuates the light floral wall paper or bedspreads. The smallest room is, by bed and breakfast standards, good size and the largest rooms are suites with sleeping quarters and separate sitting/dinning area. These larger rooms have doorwalls leading out to the yard or private deck. It's an ideal spot to watch the sun come up, the boats and ships pass by, or catch the moon shadows on the beach at night.

On the top deck, looking down from our second floor suite, we were immediately struck by Danny's and Martie's enchanting courtyard garden. Specially designed wooden pathways invite you to stroll past perfectly trimmed lawns and colorful flowerbeds raised with rocks and boulders taken from the area.

Spacious and impeccably decorated rooms

28

**Warm yourself by the fire on those cool evenings ...
or enjoy the bubbles in your Jacuzzi.**

At the end, you'll come to the spacious wood deck which overlooks the deep blue waters of Lake Huron. This section of the Huron probably has some of the finest beaches in Michigan.

Another special feature of the Huron House is the continental breakfast brought right to your room. Fresh fruits, breads, croissants or pastries with uniquely prepared toppings, juices and coffee *magically* appear outside your room each morning. This is particularly nice for those of us who prefer a little more privacy in the morning so we can lounge about, linger over that last cup of coffee or savor the view of the sparkling morning lake.

Found in a part of the state not known for many bed and breakfasts, this is one you shouldn't miss. And, considering all it has to offer, the price is certainly reasonable. If you're looking for that romantic weekend with long walks on the beach and spectacular views, the Huron House is waiting for you.

Sunnyside Resort

Greenbush, Michigan
Reservations: 517-739-5289

Located in REGION 2

Proprietors:	John & Donna Wittla
Accommodations:	7 waterfront cottages
Extras:	Equipped kitchens; private baths; linens; CATV/VCR; ceiling fans; scald proof showers; fire pit;, volleyball; shuffleboard; horseshoes; Webber BBQ grills; picnic tables; lawn furniture; light laundry facilities
Rates/Payment:	Weekly $650 (off-season rates available); check/cash
Open:	Year around

You often hear people talking about make-overs *from top to bottom*. Well for new owners, John and Donna Wittla, that's exactly what they've done with their lovely lakeside resort. Sunnyside is not new to the Greenbush area, but it is new to the Michigan Vacation Guide. We did not include it in past years simply because the resort did not meet certain standards. However, with our last visit, we were so impressed with its transformation that we are now happily including it in our book and pleased to feature it in our review section.

Scattered along the large, sandy beach are some of Sunnyside's newly renovated cottages. Upgrades are impressive. Excellent Lake Huron beach ... fun for all ages.

In just a couple of years, John and Donna have turned Sunnyside into an inviting vacation retreat. Nearly all seven units have been completely redone. Interiors and exterior have been stripped and cleaned with new ceilings and polished knotty pine walls in some units. Additional renovations include new ceramic tile on kitchen floors and counters, new carpeting, appliances, furniture, showers and windows. Kitchens even include well coordinated dishes and silverware.

Inviting knotty pine interiors with new ceramic tile floors in kitchens are just some of the nice updates made by the Wittlas.

There's room on the grounds of Sunnyside, and that's another nice feature. Guests will find cottages openly spaced on a natural wooded lot. Three units are directly on the sandy beach with absolutely breathtaking views of the clear blue water and naturally wonderful sunrises.

For those of you afraid of bugs and spiders, take heart, Donna is too. Of course, when cottages are surrounded by trees, sand and water it can be pretty hard to keep these pests out, but Donna works with a fanatical zest in an attempt to do just that.

As delightful as the current renovations are, the best is yet to come. The Wittlas tell us they have many more plans for the future. Sunnyside, with considerable work from John and Donna Wittla, has become a fresh and very pleasant surprise on the sunrise side of Michigan.

Birchwood Lodge

Paradise, Michigan
Reservations: 906-492-3320

Located in REGION 3

Proprietors:	Steve & Cathy Harmon
Accommodation:	8 waterfront cottages
Extras:	Equipped kitchens; private baths; satellite TV/ VCR; video rentals; BBQ grills; some with fireplaces; sandy swimming beach; inner tubes; bicycles and rowboats; badminton/volleyball court; swings; horseshoes; tether ball and shuffleboard; central beach house/rec room
Miscellaneous:	No pets
Rates/Payment:	Weekly $325-$500 (daily rates available); check, cash
Open:	Year around

Paradise ... an imaginary place? Not if you're traveling in Michigan's Upper Peninsula. In Michigan's Paradise, you'll feel welcomed by this scenic, friendly U.P. town where the calm, clear waters of Whitefish Bay brush across its shores.

Traditionally furnished with well maintained interiors.

Clean and homey interiors.

Its unhurried atmosphere and small town ambience make it a perfect place to relax by the water and enjoy the peace of the Up North. But don't think you'll be bored. It's centrally located to many attractions like the beautiful Taquahemon Falls, Pictured Rocks National Shoreline, lighthouses, dune rides, hiking and snowmobile tails, and much more.

Steve and Cathy Harmon, the cordial folks at Birchwood Lodge, know about the beauty of Paradise. They know because they've lived here for over 17 years. Their vast knowledge of the U.P. extends to the entire eastern side and includes places you wouldn't normally find in a travel guide. This makes a stay at Birchwood an even greater benefit for guests.

Birchwood Lodge's 8 cabins are tucked away between a sprinkling of trees and natural grounds off Whitefish Point Road. It's been around since the 1930's and has seen many renovations. The Harmons have done a very nice job maintaining the accommodations with recent improvements clearly visible in several units. Freshly upgraded bathrooms, new ceilings combine with traditional, comfortable furniture. Just like the little town of Paradise, nothing fancy at Birchwood just plenty of down-to-earth U.P. character.

Another appealing feature at Birchwood is their excellent beach which is accessed down a stairway. It's spacious (about 270 ft.) and 100% sand (minimal stones/rocks) with a very gradual water incline. Giant inner tubes help you enjoy the shoreline and rowboats are included for a tour of the bay.

Bicycles are also available for that leisurely trip into town or for exploring the surrounding area. And, if you just want to hang around the resort, there are horseshoes, swings, tether ball, badminton/volleyball and shuffleboard courts to keep you entertained. Finally, after a busy day of fun, you can kick back in your cabin and watch a video selected from the resort's own library, or checkout the latest sports game on the Satellite TV before turning in for the night.

Great sandy beach accessed through a stairway.

You may want to come back again in the fall when Paradise is a peaceful bouquet of color; or, perhaps, in winter when things really start heating up. It's snowmobile season, and Paradise's extensive trail systems are among the best in the state. Of course, in spring, the area is a birder's paradise. There have been more than 236 species of bird noted in the Whitefish Point area including bald and golden eagles.

What true Michigan vacationer can resist the experience of a U.P. adventure - winter, spring, summer or fall? Come to Birchwood Lodge in Michigan's Paradise and let the adventure begin.

Lake Shore Cabins

Silver City, Michigan
Reservations: 906-885-5318

Located in REGION 4

Proprietors:	Rick & Kitty DeaGuero
Accommodations:	6 waterfront cabins
Extras:	Equipped kitchens; private 1/2 baths; screened porches; linens; sandy swimming beach; central shower/sauna room; firepit
Rates/Payment:	Daily $39-$59 (based on double occupancy); check, cash
Open:	Year around

When people are looking for a *cabin up north*, they're looking for a place like Lake Shore Resort. Movies have been made around this type of setting – rugged log cabins nestled in virgin trees, by a beautiful lake close to majestic mountains.

Here you are literally surrounded by the sounds and colors of nature. So, be sure to take full advantage of it. In the morning go hiking, fishing or boating. Later in the day you may take in a little swimming (if you dare ... the water is cold ... it *is Lake Superior*). Nighttime brings evening bonfires and being lulled to sleep by the waves. Not far away there are charter fishing trips, golf,

Cabins rest along a beautiful sandy beach.

35

ghost towns or abandoned mines to explore. In the winter it becomes a wonderland for skiers and snowmobilers with the Porcupine Mountains just a couple of miles away.

Rick and Kitty DeaGuero are the effervescent and friendly owners of Lake Shore Cabins. They are attempting to maintain the resort's original style and beauty while ensuring the expected comforts of today. Each traditional log cabin is very clean with log and paneled interiors. One cabin dates back to about 1910. They all have screened porches and are two bedroom with comfortable furniture (some new) and full mattresses. The kitchens are well maintained, linens and towels are provided. There is a 1/2 bath in each unit consisting of toilet and sink. The shower is in the resort's shower room which also contains two authentic Finnish Saunas.

Traditionally furnished cabins are very clean with good maintenance and basic comforts.

Each cabin has indoor plumbing and private 1/2 bath (general shower available in the resort's sauna cabin).

One of the most appealing features at Lake Shore is the beach. It's about 250 feet of sand stretching well into Lake Superior. The entire resort is encased in mature trees and pines making it a fall color spectacular.

If you want a Holiday Inn, don't come to Lake Shore. However, if you are a traditionalist looking for a cabin in the U.P.'s great outdoors, Rick and Kitty have just the place for you. Make your reservations early, they book fast.

Whitetail Lodging on Lake Gogebic

Located in REGION 4

Marenisco, Michigan

Reservations: 906-842-3589

Proprietors:	**Phil and Sherri Bercot**
Accommodations:	**3 luxury, waterfront lodges and 1 apartment**
Extras:	**Equipped kitchens with microwave; private baths; linens;, gas fireplaces, TV/VCR available**
Rates/Payment:	**Weekly $500-$1,000** (Apr. 16-Nov. 30); **Daily $75-$300** (winter, 3 night min.); **Mastercard/Visa, check, cash**
Open:	**Year around**

Brand new, contemporary and squeaky clean best describes what Phil and Sherri Bercot have done to the former Sunset View Cottages on the edge of Lake Gogebic. As new owners, they have put considerable effort into making quality renovations for those seeking a more refined U.P. stay.

Spacious, open grounds on beautiful Lake Gogebic.

37

**Pleasing interior decor ... with contemporary-rustic styling
(above is their largest, two-level lodge).**

The largest of the accommodations (2 bedroom with loft and 2 full baths) sits closest to the water. Its second level loft creates an appealing, open ambiance. Kitchens are immaculate, fully equipped with gleaming counter tops and floors. Decor is warm and inviting with fresh knotty pine ceilings and walls, new tile

Kitchen/dining areas are inviting and well equipped.

and carpeted floors. A sleeper sofa and other furnishing compliment each other with a contemporary-rustic style that effectively creates a woodsy, outdoor feel. Bedrooms feature quality, queen size beds that will be a welcome relief at the end of an active U.P. day. The two additional (two bedroom) cottages sit further back on the open grounds and are similarly styled, though smaller, with well appointed interiors and a single bathroom. All three sleep from 6 to 10 and have direct water views. A fourth unit is located in the lower level of the Bercot's home. It, too, includes much of the same conveniences as the others but does not provide a direct view of the lake.

It should be noted that there is no actual beach at Whitetail. The water, however, does offer a gradual incline with no strong currents making it safe for swimming. So bring along those aquashoes to traverse the rocky beginning until you reach a natural sand bar a bit further out.

Whitetail's location is prime for the west side of the Upper Peninsula. Lake Gogebic is the largest inland lake in the state, is well known for exceptional fishing, and is considered to be one of the most beautiful.

The very natural setting of the Lake Gogebic area makes it particularly inviting to nature lovers and outdoor enthusiasts. For those seeking the serenity of nature or exciting challenges in Michigan's wilderness, come to the Whitetail Lodge where quality and comfort will ensure your next Upper Peninsula experience is a memorable one.

Northern Lights Retreat

Petoskey, Michigan
Reservations: 734-426-2874

Located in
REGION 5

Proprietors:	Mike and Jan Stagg
Accommodations:	Private cottage, 4 bedroom (sleeps 8-10)
Extras:	Equipped kitchen; private baths; fireplace, ceiling fans; CATV/VCR; wraparound deck; deck furniture; BBQ grill
Rates/Payment:	$700 (April, May, Sept., Oct.); $800 (Memorial Day-Labor Day), cash, check
Miscellaneous:	No pets, smoke-free environment
Open:	April to November

If you're looking for a trendy resort community, Petoskey is the place. If you're looking for a trendy resort home, Mike and Jan Stagg have it. Sitting on a quiet residential street is the newly acquired vacation home of Mike and Jan. They are in the process of major renovation and everything should be ready and waiting for vacationers by 1999.

Contemporary vacation home on a quiet side street.

40

Interior highlighted by open design and lots of space.

If you've had the opportunity of staying at the Stagg's "2452" property, you know they have a flare for fun decor. Though still being worked on, we could already see their unique touches adding to the charm of this home. Walls covered with snow shoes or skis, unusual and colorful paintings, fun signs here and there, very much reflect Mike's and Jan's zest.

The house itself is an open and airy two-story. Guests will first enter into the spacious main living room with tall studio ceiling, wood paneled walls with an inviting fireplace providing a warm welcome. From the fireplace, your eyes travel to the balcony of the second level where three bedrooms and 2nd floor bathroom are found. All upstairs rooms are comfortably sized with queen or bunk beds. This area, too, was under construction during our visit, but it looked like new carpeting and furniture were on the way.

To the left of the main living room, is a small formal dining room which is brightened by a doorwall that overlooks the lovely deck and yard. The kitchen, off the living room, is very clean and well equipped with everything you'll need. Also on the first floor is a second bathroom and fourth bedroom which features a very comfy king size bed.

The home is on a smaller but lovely treed lot with an enormous wraparound deck and lots of deck/patio furniture. Beaches and marinas are not far away and can be found in the lovely resort community of Petoskey which is well known for its parks, golf course, quaint shops, restaurants and, of course, sandy beaches where

41

MICHIGAN COTTAGES • CHALETS • CONDOS • B&B'S

The large wood deck, wrapping around the home, is a great place to begin or end the day.

hunting for Petoskey Stones is a favorite past time of may vacationers. Mike and Jan have priced the home very reasonably for this up scale and contemporary resort community.

Your first day there, kick back and relax, maybe build a fire in the evening or just watch TV. After that get ready for fun, water, boats, shopping, eating, sightseeing and everything else the area has to offer...happy vacationing.

Mimi's Retreat

Lake Leelenau, Michigan
Reservations: 616-941-1663

Located in REGION 5

Proprietor:	Marlene VanVoorst
Accommodations:	Waterfront cottage, 2 bedrooms with loft
Extras:	Full kitchen; private bath; screened porch; fire pit; rowboat
Rates/Payment:	Weekly (starting at) $540 (prices varies with occupancy), check, cash
Miscellaneous:	No Pets; bring linens and paper products; guests are requested to clean the cottage prior to departure.
Open:	May through September

Here you are, sitting on the back porch, sipping a cup of coffee early on a summer morning. Your eyes travel across the deep blue of Lake Leelenau to the soft, green hills on the other side. Back in your town it may be an Ozone Action Day, but at Mimi's Retreat the sun is breaking free, crisp and bright.

This small, unassuming cottage sits on a quite side street in West Bay on the beautiful Leelenau Peninsula. It has been in the VanVoorst family for years

Relaxing view of West Bay from Mimi's porch.

43

and is used as their special retreat to sneak away from life's daily chores. Today, Marlene and her son happily rent to those with simple tastes seeking the beauty and solitude the VanVoorst family has enjoyed over the years.

Built in the late 1960's, this modest, natural wood-framed cottage sits on a long lot about 60 to 70 feet wide with a small sandy beach, fire pit and boat ramp (a rowboat is included). The compact and cozy screened porch is a great spot to enjoy the sunset and a cool evening breeze.

The loft-styled interior remains basically unchanged since its initial creation. Regular maintenance has kept it in good condition with natural wood floors and

Simply furnished interiors.

area rugs adding a touch of warmth. The cottage can sleep up to six adults but is best suited for couples or young families. The main room combines a well stocked kitchen with living area furnished in simple, traditional 1960's-1970's furniture. The upstairs loft is a sleeping area with a pair of twin beds which would be particularly appealing to children. Doublebeds are found in the two first floor bedrooms. The single bathroom is clean and features a tub/shower.

Strolling outside toward water's edge, you'll find a rocky shoreline with gradual incline into the lake. It's safe for swimming, but we recommend you bring along those aqua shoes to traverse the rocky section before the smooth sandy bottom kicks-in. For people enjoying water sports, Lake Leelenau is considered an all-sports lake. Marlene tells us it's not overly crowded here so you can really enjoy

Campfire setup by the water awaits your evening s'mores roast.

your water activity. Be sure to take advantage of the rowboat included with the cottage and bring your motor to attach for a little water exploration. Perhaps later in the day you'll want to take your adventures to the land by visiting quaint, nearby villages, area wineries and, of course, Traverse City with exceptional restaurants and entertainment.

It should be noted that cleanliness is very important to Marlene. However, because she lives quite a distance from the cottage, she is not able to come by on a weekly basis to cleanup after guests depart. Therefore, she asks those staying at her place to please leave the cottage in clean condition for the next guests.

For people seeking simple accommodations at a pretty reasonable price for this scenic part of Michigan, Mimi's Retreat is a good choice.

Harold's Resort
Spider Lake, Michigan
616-946-5219

Located in
REGION 5

Proprietors:	Rolf and Kathy Schliess
Accommodations:	7 waterfront cottages
Extras:	Equipped kitchens; private baths; gas log fireplace and ceiling fans in some; screened porches; picnic tables; BBQ grills; rowboats (motor rental available); playground; fish hut; sandy swimming beach
Rates/Payment:	Weekly $320 (2 people); $650 (2 bedroom cabins, 4-6 people); check, cash
Miscellaneous:	No pets, bring linens and toiletries
Open:	Year around

Picture yourself sitting on the sandy point of your own private peninsula. The pressures of your work week left behind. You gaze at the trees, water, sun and your only concern is where to take your boat later in the day. Sipping your favorite drink, you watch your children excitedly catching what they're certain will be tonight's dinner ... thousands of minnows swimming in the warm, shallow, sandy water.

Scenic grounds at Harold's Resort on lovely Spider Lake.

All cottages offer kettle grills and picnic tables - 5 with lake views. Interiors are smaller but very homey ... clean and comfortable.

If that sounds like your type of vacation, then you need to get away to Harold's Resort. This cozy peninsula resort offers seven cottages ...all tucked away on wooded grounds overlooking beautiful Spider Lake (most units have lake views). There are stairs which take you directly to the beach or, if you prefer, you can take the steep and slopping sandy path which brings you directly to the tip of the beach's peninsula. Surrounded by tall trees in this relatively quiet section of Spider Lake, one gets the feeling of being alone.

47

MICHIGAN COTTAGES • CHALETS • CONDOS • B&B'S

Of course, as most fishing enthusiasts know, minnows aren't the only "catch" in Spider Lake where large mouth bass and a variety of pan fish are common and even an occasional muskie or pike can be found. Boats are included with all cottages so guests can take full advantage of the fishing or enjoy leisurely exploration of the lake.

Lodgings at Harold's are not new, but guests will find exteriors and interiors well maintained with several unit interiors featuring recent major renovations. Sizes vary from one room studios to two bedroom units and all but one have screened porches.

Since most of the cottages were occupied during our visit, we were only able to see the interior of a larger unit facing the water. This cottage, while not unusually spacious, was comfortably sized and very clean with two bedrooms, kitchen, dining/living area and traditional furniture. It sported new carpeting with a ceiling fan and a fully stocked kitchen.

Spider Lake is just a short distance from Traverse City, the Leelenau Peninsula, Interlochen and some great skiing and snowmobile trails. Unique shopping, wineries, live entertainment and special festivals throughout the seasons will make your stay even more enjoyable.

So, while the corporate paradigm is ticking in the city, at Harolds' Resort your only concern will be whether or not to use a lemon/butter sauce on the minnows your kids caught for dinner.

Whispering Waters B&B Retreat

Traverse City, Michigan

Reservations: 888-880-5557 • 616-941-5557

Located in REGION 5 ⑤

Proprietors:	Mark/Juliana Leslie and Brian Maynard
Accommodation:	Bed and breakfast (3 rooms, shared baths); cabin w/private bath
Extras:	On 42 acres with walking trails, streams and river; uniquely crafted interiors; outdoor hot tub; therapeutic massage; personal growth and stress management workshops; guided nature walks; small conference facilities; horse boarding; full or continental plus breakfasts
Rates/Payment:	Daily: *B&B* $80-$95; *Cabin* $150 (2 night min.); check, cash, major credit cards
Miscellaneous:	No pets
Open:	Year around

Rest and revitalization are the themes at Whispering Waters.

Whispering Waters is a perfect name for this lovely bed and breakfast where natural beauty and inviting sounds of river, streams, woods and meadows surrounds its 42 acres. Here, within its safe confines, you will find a quiet refuge where deer, small wildlife and a variety of birds, including bald eagles and blue herons, are often seen or heard.

Your experience begins as you enter the retreat's grounds and slowly drive down the narrow dirt lane. Just past their small cabin, grassy meadow and woods, you'll find the lovely, two story wood-frame home with multi-tiered deck resting beside the woods and a rippling brook.

49

MICHIGAN COTTAGES • CHALETS • CONDOS • B&B'S

Once inside you'll be wrapped in the warmth of a large, natural stone fireplace (built by manager, Brian Maynard, from specially selected stones). Dark wood logs and beams highlight tall ceilings and walls. Deep green and burgundy carpet and furniture offer an appealing contrast to brightly decorated walls and windows.

Creative interiors accented with the work of skilled artisans.

Additional natural accents are created by uniquely designed tree-branch stairways and balcony railings (also the work of Brian). To add to the charm and focused theme of nature, the eclectic owners (Juliana and Mark) have tastefully used the work of several skilled area artisans to decorate the home.

Guest rooms, though not large, are very comfortable with lovely handmade spreads and dried flower arrangements accenting each. The largest room features a private deck providing a peaceful view of the surrounding grounds.

For those seeking a more private holiday, the cozy,

Tree branches form stairways and balconies.

antique-filled one-room cabin (about a one minute walk from the main house) would be a very nice choice. It features beautifully restored cherry wood floors, tiled counters, private bath and loft sleeping area with skylight so you can sleep under the stars. Once again, the retreat's owners and manager have done a remarkable job of creating a well designed, inviting ambiance with comfortable furnishing and delightful accents.

Each morning guests are treated to freshly prepared breakfasts in the bright and cheery dining area. Brian is the skilled chef whose freshly prepared breakfast range from full to continental plus, depending on your needs. His special apple pancakes and baked muffins are a real treat ... and you must try his delicious herb tea.

Rooms are charmingly decorated.

After breakfast, your commune with nature begins. Outside you'll find well marked walking trails which also make great cross-country ski trails in the winter. Later, stroll past the horse barn (where you can stable your horse should you have one) to a sparkling section of the river near the private cabin. Here is a good spot to enjoy canoeing and tubing. Of course, downtown Traverse City with its many unique shops, entertainment and dining is just a short drive away.

Finally, after an full day, what better way to unwind than in the spacious hot tub resting near the gently rippling stream and woods by the home. Here is a perfect place to savor a glass of wine, enjoy the wind in the trees while the invigorating bubbles of the hot tub soothe away your stress and aching muscles. Around the corner, in the backyard, you'll find a beautifully crafted natural wood glider which invites quiet conversation and relaxation.

51

MICHIGAN COTTAGES • CHALETS • CONDOS • B&B'S

If you haven't already guessed, the owners, Juliana and Mark, and the manager, Brian, share a love of nature and the environment. One of their goals in creating Whispering Waters is to bring guests closer to both ... to rejuvenate the spirit and create an inner feeling of tranquillity. To help accomplish this, several special activities are offered throughout the year which include guided nature walks and workshops on personal growth, meditation and stress management.

Whispering Waters is meant to be a healing retreat far away from your hectic, everyday lives. For naturalists or those believing in the importance of holistic health, your caring hosts provide the comfortable setting and programs to put you in touch with your inner peace and harmony.

Wilkens Landing II and III

Spider Lake, Michigan
Reservations: 616-946-5219

Located in REGION 5

Proprietors:	**Rolf & Kathy Schliess**
Accommodations:	**Two Private Cottages**
Extras:	*Wilkens II*: **Full kitchen; private bath; TV/VCP; fireplace; deck; waterfront; pontoon boat; paddle boat; dock**
	Wilkens III: **Full kitchen; private bath; TV/VCP; fireplace; screened porch/deck; whirlpool tub; pontoon boat; rowboat**
Rates/Payment:	*Wilkens II*: **Summer weekly $850 (4-6 people);** *Wilkens III*: **Summer weekly $950 (4-6 people); check/cash**
Miscellaneous:	**No pets**
Open:	**Year around**

Decisions, decisions...which one to choose...by the water or in the woods. Though there are many similar features in both homes, Wilkens II and III are decidedly different. One common thread connecting them both is that the homes are managed by Rolf and Kathy Schliess.

Plenty of windows and comfortable interiors highlight Wilkens II.

53

MICHIGAN COTTAGES • CHALETS • CONDOS • B&B'S

Wilkens II is a slightly older, more traditional pine interior home that is large enough to comfortably hold 6 adults. Its most striking feature is the wall of windows that face Spider Lake. Living room or kitchen, your view is magnificent. Besides the windows, the light, over-stuffed living room furniture, fresh pine interior, and large stone fireplace will help brighten your mood. All rooms are fully carpeted and the bedrooms are ample with good firm mattresses.

Wilkens II - relaxing view of a quiet Spider Lake cove.

Just beyond the windows is a deck overlooking the grounds and Spider Lake. Waters edge has a rugged natural line of grass and reeds that's not really swimmable. However, just a short distance by boat and you will find plenty of good swimming.

In contrast, Wilkens III is a contemporary, two-story log home. It sits on a small hill surrounded by trees. Interiors are highlighted by white walls, vaulted ceiling, light carpeting, black chrome fireplace and contemporary furniture. Again, this home will comfortably handle 6 adults. The kitchen and dining room continue the trend with contemporary table, white tile floors and countertops. The staircase takes you to the second floor with ample sized bedrooms and comfortable full beds. This floor also has a full bath and continues with light contemporary styling.

Heading outside you'll find a screened front porch shaded with tall trees. It's a perfect place to relax on a warm summer afternoon. And just a short walk down the hill and through the woods is Spider Lake. Though this section of the lake is not a good swimming area, a pontoon boat will be moored ready to take you to one.

Wilkens III - a lovely log cabin with a contemporary flair. A short walk in the woods takes you to Spider Lake.

Both homes provide all the comforts you'll need to relax after a very active day on Spider Lake or Traverse City. So, whether it's a traditional cottage on the water or a contemporary home in the woods, Rolf and Kathy have a place to fit your needs.

The Beach House at Spider Lake

Located **5** in REGION 5

Spider Lake, Michigan

Reservations: 616-946-5219

Proprietors:	**Rolf and Kathy Schliess**
Accommodation:	**Waterfront private cottage, 2 bedroom/1 bath (sleeps 6-8)**
Extras:	**Equipped kitchen; private bath; fireplace; ceiling fans; CATV; beach and dock; pontoon boat; fire-pit; bunkhouse**
Rates/Payment:	**Weekly $925; check, cash**
Miscellaneous:	**No pets**
Open:	**Year around**

Vacation...we need it. We've got to have it. It's that cherished, rare break in our daily routine which allows us to think of nothing more complicated than having fun. The Beach House at Spider Lake, perched on a scenic cove of the lake in the lovely Traverse City area, will make having fun pretty darn easy.

Great setting by the water.

56

**Chalet ceilings, comfy furniture and bright interiors highlight
the Beach House at Spider Lake.**

First, its location is great. Not only does it sit directly on beautiful Spider Lake, but it's also centrally located to Interlochen and Traverse City. Both are terrific areas with plenty of quality restaurants, live entertainment, unique shops, skiing, snowmobiling and more throughout the year.

Pontoon boat is included for your leisurely tour of the lake.

57

Second, the home offers several amenities which will ensure that your stay at the lake is most enjoyable. The interior of the great room is spacious and accented with high peaked, wood-beamed ceilings and a large brick fireplace. An open picture window overlooks the deck and treats guests to a lovely view of the water. Furniture is comfortable and the T.V., tucked in the corner, is equipped with cable. Combine this with a clean, cozy kitchen/dining area with all the basics (eating/cooking utensils, stove, refrigerator and micro-wave) and ceiling fans to keep things cool (great room and kitchen), and you have the makings for a good time.

Children will enjoy the "Bunkhouse" located next to the main home. Its small, one room interior contains bunk beds and a dresser ... just the right size for children to hang out during the day or for a sleep-over.

Another nice feature at The Beach House is the large, wood deck which directly overlooks the water. It's a wonderful place to sit back and enjoy the calming view of sparkling lake and lush greenery. The deck's stairway takes you to water's edge which combines sand with natural grass. Here the water is gentle with a gradual incline making it safe for swimming. Later you'll want to take advantage of the pontoon boat moored at the dock for a leisurely tour of Spider Lake.

Of course what would a beach house be without the traditional fire pit. So bring along those marshmallows and watch the sunset as you warm yourself by the crackling lakeside campfire. Think about the fun you're going to have tomorrow ... you're on vacation!

Beechwood Manor B&B and Cottages

Saugatuck, Michigan
Reservations: 616-857-1587

Located in REGION 6

Proprietors:	Sherron & James Lemons
Accommodation:	*B&B*: 5 Rooms, private baths
	Private Cottages: 3 bedroom, kitchens, private baths
Extras:	*B&B*: Fireplaces (electric, some rooms); ceiling fans; window A/C; tandem bikes; boat slips available; continental and full breakfasts;
	Cottages: Tub/shower; ceiling fans; TV/VCR; linens; boat slips (2 waterfront, 1 side street)
Rates/Payment:	*B&B*: Daily $125-$150; *Cottages*: Weekly $895 (and up); check, cash
Miscellaneous:	No pets, smoke-free environment
Open:	Year around

Located on a quiet side street in the old Village of Saugatuck, within walking distance to shops and restaurants, this fully restored 1800's Victorian-styled home offers inviting atmosphere, appealing and comfortable rooms, and welcoming innkeepers.

Located on a quiet side street in charming Saugatuck.

59

MICHIGAN COTTAGES • CHALETS • CONDOS • B&B'S

William Perrin Sutton originally built the home in 1874. A former superintendent of Saugatuck schools, he went on to serve as U.S. Consular General in Mexico. Later, from 1893 to 1900, he practiced international law in Washington, D.C. The home remained vacant for many years and was in danger of being demolished when the Lemons took ownership in 1991.

Jim and Sherron fully appreciate the beauty of the fine craftsmanship originally created by its first builders. They want their guests to enjoy an experience in preserved Victorian era living and have taken the time to recreate a bygone era. Interior decor, antiques and furniture of the period are found throughout the home. A player piano sits in a cozy side room. Another small room, is setup for parlor games and accented with teddy bears and rag dolls.

Comfortable and well presented rooms in the Victorian style.

Each of the four guest rooms, named after the Suttons' children, feature heirloom furnishings and are decorated in warming colors of country blue, rose and cream. A welcoming split of wine and chocolates are placed in each room. In the morning, guests will be treated to a well prepared breakfast which may consist of freshly baked coffee cakes and fruit or such house specialties as appleflans or vegetable quiche. Then its off to enjoy some sailing in Saugatuck's blue waters or visit the many unique shops, beaches, and fine restaurants nearby. You may want to take advantage of the inn's tandem bicycles for a nostalgic ride through the area's scenic streets.

For those with children or other folks seeking a traditional cottage experience, the Lemons have three such lodgings available. Scattered in various locations

**One of several private cottages also available through
Beechwood. Above pictured is Sunset Dreams.**

throughout Saugatuck, each is only minutes away from sandy beaches. All cottages include 3 bedrooms, fully equipped kitchens with microwaves and dishwashers, ceiling fans, TV and VCR and one or two private baths. Two provide direct Lake Michigan or Kalamazoo Bay/Harbor access. The third is found on a quiet side street and is within walking distance to shops and restaurants.

Whether you're seeking the quiet beauty of a historic bed and breakfast or an active family getaway, one of Beechwood's accommodations will be a very nice way to enjoy your Saugatuck experience.

61

Hidden Pond B&B

Fennville, Michigan
(Saugatuck area)
Reservations: 616-561-2491

Located in
REGION 6

Proprietors:	Priscilla & Larry Fuerst
Accommodation:	2 rooms, private baths
Extras:	A/C; on 28 acres with walking trails; continental and full breakfasts
Rates/Payment:	Daily $64-$110 (plus state/local tax); check, cash
Miscellaneous:	No pets
Open:	Year around

The name Hidden Pond aptly describes this lovely, contemporary bed and breakfast concealed amongst the trees and overlooking the calm waters of a sparkling pond. Though slightly off the beaten path on a quiet country road, it is still only a short drive to the dunes, Lake Michigan beaches and the quaint villages of Fennville and Saugatuck.

Built along a sloping ravine, the home is accented with fragrant step gardens and 28 acres of natural land including, of course, a hidden pond. The 60 ft. deck or

Fragrant step gardens highlight the scenic charm of Hidden Pond.

The enclosed porch/sunroom provides a wonderful setting for morning breakfasts (weather permitting, of course).

enclosed sunroom are perfect spots to enjoy the view and relax with a glass of fine wine, a good book, or some quiet conversation.

There are well marked trails on the grounds which await your early morning or evening stroll. Deer, raccoon and a variety of birds and wildlife are frequent visitors here. Of course, you may prefer to meander down to the pond and take

Lovely, contemporary-country decor creates an inviting ambiance.

63

MICHIGAN COTTAGES • CHALETS • CONDOS • B&B'S

Cheerful rooms offer scenic views of the grounds.

advantage of the boat available for guests. The pond is not particularly large yet, Prisicilla said, guests still love to take the boat out and just sit in the middle and watch nature.

The bright and cheerful sun porch is the place where breakfast is often served. This leads the way to Hidden Pond's open styling and impeccably decorated interior. Here you'll feel right at home with its contemporary and welcoming atmosphere. Guests have complete access to the kitchen (and more importantly, the refrigerator), living room, formal dining room, adjacent sitting area with French doors overlooking the deck and scenic views beyond.

The two delightful guest rooms are located across from each other next to the dining/sitting area. The largest of their rooms, Pond View, features a king size bed, private bath and a doorwall leading to the deck with view of the pond below. Terrace View, a slightly smaller room, has a queen bed, private bath and windows with a view of the terrace and gardens. Both rooms are very comfortable and cheerfully decorated in country floral prints.

In the morning, guests will awake to the wonderful aroma of one of Chef Larry's specially chosen full breakfasts skillfully prepared and presented by Priscilla. Guests will be treated to a variety of fresh fruits, yogurt, juices and always a unique hot dish. To enhance the experience, table settings are accentuated with fresh flowers often taken from their gardens.

The friendly and exuberant hosts, being well traveled, have taken the best from their experiences and brought them all to their Hidden Pond. Rendezvous with the Fuersts to retreat from the hectic pace and discover what else life has to offer.

Riverbend Retreat

South Haven, Michigan
Reservations: 616-637-3505

Proprietors:	Bret and Pam Morgan
Accommodation:	Two luxury, cedar homes; 3 & 4 bedrooms (sleeps 12) by the Black River
Extras:	Equipped kitchens; private baths; ceiling fans; TV/VCR; fireplace (wood provided); dishwasher; laundry; private decks; hot tubs; gas grills; heated outdoor swimming pool; volleyball court; boat dock; canoes; boat; Kal-Haven Pass
Rates/Payment:	Call for current rates; check, cash
Miscellaneous:	No pets
Open:	Year around

Quiet solitude and picturesque views set the mood for visitors to Bret and Pam Morgan's beautiful Riverbend Retreat. Built into sloping grounds overlooking a calming section of the Black River, each two-level cottage is well designed and invitingly styled. The surrounding tall trees and natural greenery seen from the large windows and private decks are wonderful reminders that you're close to nature.

One of two luxury homes available.

High-peaked ceiling, fresh cedar interiors, stone fireplace ... all make for a very inviting and comfortable stay.

Upon entering the homes, guests will first appreciate the spacious, open floor design with high-peaked cedar ceilings, walls and floors. A tall stone fireplace accents the living area which also includes TV/VCR and comfortable furnishings. It is a welcoming spot to gather with friends and family.

For you cooking aficionados, be assured that the kitchens are fully equipped with dishwasher, microwave, coffeemaker, blender, toaster and even a Wok for stirring-up your favorite stir-fry. Matched sets of dishes, glassware and eating utensils can be found in the pecan wood cabinets. Well appointed upstairs bedrooms and bath are just down the hall. Lower levels include yet another sitting room with TV/VCR plus additional bedrooms and bath should members of your party want a little more privacy. Outdoor wood

Both homes overlook the Black River ... canoes/rowboats are available to guests.

Bedrooms feature king and queen size beds.

decks are highlighted by a peaceful view of the Black River. Add to this a most inviting Jacuzzi, and you have a wonderful end to an exciting day of outdoor play.

Speaking of play ... there's plenty to do at or near Riverbend. The cottages sit on 32 acres of land and, just across the road, there's an additional 38 acres with wooded trails for exploring. To ensure their guests' further enjoyment, the Morgans' have built a heated, in-ground swimming pool with private changing area and bath. Two well spaced volleyball courts are setoff to the side and, by the river, a rowboat or canoe for your water exploration.

In addition, all guests receive a pass to nearby Kal-Haven State Park with its 33.5 miles of trails stretching from South Haven to Kalamazoo. The trail is well known for excellent hiking, mountain biking, snowmobiling or cross-country skiing. Of course, Lake Michigan's beautiful beaches, shopping, golfing and great restaurants are just minutes away in South Haven.

Spoil yourself a little at Riverbend Retreat — a place where wonderful Michigan vacations begin.

The Sanctuary at Wildwood B&B

Jones, Michigan

Reservations: 800-249-5910 • 616-244-5910

Located in REGION 6 **6**

Proprietors:	Dick & Dolly Buerkle
Accommodation:	5 lodge suites/6 suites, private baths
Extras:	A/C; Jacuzzis; gas fireplaces; heated pool; private balconies; on 90 acres with walking trails; special programs: romantic, canoe, winter, golf getaways; therapeutic massages; full breakfast
Rates/Payment:	Daily $139-$179 (2 night min.); major credit cards, check, cash
Open:	Year around

"This special place is indeed a sanctuary ... a place to rest, reflect and love..." (Jan & Jerry, Canton, Michigan).

So write former guests of their memorable experience at The Sanctuary at Wildwood. We could not have said it better.

Sanctuary has its own wildlife manager to oversee the whitetail deer herd and variety of waterfowl and wild birds on its 90-acres of land.

The Sanctuary is a remarkable escape. From its spacious, uniquely inviting rooms to its beautiful landscape of meadows, woods and reflecting waters, this lovely retreat is a place of dreams. Your stay is sure to renew your spirit, revitalize your heart, and provide you with memories for a lifetime.

For those familiar with bed and breakfasts, it will come as no surprise that the innkeepers of The Sanctuary are Dick and Dolly Buerkle, owners of the popular Mendon Country Inn. They have developed a reputation for operating comfortable and appealing accommodations for over 12 years.

The Sanctuary combines a main lodge containing five spacious suites along with six additional suites located in three cottages scattered along the grounds. In designing the inn, Dick and Dolly wanted to surround their guests with the timeless beauty of nature, both inside and out. To accomplish this they brought in artisan, Andy Brown, noted for his skill at designing unique furniture from trees. In addition, they used the talents of painter, Sharon Campbell, to create wall murals supporting the individual outdoor themes of each room.

The results are incredible ... a dramatic canopied bed made from the natural branches of ironwood trees, headboards formed from dogwood branches or peeled elms. Small trees are frequently used as walls to separate the private sitting room from the sleeping area. Combine this with impressively designed murals and you'll find yourself ... in the mountains, in an evergreen grove, or in a quiet marsh during a mystical dawn.

Creative and dramatically designed rooms ... unique to The Sanctuary. Here, a canopy is formed from the branches of an ironwood tree.

In addition to its nature themes, rooms also offer private bath, fireplace, Jacuzzi for two and private deck or patio.

The interior ambiance of the rooms are effectively matched with the encompassing 90 acres of scenic land. Dick and Dolly maintain the property as a *wildlife sanctuary*. To ensure the safety and well being of their two whitetail deer herds, turkeys and vast assortment of birds, they have hired a wildlife manager. Today it's quite common to see a variety of friendly deer and fowl as you stroll through the inn's 4.5 acres of marked trails.

Yet another delightful experience at this country lodge is Dolly's full breakfasts. Each morning, guests are treated to a freshly prepared main course with a variety of delicious breads and pastries. All are served in the bright and airy dining room, surrounded by windows which overlook the pond and well groomed grounds.

After breakfast, you'll want to enjoy some of the many activities just a few minutes away. Rent a pontoon boat, go horseback riding or enjoy championship golf. You may want to take a tour of area wineries, visit the many antique shops or local Amish settlement. Charming Shipshewana, Indiana and its noteworthy shops, auction and flea market are another brief drive away. In the winter, enjoy downhill skiing at nearby Swiss Valley Ski Resort. Dick and Dolly are quite knowledgeable about things to do in the area and will be happy to provide you with a map outlining some of their recommended activities.

With life being as hectic and crazy as it sometimes is, don't we all need a sanctuary from time to time? The Buerkle's welcome you to the serenity of their Sanctuary at Wildwood.

The Seymour House B&B and Log Cabin

South Haven, Michigan

Reservations: 616-227-3918

Located in REGION 6 **6**

Proprietors:	**Gwen & Tom Paton**
Accommodation:	*B&B:* **5 Rooms with private baths**
	Log Cabin: **1920's authentic, 2 bedroom, private bath**
Extras:	*B&B:* **A/C; walking trails and pond on 11 wooded acres; some rooms with Jacuzzi, fireplace, TV/VCR; full gourmet breakfast**
	Log Cabin: **Equipped kitchen, private bath**
Rates/Payment:	**Daily $80-$145; check, cash**
Miscellaneous:	**No pets, smoke-free environment**
Open:	**Year around**

Halfway between Saugatuck and South Haven, on Blue Star Highway, sits the stately 1862 Seymour House, owned by Gwen and Tom Paton, congenial and caring innkeepers. Resting on more than 11 wooded acres, the home was originally built by William H. Seymour, prominent banker and lumber baron

Historic Seymour House, built in 1862.

71

of the 1800's. Today, Tom and Gwen Paton have taken this large estate and turned it into an inviting bed and breakfast with rooms and features to fit a variety of tastes.

During the spring and summer, guests will find the home's exterior accented with the fragrant scent of magnolia, rhododendron and other bright annuals and perennials. The backyard patio, furnished in white wicker and shaded by large maple and willow trees, offers a most picturesque view of the nearby 1-1/2 acre pond and 10 acres of woods behind. Trails through the woods are maintained to offer guests an excellent spot for nature walks and, in the winter, cross-country skiing. Tom tells us a variety of birds, deer and wildlife are frequently spotted. To add to guests' enjoyment, their pond is stocked with blue gills and large mouth bass for catch and release fishing. A paddle boat is also available for a quiet day or evening paddle.

**Bedrooms vary in size and style ... but all are
attractively appointed.**

Mornings at The Seymour House begin with one of Gwen's special full-gourmet breakfasts. Gwen prides herself in both food preparation *and* presentation. Each morning, a large centerpiece of fresh flowers accent the dining table. Smaller flowers are frequently used to decorate dishes. Gwen insists all her food is fresh with eggs, sausages, fruits and other goods collected from local farmers. Some of her breakfast specialties include Bananas Amaretto, Orange Pecan Rolls, Blueberry Buttermilk Pancakes, and Eggs Santa Fe.

After breakfast, you'll want to enjoy one of Saugatuck's or South Haven's many golf courses, beaches, shops, marinas, and fine restaurants. Then, after an exhausting day, you'll look forward to unwinding in one of the home's five

Enjoy picturesque views from the patio.

eminently comfortable rooms. Each is named after one of the Patons' favorite states which include the nautical Michigan Room, western-styled Wyoming Room with Jacuzzi, charming Vermont Room featuring a king-size bed and gas fireplace, and the rustic Colorado Room accented with a warming gas fireplace. A unique willow seat here provides an excellent view of the grounds. We also found their Arizona room very inviting with its queen size log-styled bed and spacious 2-person Jacuzzi. This room recreates a real feel of Arizona warmth in southwest colors, art and pottery pieces by Gwen.

An authentic, 1920's log cabin is also available.

Speaking of art, most of the photographs, pottery and art decorating the rooms were created by Gwen's skillful hands. Gwen is a talented artisan with her photographs frequently published in U.S. travel magazines and calendars. The Seymour House gift shop offers many of her works along with other collectibles.

73

MICHIGAN COTTAGES • CHALETS • CONDOS • B&B'S

For those who seek more rustic privacy, hidden behind trees and natural shrubbery, is the 1920's authentic log cabin. Don't expect fancy styling here. The Patons have maintained the cabin in its original state with traditional wood interiors and wood-burning fireplace. There is a small private bath and shower, two small bedrooms and a kitchen styled as it was in the 1920's. The only contemporary addition to the cabin is the inclusion of air conditioning and a skylight cut into the roof to provide additional interior light. Breakfasts are not included with rental of the cabin but are available for an additional $9.00 per person.

If you're looking for a restful retreat only minutes from Saugatuck and South Haven, The Seymour House is a very nice choice.

Tanbithn

South Haven, Michigan
Reservations: 616-637-4304

Located in REGION 6 **6**

Proprietor:	Marcia Robinson
Accommodation:	Single cottage, 1 bedroom, living area with sleeper sofa, sleeps five
Extras:	Equipped kitchen; private bath; A/C; ceiling fans; CATV; linens (bring bath towels)
Rates/Payment:	Weekly $750 (fall/winter rates negotiable); Weekends, Daily $125; check, cash
Miscellaneous:	No pets, smoke-free environment
Open:	Year around

Cute and well maintained, Tanbithn sits by the sidewalk ... great for people watching and what Marcia calls old-fashion "stooping".

Just off the sidewalk on North Shore Drive rests Marcia Robinson's small but cheery cottage, Tanbithn. Beach access is only 1/2 block, the marina 1 block. Restaurants, shopping and the park where major festivals are held are also nearby. It's definitely located in a hub of South Haven action.

Fully renovated ... new, bright and comfortably cozy interiors.

This former leather shop, delicatessen and Italian restaurant was purchased by the Robinsons in 1977. In 1994 it went through extensive renovation. Today, its comfortable, bright and airy interior reflects Marcia's talent for design. Furniture and walls are accented with splashes of color from throw pillows and wall hangings. A tall ceiling and well placed windows continue to add light to the main room which combine living and dining area. The two living room sofas open to double and twin beds. A small but efficient kitchen is located just behind the dining alcove which, in addition to stove and refrigerator, contains a microwave, coffeemaker and a good assortment of dishes and eating utensils. Down a short hallway is the bathroom with stall shower and, just across, a comfortable bedroom.

Tanbithn does not rest on spacious grounds. But for those interested, it's a fun spot to sit out, chat with passersby or just people watch. In other words, as Marcia lovingly calls it, some "good, old-fashioned stooping".

If you're seeking an accommodation providing a clean, well-designed, and comfortable interior located in a spot with easy access to the beach, marina and park, Tanbithn is a darn nice choice.

REGION 1

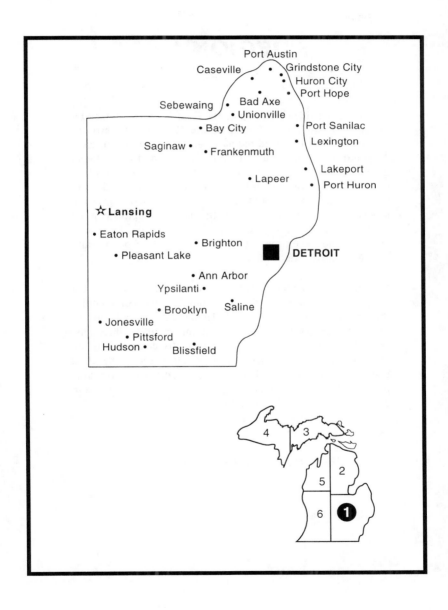

REGION 1

The southeast side of Michigan, the Heartland, is bounded by two of our Great Lakes, Huron and Erie. Here, too, the territory is agricultural with faded red barns and rolling fields of oats. As you travel along, you will see gentle hills and vails of lush green as far as your eye can see. Crystal lakes, rippling streams, waterfalls, hot air balloon races, air shows and many tours of historic homes, art fairs, unusual shops and stagecoach towns of long ago. Vibrant cities that never seem to sleep. Its treasure lies in the scenic beauty of its woods, lakes and streams made even more beautiful by the fine people and relaxed atmosphere of the area.

Shaped by the Saginaw Bay to the west and Lake Huron to the east, the "Thumb" is a world apart from the urban communities that are less than two hours away. Here the interstate highways turn to country roads and suburbs turn into distinct villages, the hectic life of the city turns into rural country charm. There are 90 miles of lake shorelines to view, small museums, beaches, country markets, antique shops, roadside parks, and picturesque bluffs, lighthouses, and an easy way of life to soothe the soul and rest the weary urban mind.

Welcome to "the gateway close to home".

BLISSFIELD & THE IRISH HILLS AREA

COVERS: BROOKLYN • HUDSON • JONESVILLE • PITTSFORD

S urround yourself with the beauty of the **Irish Hills,** a unique blend of modern and historic. Visit the Croswell Opera House, in Adrian, the oldest continuously operating theater of its kind in Michigan. It features live theater productions as well as special art exhibits. Michigan Futurity is the place to be for horse racing excitement.

Picnic by one of the Irish Hills' 50 spring-fed lakes, ride amongst its beautiful rolling hills, and take a trip to historic Walker Tavern in Cambridge State Historic Park. Enjoy a nature walk through the 670-acre Hidden Lake Gardens at Michigan State University. Of course, there's always the fun of Mystery Hill. Ready for more? Then step back in time to the 1800's and enjoy the pioneering spirit that lives on at Stagecoach Stop U.S.A. Sit back with a sarsaparilla in the saloon, pan for gold, or take a train ride ... but be careful ... we hear there's masked bandits in the area.

Join the excitement of Indy and stock car races each summer (June-August) at the Michigan International Speedway in the Irish Hills. While enjoying the beautiful fall colors, don't forget to stop in **Brooklyn** and join the fun at Oktoberfest or their arts and crafts festival. Anyone for cross-country skiing or snowmobiling? No matter what time of year, the Cambridge State Historic Park and the Irish Hills are always waiting.

BLISSFIELD

HIRAM D. ELLIS INN   **(517) 486-3155**
BED & BREAKFAST

All rooms in this 1880's, 2-story brick Victorian inn offer phones, CATV, private baths, and complementary use of bicycles. Come, relax and enjoy the many antiques and specialty shops in the area. Continental breakfast served each morning. 4 rooms. Business discounts available.

Daily $80-$100 (Corporate/Business $50)

BROOKLYN (IN THE IRISH HILLS)

THE BUFFALO INN
CAROL ZARR

(517) 467-6521
BED & BREAKFAST

Comfortable, inviting ... a uniquely different kind of home with a Southwestern charm. Enjoy your homemade breakfast by our large stone fireplace. Play pinball in our game room where smoking is allowed. 5 unique bedrooms with private and shared baths. One with fireplace. Located along "Antique Alley" in the beautiful Irish Hills.

Daily: $45-$85

CHICAGO STREET INN
KAREN & BILL KERR

(517) 592-3888
BED & BREAKFAST

Antique furnishings, original electric chandeliers, European stained glass windows, and a wicker filled veranda decorate this 1800's Queen Anne Victorian home. Wonderful full breakfasts featuring homemade baked goods are unexpected treats! Minutes from numerous lakes, golfing, hiking, antiquing. 4 suites with Jacuzzis, 3 also include fireplaces. 6 rooms w/private baths, A/C.

Daily $80-$165

DEWEY LAKE MANOR
THE PHILLIPS FAMILY

(517) 467-7122
BED & BREAKFAST & COTTAGE

Sitting atop a knoll overlooking Dewey Lake on 18 scenic acres, a "country retreat" awaits Manor guests! Picnic by the lake — enjoy evening bonfires. Hearty breakfast buffet served on the glass enclosed porch (weather permitting). At night, snack on popcorn or sip a cup of cider...there are always cookies! 5 rooms w/private baths, A/C.

Four rooms with fireplaces. Also lakefront home near B&B rented weekly in the summer. *Website: www.getaway2smi.com/dewey*

Daily $55-$75

DUANE LOCKE
(734) 971-7558
COTTAGE

Lakefront cottage on Wamplers Lake, in the Irish Hills, sleeps up to 6. Features large enclosed porch, excellent swimming and fishing boat. No pets.

Weekly $500

JANET WITT
(419) 878-7201
COTTAGES

On Clock Lake, 2 fully furnished cottages, 1 lakefront/1 with lake access. Clean and comfortable home-away-from home. Both have equipped kitchens, microwave, CATV, VCR, picnic table, gas grill, campfire ring and boat. The cottage with direct lake frontage has a screened porch and pier.

Weekly $800 (lakefront); $550 (lake access)

HUDSON

SUTTON'S-WEED FARM B&B
(517) 547-6302 • (800)-826-FARM
BED & BREAKFAST

You'll step back in time when you're a guest at this 7 gable Victorian farmhouse (built 1874) decorated with five generations of antiques. Stroll along the 170 acres of wooded trails and watch for deer and wildlife. Breakfast to your taste— reservations, please. No, smoking. No pets. 4 rooms.

Daily $55-$70

JONESVILLE

THE MUNRO HOUSE
JOYCE YARDE
(800) 320-3792 • (517) 849-9292
BED & BREAKFAST

☆ EDITOR'S CHOICE ☆

This 1840 Greek Revival home was a station on the underground railroad. Enjoy an old fashioned stroll in our small town, or snuggle in front of the fireplace in your room. Coffee and dessert in the evening and a full breakfast in the morning. Golf, x-country skiing, theater and antiquing. 7 rooms with private baths, phones, TV. 2 rooms with Jacuzzi.

Daily $75-$150

Editor's Note: The history associated with this lovely B&B and its charismatic owner combine to make the Munro House an excellent choice.

PITTSFORD

THE ROCKING HORSE INN   (517) 523-3826
MARY ANN & PHIL MEREDITH   BED & BREAKFAST

This Italianate-style farmhouse, sits on two acres. Our guests love spending peaceful moments on the lovely wrap around porch, and say they "never go away hungry" from Mary Ann's evening desserts to the full breakfast next morning. 3-4 air conditioned guest rooms with TV, private bath, full and queen beds.

Daily $50-$75

ANN ARBOR • BRIGHTON • SALINE • YPSILANTI

Ann Arbor, home of the University of Michigan. This cosmopolitan area offers year around activities for its visitors — from arts and crafts to live theater and entertainment. While here, be sure to stroll the many unique shops, visit the University of Michigan planetariums, canoe, swim or hike in Gallup Park. In late July, arts and craft enthusiasts never miss the Ann Arbor Art Fair featuring noted artisans from across the country. Only 10 miles from Ann Arbor rests **Saline**. Noted for its historic homes and antique shops, the area hosts nationally recognized antique shows from April through November. **Ypsilanti**, home of Eastern Michigan University, is also a city of diverse activities. Among its many points of interest include Wiard's Orchard which offers fresh cider, tours and hayrides. Enjoy the festivities for a yearly Heritage Festival (celebrated each August) commemorating its early French settlers.

Surrounded by lakes, the **Brighton** area offers excellent golf courses, parks, downhill and cross country skiing. In the summer, Independence, Folk Art and Farmer's Market festivals abound at Mill Pond located in the heart of the city.

ANN ARBOR

THE URBAN RETREAT BED & BREAKFAST   (734) 971-8110
          BED & BREAKFAST

Contemporary ranch-styled home, antique furnished, set in a quiet neighborhood, it is only minutes away from downtown and UM/EMU. Walking and jogging trails. A National Wildlife Federation "Backyard Wildlife Habitat". Full gourmet breakfasts. A/C. 2 rooms.

Daily $55-$65

BRIGHTON

BRIGHTON HOME
(810) 227-3225
VACATION HOME

Built in 1990, this home sleeps 8 and is completely furnished. Located in a secluded area. The balcony overlooks the water only 10 ft. away. Features fully equipped kitchen, microwave, freezer, dishwasher, washer and dryer, use of rowboat and dock.

Weekly   (summer) $800   (off season rates available)

ISLAND LAKE RESORT
CHARLOTTE BAPRAWSKI
(810) 229-6723
DUPLEX/COTTAGES

Fronts both Briggs and Island Lakes. Year around resort offers 1-3 bedroom housekeeping cottages and duplex units. Completely furnished and equipped (bring bed linens and towels). Use of boat is included. Excellent fishing. Beautiful sandy beach, playground, picnic tables and more. 50% deposit required. Pedestrian underpass below Academy Road.

Weekly $225-$500   (duplex units less)

SALINE

THE HOMESTEAD BED & BREAKFAST
SHIRLEY GROSSMAN
(734) 429-9625
BED & BREAKFAST

1851 circa brick farmhouse filled with period antiques, features comfort in Victorian elegance. Cross-country ski, stroll or relax on 50 acres of farmland. Only 10 minutes from Ann Arbor. A/C. Corporate rates. 5 rooms.

Daily $35-$75

YPSILANTI

PARISH HOUSE INN
CHRIS MASON
(800) 480-4866 • (734) 480-4800
BED & BREAKFAST

1893 "Queen Anne" styled home first constructed as a parsonage. Extensively renovated in 1993. Victorian styled with period antiques. Fireplace, Jacuzzi, CATV, central A/C, and telephones. Hearty breakfast. Enjoy near-by golfing, antiqueing, biking and restaurants. No smoking. 9 rooms w/private baths.

Daily $89-$124 (Corporate Rate $79)

LANSING

COVERS: EATON RAPIDS • PLEASANT LAKE

Lansing, home of our State Capital since 1847. Visiting the Capitol building is an absolute "must do" for travelers in the area. Guides conduct free tours daily! Also take some time to visit the Michigan Historical Museum and explore the state's dynamic and exciting past. Relax on a riverboat cruise of the Grand River. There's also plenty of excellent golfing, shops, galleries, live theater and restaurants. The Boars Head Theater (Michigan's only resident theater) and Woldumar Nature Center are additional attractions.

If you're looking for an intimate and distinctive dining experience, you'll want to try Dusty's English Inn in **Eaton Rapids** — only a short drive from Lansing. For simpler yet well prepared homemade meals, you'll enjoy *Ellie's Country Kitchen* on East Grand River in Williamston for breakfast, lunch and dinner. Just down the street, is the *Red Cedar Grill* with its casually upscale atmosphere.

LANSING & EATON RAPIDS

DUSTY'S ENGLISH INN   **(517) 663-2500 • (800) 858-0598**
                            BED & BREAKFAST

Resting along the Grand River, amidst lovely gardens and woodland trails, this elegant English Tudor-style home is decorated throughout with antiques and reproductions. Its intimate restaurant offers fine dining and cocktails in the European tradition. Full English breakfast is served each morning.

Daily $85-$155 (dbl., plus tax)

PLEASANT LAKE

"2452"
JAN/MIKE STAGG

(734) 426-2874 • EMAIL: 2staggs@ameritech.net

COTTAGE

★ EDITOR'S CHOICE ★

Vacation cottage on all sports lake with sandy bottom. 3 bedrooms, sleeps 5-7, one bath, fully carpeted, with large fully equipped kitchen. Walk to fine dining, playground and 18 hole golf course (x-country skiing in winter). Enjoy fabulous sunsets, grassy sunbathing area, private dock, boat hoist, TV with VCR. Grill provided, linens extra. Open year around.

Weekly $450-$475 (call for weekend, monthly and off-season rates)

Editor's Note: Well maintained cottage on narrow lot. The new wood deck offers a great view of lake. Good value.

PORT HURON • LAPEER

Port Huron, where Lake Huron's waters become the St. Clair River. This port town is the home of the Blue Water Bridge, arts and craft fairs, waterfront dining and wonderful views from the shoreline. While in the area, visit Fort Gratiot Lighthouse and the Knowlton Ice Museum. In July, enjoy the excitement of the Blue Water Festival and the 3-day Port Huron to Mackinac Island Yacht Races.

Approximately 35 miles west of Port Huron is the scenic countryside of **Lapeer**. Surrounded by orchards, the area is known for its blueberry farms. The many lakes and streams in this region offer good fishing. In the winter, enjoy one of Lapeer's groomed cross-country ski trails.

LAPEER

HART HOUSE
ELLIE HAYES

(810) 667-9106
BED & BREAKFAST

Listed on the National Historic Register, this Queen Anne B&B was home of the first Mayor, Rodney G. Hart. Full breakfasts served each morning. Private baths. 4 rooms. No smoking.

Daily $30-$35

PORT HURON

THE VICTORIAN INN
MARVIN/SUSAN BURKE

(810) 984-1437
BED & BREAKFAST

Queen Anne styled inn, authentically restored, offers guests a timeless ambiance. Each room uniquely decorated. Enjoy the Inn's classically creative cuisine and gracious service. One hour from Detroit. 4 rooms, private/shared baths.

Daily $85-$125

LEXINGTON • PORT AUSTIN • CASEVILLE • BAD AXE

Covers: Grindstone City • Port Hope • Port Sanilac Sebewaing • Unionville

Known for its historic homes, **Lexington** has excellent boating, fishing and swimming. Visit the general store (dating from the 1870's) and indulge in the tasty nostalgia of their "penny candy" counter. Walk to the marina and visit the old lighthouse which was built in 1886.

Further north is **Port Hope**, home of the Bottom Land Preserve. The Lighthouse County Park, just outside town, is an ideal spot for scuba diving enthusiasts to view the under water wrecks of 19th Century vessels.

Take the turn off to Huron City, and stroll among the historic recreations of a 19th Century village. Visit **Grindstone City** and see if you can spot some of the original grinding wheels made from sandstone. We understand the general store in Grindstone serves ice cream cones big enough to satisfy the hottest and hungriest of visitors.

Celebrate both outstanding sunrises and sunsets at the tip of the thumb in **Port Austin**. Stop at Finan's Drug Store's nostalgic soda fountain in the area's restored business district. Discover the rolling sand dunes hidden behind the trees at Port Crescent State Park. Relax on its excellent 3-mile beach. This is also a bird watcher's haven with abundant numbers of hawk, oriole, osprey and bluebird populations.

LEXINGTON • PORT AUSTIN • CASEVILLE • BAD AXE

(continued...)

Moving around the thumb is **Caseville**. Drive along its half-mile stretch of Saginaw Bay Beach. Here's a great area for perch fishing, boating, swimming and just plain relaxing.

For a unique dining experience in Port Austin, try *The Bank* on Blake Street ... a little pricey, but worth it. This historic former bank is now an excellent restaurant, noted for its sourdough bread with herb butter and freshly prepared meals. Another excellent dining treat is offered at the *Garfield Inn* on Lake Street that serves as both a B&B and elegant restaurant. For more casual, relaxed dining you'll want to stop at the *Port Hope Hotel Restaurant* (in Port Hope) where we understand they prepare some hearty and very tasty hamburgers and other basics at affordable prices.

BAD AXE

GRAYSTONE MANOR   **(517) 269-9466**
BOB & JO VANSCHEPEN   **BED & BREAKFAST**
In town on 2.5 acres. 6 traditionally furnished rooms with private baths, A/C and CATV. Suite with queen half-poster bed. Perfect for weddings, special occasions. Princess room with king-size bed and whirlpool tub. Open Year around. Children 12 yrs. and up welcomed. MC/Visa. Business rates.

Daily $65-$85

CASEVILLE

BELLA VISTA MOTEL & COTTAGES   **(517) 856-2650**
         COTTAGES/EFFICIENCIES/MOTEL
1 bedroom efficiencies with kitchenettes, 2 bedroom cottages with full kitchens. Motel and cottages have lake views from picture windows and include screened porch, linens, tiled bath, CATV w/HBO. Heated outdoor pool, grills, picnic tables, sun deck, shuffleboard courts, swings, 400 ft. of beach.

Daily $69-$79 (motel)   Weekly $640-$940 (cottages)

CARKNER HOUSE   **(517) 856-3456**
         BED & BREAKFAST
Built around 1865, President McKinley stayed in here while visiting the area. 4 rooms, A/C, king size beds with private entrance. An efficiency apartment with kitchen, private entrance and bath; and 2 rooms share a living room, full kitchen and bath. No pets. Major credit cards. Open June-October.

Daily $60-$140

MICHIGAN COTTAGES • CHALETS • CONDOS • B&B'S

SUNSET BAY   **(517) 856-4400**
MOTEL/COTTAGES

Year around waterfront facility offers pool, A/C, and CATV. King and queen size beds available. Most major credit cards accepted.

Daily $84 (and up)

GRINDSTONE CITY

WHALEN'S GRINDSTONE SHORES   **(517) 738-7664**
CABINS

Located in historic Grindstone City at the top of the thumb on a harbor waterfront, Small and nicely wooded area features 11 units, 5 of them cabins with kitchen facilities. Beautiful Lake Huron view and good fishing. Hannicap accessible. Major credit cards accepted.

Call for Rates

LEXINGTON

BEACHCOMBER MOTEL & APARTMENTS   **(810) 359-8859**
COTTAGES/MOTEL

Spacious grounds feature motel, efficiencies, family units, cottages with fireplaces. Sandy beach, pool, fishing, tennis court, A/C, color TV. Beach house bed and breakfast offers continental breakfast served at your door. Open all year. No pets.

Daily $45 (and up)

BRITANNIA BEACH HOUSES   **(810) 359-5772** • EMAIL: windsor@greatlakes.net
HUGH & HANNAH LIDDIARD   COTTAGES

Six spacious, comfortable, 1-3 bedroom cottages on sandy Lake Huron beach. Low bluff with ramp; lakeside patio. Clean, stylishly decorated. Heated, carpeted with living rooms and complete kitchens (including microwave). CATV/VCR, grill, play structure, canopied picnic area. Golf, harbor nearby. Family oriented, peaceful relaxation. No smoking/pets. April-October.

Weekly $325-$875   Daily $70 (and up)

Editor's Note: Operated by the former owners of the Britannia House Bed and Breakfast. The Liddiards are completing major renovations to these older cottages.

COZMA'S COTTAGES   **(810) 359-8150** • **(313) 881-3313**
COTTAGES

These cottages, located on 2 acres in a secluded, beautiful, park-like setting along 200 ft. of private, sandy beach ... ideal for family reunions. Volleyball/badminton court, shuffleboard, horseshoes, kiddie swings, stone BBQ grills, picnic tables, ceiling or wall fans. Showers in all units. Bonfires on the beach nightly.

Weekly $345 (and up)

GLENVIEW
LINDA & CHUCK PHIPPS

(810) 359-7837
COTTAGE

✱ E D I T O R ' S   C H O I C E ✱

Fully renovated and charmingly decorated cottage in quiet neighborhood. Private beach access across the street. Cottage features cedar interior, ceiling fan, fireplace, TV (no cable) and VCR. Fully equipped kitchen. Webber grill and bicycles. Two bedrooms (sleeps 6). No pets. Open year around.

Weekly $500

Editor's Note: Appealing decor and good use of space make this small cottage a winner. No direct view of water, but beach access is available through a stairway across the street.

LITTLE WHITE COTTAGES

(616) 669-5187
COTTAGES

Two private cottages. Both completely furnished except linens, no pets/smoking:

Seadog: Charming, old-fashioned cottage on water's edge, 50 ft. beach in quiet area. 823 sq. ft. cottage, 7 rooms, 2 bedrooms, fireplace, kitchen, large screened porch overlooking Lake Huron. Beautiful view, nice for swimming and relaxing. Limit of 8.

Weekly $595 (June /Sept.)
$795 (July /Aug.)

Nymph: Cozy, antique cottage set 60 yards from Lake Huron at woods edge. 720 sq. ft., 1 bedroom, screened porch, partial view of lake. Glassed wood stove. Limit 6.

Weekly $495 (June /Sept.);
$550 (July /Aug.)

Exterior of *Seadog*

Editor's Note: On a small but quiet lot. Owners continue to make significant upgrades to add to the comfort and appearance of these older cottages.

MICHIGAN COTTAGES • CHALETS • CONDOS • B&B'S

**LUSKY'S LAKEFRONT
RESORT COTTAGES**

TOLL FREE: (877) 327-6889 • (810) 327-6889
COTTAGES

The friendly owners of Lusky's have completely refurbished all cottages! Clean, cozy and comfortable, each comes w/ceiling fans, cable TV, picnic tables, BBQ grills, fully equipped kitchens, private toilets (private showers). Screened porches have good view of lake and play area. Play area features airplane swings, play boats, tire swirl, gymset with tube slide, large sandbox. Also volley ball, basketball, shuffle-board, paddle-boats and rowboats. Stop at our novelty store for candy, pop, ice cream and trinkets galore — at old fashioned prices! All this makes for a fun, relaxing and affordable family vacation place where memories are made and treasured. Rentals available daily-weekly. Pets allowed.

Weekly $390-$480   Daily $55-$80

Editor's Note: The friendly owners continue to do a very nice job maintaining this traditional resort. Cottages with cozy decor. Very nice beach.

**THE POWELL HOUSE
NANCY POWELL**

(810) 359-5533
BED & BREAKFAST

★ E D I T O R ' S   C H O I C E ★

This charming B&B is located on beautifully landscaped grounds. Each of the four rooms offers their own separate charm and features king and queen size beds. Two rooms w/private baths, two rooms (suite) share a bath. Bicycles available for your leisurely tour of historic Lexington. Full breakfast included.

Daily $65-$75 (depending on room)

Editor's Note: Charmingly decorated, historic home maintained in very good condition by a delightful proprietor. See our review.

MARLENE WILSON

(517) 635-2911
VACATION HOME

3,000 sq. ft. home on 4 acres of wooded land and 250 ft. of beach front. Stairway leads to the beach. Four bedrooms (sleeps 8), completely furnished with fully equipped kitchen (stove, refrigerator, coffee maker, washer, dryer, etc.). Enjoy the scenic view of the Blue Water Bridge at night. Only 20 minutes north of Port Huron. Advance security deposit and payment required.

Weekly $1,250-$1,500 (seasonal rates)

Editor's Note: This older home on a scenic bluff overlooks the lake and offers plenty of room for those who crave it. See our review.

PORT AUSTIN

GARFIELD INN

(517) 738-5254
BED & BREAKFAST

Visited by President Garfield in 1860, the inn features period antiques and one of Michigan's premier restaurants! For that special occasion ask about the "Presidential Room". Rooms feature double and queen size beds. Complementary bottle of champagne. Breakfasts served between 9 am-10 am. Six rooms (private/shared baths).

Daily $95-$110 (May-Oct.); $85-$95 (Off-season)

HARBOR PINES/NORTH SHORE BEACH

(248) 650-9888
CONDOS

Two luxury condominiums, available year around, on 300 ft. of Lake Huron — tip of Michigan's thumb! Includes 2 bedrooms, 2 baths, sleep 6, fully furnished. Heat, air conditioning, CATV, VCR, and fireplaces. Playground area. Rental available weekly, monthly, or yearly. No pets.

Call for Rates

KREBS BEACHSIDE COTTAGES
MARV & SALLY KREBS

(517) 856-2876
COTTAGES/EFFICIENCIES

* E D I T O R ' S   C H O I C E   *

8 cottages (1-4 bedroom) on open, landscaped grounds with a scattering of trees. Fully furnished with living area, private baths, equipped kitchens with microwaves. Picnic tables and grills. Large wooden deck overlooks 200' of sandy beach with a great view of Saginaw Bay. Open May-Nov. 15. Heated. Hunters welcome. Pets allowed off-season.

Weekly $495 (and up) Reduced/daily rates spring/fall
Editor's Note: Simple, clean, comfortable cottages on spacious grounds, affordably priced with warm and caring owners make this a choice spot to stay — reserve early.

KREBS LANE COTTAGES/MOTEL

(313) 886-5752 • (517) 738-8548
MOTEL/COTTAGES/EFFICIENCIES

Set vertically to the water, these 6 clean, well maintained, 2 bedroom cottages sit on a 300 ft. x 50 ft. lot of sandy beach on Saginaw Bay. Includes equipped kitchens (all with microwaves) and hook-up for cable TV. Some units offer knotty pine interiors and lake views. Open year around. No pets.

Weekly $500-$575

MICHIGAN COTTAGES • CHALETS • CONDOS • B&B'S

THE CASTAWAYS BEACH RESORT & MOTOR INN   (517) 738-5101
MOTEL
Located along 400' of Lake Huron shoreline, this resort offers 46 rooms, dining room and lounge. Several rooms feature kitchenettes (refrigerator, stove and sink). Swimming pool, A/C, hot tub, CATV and handicap accessibility. MC/ Visa accepted. Open April-October.

Daily $91-$102

LAKE STREET MANOR   (517) 738-7720
BED & BREAKFAST
Built in 1875 by a lumber baron. Furnished with antiques and features large bays, high peaked roof and gingerbread trim. Hot tub and in-room movies, private and shared baths. Brick BBQ's and bikes offered for guests' enjoyment. Fenced 1/2 acre. 5 rooms

Daily $42-$49 ($55-$65 Weekends)

LAKE VISTA MOTEL & COTTAGE RESORT   (517) 738-8612
RON & MARY GOTTSCHALK   MOTEL/COTTAGES
On the shores of Lake Huron and Saginaw Bay, motel units feataure CATV and A/C. Efficiencies with ceiling fans, two double beds and queen size sofa sleeper. Equipped kitchens include microwaves. Recreational area, heated pool, snack bar on premises. Bait and tackle. Fishing licenses. Major credit cards.

Weekly $520 (and up, for cottages)

OSENTOSKI REALTY/LAKEFRONT   (888) 738-5251 • (517) 738-5251
ACCOMMODATIONS   CONDOS/COTTAGES
Spacious condos and cottages located on the beautiful shores of Lake Huron and Saginaw Bay. 1 and 2 bedroom units feature fireplaces, CATV, fully equipped kitchens and much, much more. Open all year.

Weekly $600 (and up)

TOWN CENTER COTTAGES   (517) 738-7223
COTTAGES
In the heart of it all! Comfortable two bedroom cottages with fully equipped kitchens, CATV, screened front porch and a very private outdoor area with picnic tables, grills and a fire ring for family fun. Short stroll to beach, shopping, dining, and all the fun.

Weekly $375   Daily $65

PORT HOPE

STAFFORD HOUSE   **(517) 428-4554**
GREG & KATHY GEPHART   **BED & BREAKFAST**

Only one block from Lake Huron, this nicely maintained B&B sits on an attractive open treed lot with a lovely backyard wildflower garden. Open year around. Full breakfasts served each morning. 4 rooms (one suite overlooks garden and is air conditioned) with private baths and CATV.

Daily $60-$85

PORT SANILAC

RAYMOND HOUSE INN   **(800) 622-7229 • (810) 622-8800**
RAYMOND & SHIRLEY DENISON   **BED & BREAKFAST**

500 ft. from Lake Huron and lighthouse, 1871 Victorian Home. 7 large, high-ceiling bedrooms, private baths, A/C. All in period furnishings. CATV-VCR, in-room phones. Old fashioned parlor/dining room adds to charm. Open May-Dec. "Pamper" room with fitness and massage. No smoking/pets.

Website: www.bbonline.com/MI/raymond

Daily $65-$115

Editor's Note: Antiques and lovely decor highlight the Raymond House and make it a very nice choice for the area. You'll want to check out the dolls created by Shirley (featured in Michigan Living) on display at the Inn.

SEBEWAING

RUMMELS TREE HAVEN B&B　　　　　　　**(517) 883-2450**
CARL & ERMA RUMMEL, JR.　　　　　　　**BED & BREAKFAST**
A 2 room bed & breakfast with full breakfast. Features private baths, cable TV, A/C, refrigerator and microwave. Fishing for perch and walleye. Very good area for hunting duck, goose, deer and pheasant. Personal checks accepted. Open all year. Pets allowed in garage area.

Daily　　　$35-$50

UNIONVILLE

FISH POINT LODGE　　　　　　　　　**(517) 674-2631**
　　　　　　　　　　　　　　　　　　　LODGE
Located near Fish Point game reserve this lodge, built in 1902, offers 4 bedrooms, shared bath and a huge fireplace. Kitchen facilities are available. Lodging accommodates up to 20 people. Breakfast included. Two cabins and R.V. sight also available. Credit cards accepted. Open year around.

Call for Rates

BAY CITY • FRANKENMUTH • SAGINAW

Bay City, well known for its water sports, features a variety of events including speedboat and offshore power boat races. Tour the city's historical sites and view the many stately homes on Center Avenue, Wenonah and Veterans Memorial parks. Come south from Bay City and explore the historic district of **Saginaw**. Take a four-mile river walk, visit a museum or the zoo and stroll among the fragrant rose gardens in downtown parks.

Traveling south from Saginaw, you'll reach the historic town of **Frankenmuth**. The classic Bavarian stylings of its original settlers can be seen throughout the town's homes, buildings and craft shops. For many it has become a traditional yearly visit. They come to the more than 100 shops and attractions, stroll the streets, tour the wineries and brewery, sample traditional German cuisine or their famous *all you can eat* chicken dinners. While there are many good places to eat in the area, the *Bavarian Inn* and *Zehnder* are still the most popular...and *beware* their bakeries are *too* tempting.

While you're in Frankenmuth, be sure to take a horse-drawn carriage ride or a river tour. And, of course, you must visit Bronner's Christmas Wonderland where holidays are celebrated 363 days a year. Spend the night, because you'll want to start shopping early the next morning at the areas largest designer outlet shopping mall located only a few minutes away in Birch Run.

BAY CITY

CLEMENTS INN   **(800) 442-4605**
DAVID & SHIRLEY ROBERTS   **BED & BREAKFAST**

This 1886 Victorian mansion offers 6 comfortably elegant rooms with private bath, TV/VCR and phone. Six fireplaces, central A/C. Enjoy a romantic evening in 1 of 2 whirlpool suites with in-room fireplaces.

Daily $75-$190

FRANKENMUTH

BED AND BREAKFAST AT THE PINES   **(517) 652-9019**
RICHARD & DONNA HODGE   **BED & BREAKFAST**

Welcome to our casual ranch-style home in a quiet residential neighborhood, within walking distance of famous restaurants and main tourist areas. Double and twin beds. Wholesome nutritious breakfast featuring homemade baked items, fresh fruit, jams and beverages. Open year around. 2 rooms. No smoking.

Daily $40-$50

Editor's Note: Charming owners create a real "homey" experience in this traditional, ranch-styled home. Small but very comfy rooms.

POINT OF VIEW   **(517) 652-9845**
ED AND BETTY GOYINGS   **COTTAGE**

* EDITOR'S CHOICE *

Completely remodeled one-room cottage plus Florida Room ... has lots of history. Features open great room with original maple floors and paneled walls, fireplace, bar, dinette, furnished kitchen, private bath. Includes CATV, phone, A/C, grill and picnic table. Linens included. No pets. Children under 12 FREE.

Weekly   *$400 ($35 each add'l. person)   Daily *$65 ($25 each add'l. person)
* Rate based on single occupancy

Editor's Note: Betty has a talent for interior design and it shows in this delightfully cozy one room cottage. Lovely location.

SAGINAW

BROCKWAY HOUSE BED & BREAKFAST
(517) 792-0746
DICK & ZOE ZUEHLKES
BED & BREAKFAST

On the National Register of Historic Homes, this 1864 B&B was built in the grand tradition of the old southern plantation. Near to excellent restaurants and antique shops. 4 rooms, private baths, A/C. Two-person Jucuzzi suite. Full gourmet breakfast served each morning.

Daily $85-$225

HEART HOUSE INN
(517) 753-3145
KELLY ZURVALEC
BED & BREAKFAST

This 8,000 sq. ft. mansion, built during the Civil War, features black walnut beams and lumber throughout. All 8 rooms with private bath, phones, TV, A/C, complimentary local daily paper. "Continental Plus Breakfast". Liquor License. Major credit cards accepted.

Daily $65-$80

REGION 2

REGION 2

Progressing northward, the forest grows denser, filled with sparkling lakes and streams. Here is canoeing, skiing and abundant fishing, fine places to eat, festivals, art fairs and scenic beauty as far as the eye can see.

Going east, to Lake Huron, we enter the land where lumber once was *King*, the land of the *River Rat* and the *Legend of Paul Bunyan*. More money was made here on lumber than miners made in the Klondike during the Gold Rush. Stripped bare by the lumbering frenzy, in 1909 the reforestation began. Today the forests are tall and stately and the forest floors are deep again with pine needles and teaming with wild life. Throughout the forest there are lakes, trout streams and fishing at its best. In the winter, when the forests floor is covered by snow, you will see not only the markings of elk, deer and moose, but also those of snowshoe, snowmobile and ski trails.

The days along the Huron are filled with activities throughout the seasons — sandy beaches, good swimming, tournaments, museums, lighthouses, historic sights, but most of all the scenic beauty and wonders of nature. The morning is a gentle symphony as the sun rises, a golden globe, out of the Huron and the breezes whisper through the pines mingling with the sound of the birds.

Yes, here is the excitement, beauty, peace and tranquillity.

OSCODA & THE AUSABLE AREA

COVERS: EAST TAWAS • GREENBUSH • MIO

Experience the open hospitality of AuGres as you continue to travel north on Michigan's east side. The restaurants and bake shops here are truly homey with freshly prepared meals. Considered the "Perch Capital", this small town has more than 1,000 boat docks and waters well stocked with perch, walleye and a large variety of pan fish. The best scenic views can be found along the lake shore roads, from Point AuGres and Point Lookout. Take your boat to Charity Island and explore its "most photographed" lighthouse. Excellent golf is available at Huron Breeze Golf & Country Club or, for the whole family, visit Lutz's Fun Land featuring waterslides, go-carts, and a variety of games and rides.

Settled where the AuSable River meets Lake Huron, these series of communities offer a variety of activities from canoeing and fishing to hiking, hunting, cross-country skiing, and snowmobiling. **Oscoda** is considered the gateway to the River Road National Scenic Byway that runs along the south bank of the AuSable River. **Tawas City** and nearby Huron National Forest offers lakes, beaches and great trails. During winter season, cross-country ski enthusiasts can enjoy the well-groomed trails at Corseair. In February, the Perchville U.S.A. Festival takes place — be there to enjoy the festivities.

The quaint harbor town of Harrisville offers terrific trout and salmon fishing. The Sturgeon Point Lighthouse Museum, a summer concert series, art and craft fairs, festivals and the Harrisville State Park provide a variety of both summer and winter recreational fun.

Mio, the Heart of the AuSable River Valley, excels in canoeing and winter sport activities. In June they host the Championship Canoe Race and the Great Lakes Forestry Exposition in July. While there, tour the Kirtland warbler nesting area.

To sample some of the area's down home cooking, try *The Bear Track Inn* (AuGres) noted for outstanding breakfast buffets plus a diverse menu including, of course, excellent fish. *H&H Bakery* (AuGres) has developed a proud reputation for their delicious, fresh baked goods with one of their specialties being pizza. *Charbonneau* (on the AuSable in Oscoda) offers a waterfront setting with a diverse menu; *and Wiltse's* (Oscoda) for some of the best blueberry pancakes around. Also, we've heard the *Greenbush Tavern* offers up some pretty good pizza and "all you can eat" fish on Friday.

EAST TAWAS

RIPTIDE MOTEL & CABINS   **(517) 362-6562**
EMMA & LARRY, MANAGERS   **MOTEL/CABINS**

On Tawas Bay, this year around motel/cabin resort features large sandy beach, picnic tables, play area, CATV and BBQ grills. In addition to motel rooms, Riptide offers 4, 2-bedroom cabins with equipped kitchens, private baths, linens provided. No pets in summer.

Weekly $270-$540 (cabins assume 6 days)   Daily $45-$90

GREENBUSH

SID'S RESORT   **(517) 739-7638 • (810) 781-3845**
        COTTAGES

✻ E D I T O R ' S   C H O I C E ✻

Property reviewed and featured in the 1997/98 *Michigan Vacation Guide* as a *"highly recommended Premiere Resort"*. 11 cottages set along a sandy stretch of Lake Huron and wooded grounds near many golf courses. 1, 2 or 3 bedroom cottages sleep

2-8. Renovations include cathedral ceilings, knotty pine walls, lofts, color coordinated new furnishings, remodeled kitchens and much more. Amenities: CATV, gameroom, shuffleboard, badminton, playgrounds and picnic areas; watercraft rentals. Open May-Oct. No pets.

Weekly $450-$1,250 (Off-season - weekly or daily rental available)

Editor's Note: Sid's continues to be a favorite of ours on Michigan's sunrise side. Highly recommended. Make reservations early.

SUNNYSIDE COTTAGES
JOHN & DONNA WITTLA

(517) 739-5289
COTTAGES

★ EDITOR'S CHOICE ★

On the sunrise side of Michigan you will find these charming, knotty pine cottages. They offer equipped, tiled kitchens with microwave, stove, refrigerator, coffee maker and all utensils. Large living room (some with sofabed), two bedrooms or two bedrooms and loft. Gas heat, CATV, VCR, BBQ grills, picnic tables and lawn furniture. Close to area activities.

Weekly $650

Editor's Note: Recent major renovations have made this resort a winner. See our review.

MIO

HINCHMAN ACRE RESORT

(800) 438-0203 (MI) • (517) 826-3267
COTTAGES

★ EDITOR'S CHOICE ★

AAA Rated Family Resort. A place for all seasons—something for everyone. Summer—weekly family vaca-tions. Rest of year — secluded getaway weekends. 13 cottages (1-2-3 bedrooms), CATV, A/C, fireplaces, phones, kitchens, cribs, swimming, beach, fishing. Enjoy campfires, playground, gameroom, hiking and mountain bike trails. Canoe trips on AuSable River, canoe, tube, raft and kayak rentals. Cross country ski on groomed tracked trails, ski and snowshoe rentals. Golf, horseback riding, antique shops. Amish community nearby. 3 hours from Detroit. No Pets. Brochure. *Website: www. hinchman.com*

Weekly $275-$525   Daily $50-$150

Editor's Note: Spacious grounds in a natural setting. The resort offers diverse activities with very clean and well maintained lodgings. Good location for a very good price.

OSCODA

ANCHORAGE COTTAGES
CHARLEY & SUE MOSS

(517) 739-7843
COTTAGES

Unpack and relax on our sugar sand beach on Lake Huron. Six clean, comfortable, fully furnished cottages (2-4 bedrooms). CATV, grills, picnic tables, shady backyard, fire pit, horseshoes, swing set. AuSable River nearby. Fish, golf, canoe, hunt, etc. Friendly atmosphere! Pet w/approval/Fee. April-Dec. Major credit cards accepted.

Weekly $450-$650

AUSABLE RIVER RESORT

(517) 739-5246
COTTAGES

Located on the AuSable River. Two bedroom cottages with kitchen and color TV. Only a half mile west of downtown Oscoda and five blocks from the lake. Boat dockage available. No pets.

Call for Rates

BAREFOOT BEACH COTTAGES
PAUL DAVIES

(517) 739-1818
COTTAGES

8 furnished, knotty pine cottages (sleep 4-6) with private showers on 200 ft. of sandy beach along Lake Huron. Safe swimming. Resort features swings, loungers, rowboats, paddleboats, grills, bonfire pit, shuffleboard and volleyball. Linens supplied. Gift shop. Bring towels. $100 deposit. No pets.

Weekly $400-$550   Daily $26-$70

EAST COAST SHORES RESORT
ROY WENNER

(517) 739-0123
CABINS

✸ EDITOR'S CHOICE ✸

New Owner—major renovations completed in 1993-94. Resort rests on 200 ft. of sandy beach, fully furnished, 2-4 bedroom beach front cabins with equipped kitchens (includes microwave, automatic coffeemaker), CATV w/HBO, ceiling fans and screened porch. Enjoy volleyball, badminton, horseshoes, bonfires and swimming. No pets.

Weekly $525-$742   Daily $75-$106

Editor's Note: New owners have done a great job in renovating this older, traditional resort. See our review.

El Cortez Beach Resort

(517) 739-7884
COTTAGES

On Lake Huron, these 1-2 bedroom cottages offer equipped kitchens, gas heat, city water. Some cottages have CATV w/HBO. Linens provided. Enjoy the family fun area, BBQ's, picnic tables and large sandy beach. Fish cleaning station on premises. Wave runner rentals. No pets.

Weekly $445-$1,000   Daily $45 (and up)

Editor's Note: New owners have put major effort into updating this older, cottage resort with good results. The new beach homes were luxurious and were a favorite of ours. Also, great beach. See our review.

Huron House

(517) 739-9255
BED & BREAKFAST

★ EDITOR'S CHOICE ★

Located between Tawas and Oscoda, on a beautiful stretch of sandy Lake Huron beach. Accommodations feature panoramic views of Lake Huron, fireplaces, private hot tubs, in-room Jacuzzis and continental breakfast at your door. Glorious sunrises, romantic moonrises, lighted freighters passing in the night. Perfect romantic getaway!

Daily $75-$145

Editor's Note: Beautifully designed rooms, most with excellent lake views. Charmingly landscaped courtyard. Treat yourself! Highly recommended. See our review.

New AuSable Beach Resort
Ron Teasley

(800) 231-1875
CONDOS/COTTAGES

Located 2 miles south of Oscoda on Lake Huron, these 1-3 bedroom cottages and condos offer fully equipped kitchens, showers, carpeting. Some cottages w/fireplaces. Enjoy horseshoes, playground and sandy beach.

Weekly   Condos $660-$670   Cottages $360-$765

Sand Castle
Karen/Alex Ragia

(517) 739-9881
COTTAGES/MOTEL

New Owners! Nine, 1-2 bedroom cottages are located on the beach. Includes fully equipped kitchen (linens provided), CATV, shuffleboard, volleyball, fish cleaning area and more.

Weekly $475 (and up)

Shady Shores Resort
Kent & Jeanne Lang/Jim & Maryann Gross

(248) 852-1103 • (810) 751-1835
COTTAGES

Six cottages 3 miles south of Oscoda on 200 ft. of sandy beach. Furnished, 2 bedroom cottages with CATV. Kitchens include refrigerator, range and dishes. Linens provided (bring towels). Most have glassed-in porch. Picnic tables, BBQ's, swings, horseshoe pits, basketball and shuffleboard courts. No pets.

Call for Rates

MICHIGAN COTTAGES • CHALETS • CONDOS • B&B'S

SHENANDOAH ON THE   (517) 739-3997 • (941) 352-4639 (WINTER)
LAKE BEACH RESORT   COTTAGES
Six cottages, 2 miles south of Oscoda on Lake Huron w/300' sandy beach.
Features 1 and 2 bedroom cottages and 3 bedroom beachhouses. Each has
fully equipped kitchen (some w/fireplaces), decks, CATV, recreation area,
campfires. Open May-October.

Daily $45-$150 (call for weekly rates)

THOMAS' PARKSIDE COTTAGES   (517) 739-5607
                                              COTTAGES
On Lake Huron with 333 ft. of private beach, the cottages are near the AuSable
River. Includes 2, 1 bedroom and 11, 2 bedroom cottages facing the lake with
enclosed porches, kitchen with stove and refrigerator, CATV. Bring radio and
linens. $100 deposit. No pets.

Weekly $400-$500

ALPENA & THUNDERBAY

COVERS: ATLANTA • HAWKS • HILLMAN • OCQUEOC • ONAWAY •
PRESQUE ISLE • ROGERS CITY

Located on the beautiful sunrise side of Michigan, visitors can enjoy a
variety of activities — summer through winter. Explore **Thunder
Bay's** underwater ruins of sunken ships from another era. Or, for
something a little less exerting, enjoy **Alpena's** "live" theater which presents
year around plays and musicals. The area also offers a wildfowl sanctuary,
lighthouses, and excellent hunting, fishing, cross-country skiing, and golf.
Don't miss July's Brown Trout Festival which lures (excuse the pun...) over
800 fishing contestants to this nine-day event featuring art, food concessions
and nightly entertainment.

While in the area, don't forget to visit one of the Lower Peninsula's largest
waterfalls, Ocqueoc Falls, in **Rogers City**.

ALPENA

GLORIA HASSETT   (517) 734-2066 (AFTER 4 P.M.)
                                               COTTAGE
One, two-bedroom cottage located on US 23 South. It is midway between
Alpena and Rogers City on Grand lake.

Weekly $300

TRELAWNY RESORT

(517) 471-2347
COTTAGES

Resort features 9 attractive, clean and comfortable cottage homes. They have 200 ft. of white sugar sand beach on Lake Huron's beautiful Thunder Bay with 3 acres of restful grounds and tall pines. On-site laundromat and game room. Cottages have fully furnished kitchens and shower bath. No pets.

Weekly $399-$485   Daily $65-$80

ATLANTA

BRILEY INN
CARLA & BILL GARDNER

(800) 824-7443 (RES.) • (517) 785-4784
INN

Elegant redwood inn with impressive windows overlooking Thunder Bay River. Rooms are decorated in Victorian Antique. Great Room, cozy den with fireplace, Jacuzzi, full country breakfast. Canoes and paddleboat available. Central A/C, CATV. Minutes from Elk Ridge, Garland. Golf packages available. Private baths. 5 rooms.

Daily $60-$70

RIVER CABINS

(517) 785-4123
CABINS

One mile west of Atlanta on M32, 1/2 mile south on McArthur and Thunder Bay River. Five, 1-2 bedroom cabins offer furnace heat, cooking facilities, linens, plus a boat with each cabin. Bathhouse w/shower, picnic tables, games and fire ring on premises. One day FREE with a week stay.

Daily $25-$40

HAWKS

NETTIEBAY LODGE
MARK & JACKIE SCHULER

(517) 734-4688
COTTAGES & LODGE

★ EDITOR'S CHOICE ★

Year around on beautiful Lake Nettie. One to 4 bedrooms with full kitchens, living room, private baths (linens available) and lake views. Into bird watching? NettieBay is where you want to go. Join them in classes, seminars and their birding walks. Also enjoy excellent fishing and x-country skiing. No pets.

Weekly $389-$548

Editor's Note: Excellent programs available on birding and other outdoor activities. Natural and picturesque setting. Accommodations basic, clean and comfortable.

HILLMAN

THUNDER BAY RESORT-BEST WESTERN

(800) 729-9375
CONDOMINIUM/VILLAS

* E D I T O R ' S   C H O I C E *

Golf resort featuring luxury suites, whirlpool suites and villas. Each includes bedroom(s), bathroom(s), kitchen, living room, and deck overlooking golf course. 2 restaurants on premises. During winter, Elk viewing sleight ride with gourmet dinner packages, cross-country skiing, snowmobiling, ice skating and romantic getaways.

Call for Rates

Editor's Note: Premiere resort with unique golf course and interesting year around package programs. Wintertime Elk viewing/gourmet dinner program has become very popular.

OCQUEOC

SILVER ROCK RESORT ON OCQUEOC LAKE
STEVE & VICKI KELLAR

(810) 694-3061
COTTAGE

Ocqueoc Lake is a 132 acre lake twenty miles north of Rogers City and three miles west of Lake Huron. 2 bedroom cottage with boat, color TV. ORV and snowmobile trails nearby. Great fishing for bass, walleye, pike, trout and salmon. Open all year. No pets.

Call for Rates

ONAWAY

STILLMEADOW B & B
CAROL LATSCH

(517) 733-2882
BED & BREAKFAST

Flower beds, kitchen garden and berry patch add to the charm of this simple country home, nestled at woods edge, with deck for relaxing and enjoying the view. Four rooms, private baths, queen beds and a country breakfasts. Radios, CATV and stereo in public room. Smoke-free. Pets allowed leashed outside. Major credit cards.

Weekly $350* (and up)   Daily $65* (and up)   *Per Couple

Editor's Note: This charming B&B offers a comfortable and relaxing country atmosphere with freshly prepared, hearty breakfasts. Carol is truly knowledgeable about things to do and see in the area.

PRESQUE ISLE

FIRESIDE INN
(517) 595-6369
COTTAGES/LODGE

Densely wooded surroundings, built in 1908. 17 cottages/cabins and 7 lodge rooms. Some are newly renovated, others maintain a "rustic" image. Private baths. Some kitchens and fireplaces. Lodge offers small sleeping rooms, some with private baths. Tennis, volleyball, ping-pong, horseshoes, shuffleboard. Price includes 2 meals per day. Open Spring through Fall. Pets O.K.

	Rooms	Cabins/Cottages
Daily*	$30-$40	$40-$75
Weekly*	$160-$210	$240-$350

* Price based per adult (children rates somewhat less)

Editor's Note: Historic resort located in a quiet, wooded setting. Cottages range in size with several maintained in rustic condition - sparse and basic furnishings. Several cottages have been renovated/updated.

ROGERS CITY

MANITOU SHORES RESORT
BRUCE/COLLEEN GRANT
(517) 734-7233
COTTAGES/CABINS/MOTEL

Resting along 600 ft. of Lake Huron, this 12 acre resort features 4 cottages, 4 motel units and 3 large log cabins — all with wood decks overlooking the lake. Cottages and cabins include fully equipped kitchens. Log cabins also feature microwave, dishwasher, fireplace with glass sliding doors. A/C and TV/VCR. Evening campfires. Linens provided. One unit with limited handicap access. No pets.

Weekly $450-$900   Daily $60-$200

MACKINAW CITY • MACKINAC ISLAND

Near the tip of the mitt, **Mackinaw City** is located at the southern end of the Mackinac Bridge and offers ferry service (May-October) to Mackinac Island. Known for its sparkling waters and natural beauty, it is visited by thousands of vacationers each year. While in the City, be sure to visit Fort Michilimackinaw. Built in 1715, the Fort was initially used as a trading post by early French settlers before becoming a British military outpost and fur-trading village. Today its costumed staff provide demonstrations and special programs. You'll also want to stop by Mill Creek Park (just east of town). Visit the historic water-powered sawmill and gristmill which re-create one of the first industrial sites. You'll also find ongoing archeological digs and reconstructed buildings here.

Perhaps one of the newest attractions in Mackinaw City is Mackinaw Crossings & Center Stage Theatre. It's northern Michigan's largest entertainment complex. This brightly painted, Victorian-themed outdoor complex boasts over 50 retail shops, six restaurants, a five-plex theatre, unique butterfly house and an arcade. Every hour (during the season) the outdoor amphitheater offers live entertainment plus a free laser light show every night. To add to this is the 850-seat Center Stage Theatre which features live, Broadway-style shows (tickets: 616-436-4053). If you enjoy miniature golf, check out the one right next to the Crossings. The whole family will love it. Then, for another unique treat, try the century-old *Detroit-to-Mackinac Depot Pub & Grill* which has been charmingly restored to reflect the railroad era of yesteryear.

If you're a walker, don't forget the famous Mackinac Bridge Walk on Labor Day. Join in the joy and celebrations with Michigan's Governor and thousands of others who walk the world's longest total suspension bridge.

Visit **Mackinac Island** and step back in time. This vacation land is a haven for those seeking a unique experience. Accessible by ferry, the Island allows only horse-drawn carriages and bicycles to be used as transportation. Historical and scenic, the Island is filled with natural beauty and boasts a colorful past. Explore Old Fort Mackinac where costumed staff perform period military reenactments and demonstrations. In addition, the Fort has an interpretive center that traces military life on the island during the 1800's. Stop for a refreshment or lunch at the fort's *Tea Room* which offers a wonderful, panoramic view of the straits.

Take a carriage tour, visit nearby historic buildings and homes, browse the many shops, and dine at the many restaurants. Enjoy nightly entertainment, golfing, swimming, hiking, horseback riding, and just relaxing on this Michigan resort island. There are also several fine restaurants on the island. For an elegant dining experience, try the 107 year old Grand Hotel's formal dining room. Or, on the northwest side of the island, *Woods* is the spot for a romantic, candlelight dinner

MACKINAW CITY • MACKINAC ISLAND

(continued...)

(located in Stonecliffe, a mansion built in 1905). For more casual dining with very good food, try the *Point Dining Room* at the Mission Point Resort. Hangout with the locals, and try the down-to-earth *Mustang Lounge* (one of the few places open year around). Enjoy your trip to the island ...oh, by the way, don't forget to bring home some fudge.

MACKINAW CITY

THE BEACH HOUSE   (800) 262-5353 • (616) 436-5353
COTTAGES

Situated on 250' of Lake Huron frontage, view the Bridge and Island from these 1-3 bed cottages in Mackinaw City. Units include kitchenettes (no utensils), electric heat, A/C, CATV w/HBO. Coffee and homemade muffins available each morning! Playground, beach, indoor pool and spa on the premises. Small pets O.K.

Daily $39-$125

Editor's Note: Good, clean, comfortable accommodations.

CEDARS RESORT   (616) 537-4748
COTTAGES

Four, 1-2 bedroom cottages on Paradise Lake, just 7 miles south of Mackinaw City. Each unit includes full housekeeping, equipped kitchen, bathroom, gas heat and CATV. 2 units with fireplace (wood furnished). Sandy beach - great for swimming. Boat and dock included. Open year around. $100 deposit.

Weekly $335 (and up)

CHIPPEWA MOTOR LODGE - ON THE LAKE   (800) 748-0124 • (616) 436-8661
MOTEL/COTTAGES

Motel and 2 bedroom cottage units (double/queen size beds) offered. Features sandy beach, CATV, direct dial phones, indoor pool/spa, sun deck, shuffleboard, picnic area. 1 block from ferry docks.

Weekly $250-$750*   Daily $29-$99*

*Based on double occupancy. Rates will vary depending on season.

Editor's Note: Clean and very nicely maintained. Many rooms have cozy, paneled interiors.

MICHIGAN COTTAGES • CHALETS • CONDOS • B&B'S

LAKESHORE PARADISE   **(616) 537-4779 • (810) 268-9119**
                                                                    COTTAGES

Approximately 5 miles south of Mackinaw with 250' lake frontage. Featured are 6, 2 bedroom housekeeping cottages plus one studio with heat, stoves and refrigerators. Some tubs and TV's. Playground, picnic tables, grills on premises, raft in water, boats/dock facilities and bonfire on beach. May 15 to Sept. 15.

Call for Rates

WATERFRONT INN   **(800) 962-9832 • (616) 436-5527**
                                                              MOTEL/COTTAGES

Sitting on 300 ft. of sandy beach, this facility offers full housekeeping cottages along with its motel units. Amenities included CATV w/HBO, A/C and indoor pool. Picnic and playground area on premises. Bridge and Island view.

Weekly $250-$750*   Daily $29-$99*
*Based on double occupancy. Rates will vary depending on season.

MACKINAC ISLAND

BAY VIEW AT MACKINAC   **(906) 847-3295**
DOUG YODER   BED & BREAKFAST

☀ E D I T O R ' S   C H O I C E ☀

This Victorian home offers grace and charm in romantic turn-of-the century tradition along with the comfort of today. It is the only facility of its type and style sitting at the water's edge. Deluxe continental breakfast served from harbor-view veranda. Private baths. Open May 1-Oct. 15. 17 rooms. Major credit cards.

Daily $95-$290

Editor Note: Located in a quiet section on the Island's main road. This lovely B&B directly overlooks the water. All rooms have views. It's a bit of a walk from the docks...but that's Mackinac.

CLOGHAUN   **(906) 847-3885 • WINTER (313) 331-7110**
JAMES BOND   BED & BREAKFAST

This large Victorian home is convenient to shops, restaurants and ferry lines. Built in 1884, it was the home of Thomas and Bridgett Donnelly's large Irish family. Today guests enjoy the many fine antiques, ambiance and elegance of a bygone era. Open May-Nov. 11 rooms.

Daily $90-$140 (plus tax)

GREAT TURTLE LODGE
NORM BAUMAN

(800) 206-2124 • (906) 847-6237
CONDOS/APARTMENTS

Newly renovated in 1993, these two condos/apartments offer fully equipped kitchens, Jacuzzis (TV and VCR available). One bedroom sleeps 4-5, two bedroom sleeps 7-8. Located in a quiet wooded area of the Island — close to town. Minimum 2-3 night stay. Open year around.

	1 Bedroom	2 Bedroom
Daily	$180	$200
Weekly	$1,000	$1,200

HAAN'S 1830 INN   SUMMER (906) 847-6244 • WINTER (847) 526-2662
NICHOLAS & NANCY HAAN
BED & BREAKFAST

Historic home, built in Greek Revival style, furnished in period antiques. The earliest building was used as an inn in both Michigan and Wisconsin. Continental breakfast on the wicker filled porch. Featured in <u>Detroit Free Press</u>, <u>Chicago Tribune</u>, <u>Chicago Sun Times</u> and <u>Sears Discovery Magazine</u>. Open May 21-Oct. 18. 7 rooms (5/private baths, 2/shared baths).

Daily $80-$150

JOE'S ISLAND GETAWAY
JOE DRESSLER

(800) 631-5767
PRIVATE CONDOMINIUM UNIT

Enjoy your romantic Mackinac Island stay in our luxurious condo. Old World charm with all of today's amenities. Breathtaking view, jacuzzi, fireplace, balcony. Hiking, biking, tennis and Grand golf course nearby.

Call for Rates

LAKEBLUFF CONDOS AT STONECLIFFE -   (800) 699-6927 • (847) 699-6927
PENTHOUSE STUDIO SUITE (OAKWOOD BLDG.)
PRIVATE CONDOMINIUM UNIT

Located high atop the West Bluff of Mackinac Island. Beautiful one room suite sleeps two with a solarium overlooking a breathtaking view of the Straits of Lake Huron and the Mackinac Bridge. Cathedral ceiling with skylights, Jacuzzi next to fireplace, private balconies, queen size bed. Small dining area. Kitchen with microwave, bar refrigerator,

CATV, TV/VCR. Golf course. Daily maid service. No smoking. *Website: www.mackinac.com/lakebluff/*

Daily: $225 (In Season); $205 (Off Season) Mid-week, 2 Night Minimum

MICHIGAN COTTAGES • CHALETS • CONDOS • B&B'S

LAKEBLUFF CONDOS AT STONECLIFFE - **(800) 699-6927 • (847) 699-6927**
GARDENVIEW STUDIO SUITE (OAKWOOD BLDG.) **PRIVATE CONDOMINIUM UNIT**

Located high atop the West Bluff of Mackinac Island. Charming one room suite, sleeps two, features small kitchenette, wet bar, microwave and small refrigerator. Queen size bed, sofa, Jacuzzi with separate shower. Bayed sliding patio doors take you to balcony and overlook of Stonecliffe's gardens and grounds. CATV, TV/VCR. Golf course. Daily maid service. No smoking. *Website: www.mackinac.com/lakebluff*

Daily: $165 (In Season); $155 (Off Season) Mid-week, 2 Night Minimum

METIVIER INN **SUMMER (906) 847-6234 •** **EMAIL: metinn@light-house.net**
GEORGE & ANGELA LEONARD **BED & BREAKFAST**
Originally built in 1877 and recently renovated, the Inn offers bedrooms with queen size beds, private baths, and one efficiency unit. Relax on the large wicker filled front porch and cozy living room with a wood burner. Deluxe continental breakfast served. Open May-October. 22 rooms. *Website: www.mackinac.com/metivier.index.html*

Daily $115-$255

HOUGHTON LAKE • CHEBOYGAN • BOIS BLANC ISLAND

COVERS: BURT LAKE • GAYLORD • GRAYLING • HARRISON • HIGGINS LAKE • LEWISTON • MULLETT LAKE

Houghton Lake, where hunters and vacationers thrive on one of Michigan's largest inland lakes. Enjoy hunting, boating, water skiing, cross-country skiing, and snowmobiling. Ice fishing for walleyes, bass and bluegill is so good it merits its own annual event. Each year, the Tip-Up-Town U.S.A. Festival (held mid to late January) offers a variety of events including contests, parades and games for the entire family.

Known as the "Alpine Village", **Gaylord** has more to offer than just great downhill and x-country skiing or groomed snowmobile trails. Try their championship

HOUGHTON LAKE • CHEBOYGAN • BOIS BLANC ISLAND

(*continued....*)

golf courses or terrific year around fishing. Nearby, in the Pigeon River State Forest, roams the largest elk herd east of the Mississippi.

Grayling's historical logging background is preserved at Crawford County Historical Museum and Hartwick Pines State Park. Grayling is also the area for canoeing and trout fishing enthusiasts. In fact, the area is known as the Canoe Capital of Michigan. It is the spot for the internationally famous Weyerhaeuser Canoe Marathon which takes place the last week of July. During this event, up to 50 teams of paddlers attempt to finish a gruelling 120-mile course which can take up to 18 hours to complete. This event is considered one of the most demanding endurance races in any sporting event. Televised broadcasts reach over 150 countries worldwide. The popular AuSable River Festival takes place the week of the Marathon. The festival abounds with numerous activities which include a major parade, juried art shows, antique car shows, ice cream socials, special canoe tours, and several amateur and youth canoe races.

Cheboygan continues the chain of great year around fishing, skiing, snowmobiling, swimming and golf. Be sure to visit Cheboygan's Opera House built in 1877. This restored Victorian theater still offers great entertainment on the same stage that once welcomed Mary Pickford and Annie Oakley!

Seeking an island retreat without all the crowds? **Bois Blanc Island** is your spot. Referred to as *Bob-lo* by the locals, this quiet, unspoiled island is only a short boat ride from Cheboygan and Mackinac Island. One main road (unpaved) takes you around the Island (cars are permitted). Great for nature hikes, private beaches, boating and relaxing. Here is a community of century homes and a remote lighthouse. While visiting, stop at the *Boathouse Restaurant* or the *Bois Blanc Tavern* and meet some of the warm and friendly year around residents.. The Island is accessible by two ferry boat services (runs several times per day). Be sure to call ahead and reserve a spot if you plan on bringing your car (Plaunt Transportation: (616) 627-2354 or The Island Ferry Service (616) 627-9445 or (616) 627-7878).

BOIS BLANC ISLAND

BOIS BLANC ISLAND RETREAT
GRAM/LINDA MCGEORGE

(616) 846-4391
COTTAGE

* E D I T O R ' S   C H O I C E *

Secluded, four bedroom, waterfront cottage on quiet protected bay. Surrounded by white pines and cedar forest. Beautiful view of Lake Huron and the Straits Channel. Cottage offers all the conveniences in a private setting — just bring groceries and fishing pole. Relax, fish, hike, swim, explore, boat mooring. Mackinac Island 8 Miles. Open May-Nov. Car ferry. No pets.

Weekly $525-$750
(Off-season weekend $300)

Editor's Note: Comfortable and clean cottage with renovations completed in 1995. Great island retreat with natural grounds and sandy beach.

BURT LAKE

MILLER'S GUEST HOUSE ON BURT LAKE
JESS & PAM MILLER

(616) 238-4492
VACATION HOME

One-of-a-kind spacious Burt Lake guest house. Recently built to exacting standards for our personal friends and family. Now available for up to 4 non-smoking guests. Complete kitchen, private sandy beach. Brilliant sunsets, quiet wooded atmosphere. Ideal for swimming, sailing, canoeing, bicycling. No pets. Open year around.

Weekly $600 ($350 off-season)

SHARON PRESSEY   **SUMMER (906) 643-7733 • WINTER (561) 229-1599**
COTTAGES/HOME

2 and 3 bedroom cottages. 150' water frontage. One with loft, one with fireplace, one with dishwasher. All have decks overlooking water, fully equipped kitchens, cable TV, gas grills & row boat. Bedding provided. Terrific walleye and bass fishing. Smoking allowed, pets upon approval. Open April-Oct.

Weekly $700-$850 ($375-$475 off-season)

CHEBOYGAN & MULLETT LAKE

LAKEWOOD COTTAGES   **SUMMER (616) 238-7476 • WINTER (248) 887-5570**
KEITH R. PHILLIPS
COTTAGES

Clean comfortable 2-3 bedroom cottages located on Mullett Lake, with lake frontage. Screened porches, CATV, carpeted, fully equipped kitchens, showers, picnic tables, grills, boats and motors for rent. Buoys for private boats, swimming, fishing, 24' pontoon boat and evening bonfires. Pets allowed. Open May-Sept.

Weekly $340-$400   Daily $60-$65

THE PINES OF LONG LAKE   **(616) 625-2121 • (616) 625-2145**
COTTAGES

Year around resort, 1-3 bedroom cottages. 2 bedroom cabins with 2 double beds face the lake, shared shower building. 1 & 3 bedroom cottages with private showers. All have stoves, refrigerators, limited utensils, gas heat, blankets/pillows (bring linens). Bar/restaurant on premises. Pets allowed ($10 add'l).

Weekly $225-$275   Daily $50-$60

VEERY POINTE RESORT ON MULLETT LAKE   **(616) 627-7328**
FRED SMITH & DEBBIE SOCHA
COTTAGES/MOTEL

Lakefront cottages, open year around. Fully furnished (except linens—linens available), includes microwave, CATV/HBO & Disney. Picnic area. Motel with efficiencies (some with A/C) across from lake, beach privileges. Docks. Good fishing, x-country skiing, skating and snowmobiling. Ask about pets.

Weekly $300-$1,000 (Motel: $25-80 Daily)

GAYLORD

BEAVER CREEK RESORT   (877) 295-3333
LARRY BOWDEN   CABINS
Four Season Resort. Sometimes the best cure for cabin fever is a better cabin. Beautiful 1 and 2 bedroom fully furnished log cabins. Enjoy our indoor pool, Jacuzzi, sauna, 18 hole championship golf course, waterslide and putt-putt golf. No pets. *Website: www.bcrthenatural.com*

Daily $51-$136

MARSH RIDGE   (800) 743-PLAY
HOTEL/TOWNHOUSES/CHALET(LODGE)
Unique decor and themes throughout. Some Jacuzzi rooms, king size beds, microwaves, refrigerators and remote TV's. Townhouses with full kitchen, living room, bath and bedroom downstairs (upstairs sleeping loft) and 2nd bath. Swimming pool, shops and more on premises. No pets.

	Hotel/Suites	Townhouses/Lodge
Daily	$89 (and up)	$120 (and up)

POINTES NORTH   (517) 732-4493
BETSY BERRY   VACATION HOMES
Five private, lakefront vacation homes for day, week or month rental. Sizes vary from 3 to 4 bedrooms. Properties vary from sophisticated country to cozy, log cabin and chalet styling. All are set in secluded locations and come fully furnished and equipped, including rowboat, CATV and telephone. No pets.

Weekly $700-$1,200

Editor's Note: All of Betsy's lodgings are very comfortable with good locations.

TREETOPS SYLVAN RESORT   (888) TREETOPS • (517) 732-6711
CONDOS/CHALET/EFFICIENCY
Standard, deluxe accommodations—condominiums, efficiencies and chalets. 81 holes of championship golf, 19 downhill ski runs and 14 km. of groomed, x-country trails. Dining room, grill and sports bar on premises. Plus indoor/outdoor pools, spas, fitness center, state licensed day care, Edelweiss Ski and Sports Shop.

Daily $69 (and up)

GRAYLING

BORCHERS BED & BREAKFAST   **(800) 762-8756 • (517) 348-4921**
MARK & CHERI HUNTER   **BED & BREAKFAST**

* E D I T O R ' S   C H O I C E *

The friendly hosts at Borchers invite you to enjoy a unique riverfront experience on the banks of the AuSable. Six rooms, twin/double beds (shared baths) and queen beds (private baths). Full breakfasts. Canoe rentals. Smoking permitted on porch. Open year around. *Website: www.borchers.com*

Daily $59-$69 (shared bath); $64-$89 (private bath)

Editor's Note: This delightful retreat will make a great place to begin your AuSable River vacation.

HARRISON

LAKESIDE MOTEL & COTTAGES   **(517) 539-3796**
BOBBIE & GARY SAGER   **MOTEL/COTTAGES**

Modern cottages located on Budd Lake. Private beach and picnic area. 2 cottages with 2 bedrooms (sleeps 5); 1 with 1 room (sleeps 2). Available nightly or weekly from April-November. Great fishing, hunting, golfing nearby. Casino gaming 28 expressway miles away. No pets.

Weekly $275 (+ tax per week)

SNUG HAVEN LAKESIDE RESORT AND   **(517) 539-8117**
WATERCRAFT RENTAL   **COTTAGES**

Fully furnished housekeeping cottages on Budd Lake, a 175-acre all sports lake. Located on 200 ft. of sandy beach, all cottages have decks, picnic tables and gas grills. Open May-November. Jet skis, pontoons and fishing boats available for rent. Excellent bass, muskie and pan fishing. Pets welcome with cleaning fee.

Weekly $450-$525

HIGGINS LAKE

BIRCH LODGE   **(517) 821-6261**
    COTTAGES

This 50 year old resort rests along the shores of Higgins Lake. The 17 cottages (1-3 bedroom/no kitchens) are simply furnished, maintained in great condition and sit in a semi-circle facing the water. Sandy beach. Gathering room features TV w/VCR. Meals are included in price. Open May-Oct.

Weekly $555*   Daily $90*
(* per adult; children less)

Editor's Note: We understand from guests that pretty tasty meals are served here.

CEDAR SHORE CABINS   (810) 629-6657
RICK DIXON   Email: reservations@higginslake.com

CABINS

Enjoy one of the most beautiful lakes in the world! At the Cedar Shore, you can choose the cabin that's right for you. We have small, medium, or large depending on your needs. All of this located on 100 ft. of lakefront on the northwest shore of Higgins Lake. There is a gravel road that separates the cabins from the beach.

Website: www.higginslake.com

Weekly: $600-$1,200

MORELL'S HIGGINS LAKE COTTAGE   (517) 821-6885
COTTAGE

Overlooking the south end of beautiful Higgins Lake, this immaculate, cozy cottage sits on a nicely wooded lot and is fully furnished w/equipped kitchen, two bedrooms and nursery. Cottage sleeps 5-6. Includes use of rowboat and a 4000 lb. hoist. No pets.

Weekly (Summer) $742   (After Labor Day thru Memorial Day — special rates.)

REZNICH'S COTTAGES   (517) 821-9282
COTTAGES

Clean, comfortable 3, 2 bedroom cottages on Higgins Lake. Tiled floors, private bath, gas heat and equipped kitchen. BBQ, picnic table and rowboat included in rental price. All cottages are close to the water, one directly overlooks the lake and features knotty pine interior.

Weekly $500-$550

HOUGHTON LAKE

BAY BREEZE RESORT & MOTEL   (517) 366-7721
MANFRED & DIANE BOEHMER   COTTAGES/MOTEL

2 large cottages (sleep 6) and spacious kitchenette motel rooms with 2 double beds on Houghton Lake. Private sandy beach, CATV, picnic tables, BBQ grills, horseshoes, boat dockage. Linens provided. Pontoon, boat/motor, wave runners and bicycle rentals available. Open year around.

Weekly $315-$485   Daily $50-$75

BEECHWOOD RESORT

(517) 366-5512
COTTAGES

2-3 bedroom, fully furnished, log cabins with fireplaces (wood provided), equipped kitchens (linens provided), private baths. Boat included with each cabin. Shuffleboard, horseshoes, swings. Good swimming beach and very good fishing.

Weekly $400   Daily $60

THE CREST

(517) 366-7758 • (248) 363-9485
COTTAGES/EFFICIENCIES

Lakefront lodgings (3 cottages/3 efficiencies) feature nicely maintained, very clean facilities inside and out! Furnishings in good condition and comfortable. Complete kitchens, picnic table and grill. Ping pong, horseshoes, basketball, paddlewheeler and swim raft. No pets.

Weekly $305-$485

Editor's Note: Cute cottages ... nicely maintained.

DRIFTWOOD RESORT   RESERVATIONS: (800) 442-8316 • (517) 422-5229
BOB & SHEILA BLESSING   CABINS

Modern lakefront resort on 2 wooded acres on the north shore. 7 housekeeping cabins (4 log cabins with fireplaces and microwaves) include porches, swings, color TV, full kitchens, electric coffeemakers, 14 ft. boat, picnic table and grill. Excellent playground with basketball, volleyball, horseshoes, swings, etc. Motor and paddle boat rental. Open all year. No pets.

Weekly $375-$575 (Call for daily rates.)

HIDEAWAY RESORT

(517) 366-9142
MARYANN PRZYTULSKI   COTTAGES

A clean and well kept resort on Houghton Lake features 4 cottages (2 bedrooms) with full kitchens. 3 cottages directly face the water. Sandy swimming beach. Rowboat included, dock available. Pets allowed.

Weekly $400-$425

LAZY DAYS ASSOC. COTTAGES

(810) 979-2819
COTTAGES

Near Tip-Up-Town site on the shores of Houghton Lake. Features 100 ft. sandy beach with 124 ft. dock. Cottages fully furnished and equipped. Kitchens include microwaves. Queen size beds, CATV. Boats available.

Call for Rates

MICHIGAN COTTAGES • CHALETS • CONDOS • B&B'S

LAGOON RESORT & MOTEL (517) 422-5761 • RESERVATIONS: (888) 215-4711
DON & ELLEN THOMAS COTTAGES/MOTEL

A Houghton Lake favorite. This resort offers 8, 2 and 3 bedroom cottages; 4, 2 bedroom apartments; and 3 motel rooms. It features 260' water frontage with a sandy beach, water slide, boat ramp and dockage, huge lighted playground, shuffleboard, and horseshoe court. Pontoon, outboard motors, jet ski, hydro-bikes and ice shanty rentals. Free use of rowboat. Walking distance to 2 amusement parks and restaurant. Open all year. Call for daily rates and off-season rates. No pets.

Weekly $280-$620

MILLER'S LAKESHORE RESORT (248) 652-4240
DOUG MILLER COTTAGES/CHALET

Open all year. Good swimming, fishing, hunting, snowmobiling and ice fishing. New chalet with fireplace. Modern lakefront housekeeping cottages. Large unit with fireplace. Boats with cottages. Motor rentals. Dockage. Safe sandy beach. Large playground. Grill and picnic tables. Ice shanty. On snowmobile trails. Located at Tip-Up-Town, Zone 10. 306 Festival Drive. Visitors by approval. No pets.

Weekly $420-$560

MORRIS'S NORTHERNAIRE RESORT (517) 422-6644
WES & MARY MORRIS COTTAGES

1-2 bedroom housekeeping cabins on Michigan's largest inland lake. Dock and 14' boat included. Cabins feature all kitchen items, microwave and drip coffeemaker, HBO TV. Open all year. Hunting, fishing, snowmobiling, cross-country skiing, water activities. No pets. Mobile Travel Club quality rated.

Weekly $250-$550 Daily $50-$100

SHADY VALLEY RESORT (517) 366-5403
COTTAGES

Fully furnished 2, 3 and 4 bedroom cottages. Equipped kitchens, color TV and carpeting. Some with screened porches. Newly built cottages available. Boat included. Motors, pontoons, canoes, snowmobile, ice shanty rentals available. Playground, grills, lawn furniture, fire pit on beach. Handicap access. Laundry facilities. Open all year. Pets allowed.

Weekly $450-$600 Daily $65-$100

Editor's Note: Traditional cabins nicely maintained. Cottage closest to the water has great view of Houghton Lake.

SONGER'S LOG CABINS
KATHY

(517) 366-5540
COTTAGES

★ EDITOR'S CHOICE ★

Open year around, these clean and well maintained log cabins are located on the north shore of Houghton Lake with 150' lake frontage. Each two bedroom cabin features fully equipped kitchens, cable TV, private baths, screened porches and use of 14 ft. boat. Several have natural fireplaces. Paddle boat, pontoon boat, tether ball, swimming and more. No pets (except for fall).

Weekly   *$475-$570 (summer)   Daily $65-$85 (winter)
*Rates reduced in winter

Editor's Note: Clean and cozy log cabins by the water...good choice for the area.

TRADEWINDS RESORT
PAUL & KIM CARRICK

(517) 422-5277
COTTAGES

Year around resort. Cottages are carpeted, fully furnished with equipped kitchens, private bath/showers, double beds, CATV. Boats included with rentals. Motors and pontoon boats available. Facilities set on spacious grounds with sandy beach. Horseshoes, volleyball, shuffleboard, playground on premises. Provide your own linens and paper products.

Weekly $450-$500 (off-season rates available)

WEST SHORE RESORT

(517) 422-3117
COTTAGES

★ EDITOR'S CHOICE ★

Nicely maintained, clean and comfortable, small 2 bedroom (sleep up to 6) cottages are fully furnished with equipped kitchens. The cottage closest to the water is more spacious with a direct water view. Provide your own linens/towels during prime season (June-Aug.). $150 deposit. No pets.

Weekly $385-$676

Editor's Note: Mostly smaller but well maintained, clean cottages. The cottage nearest to the lake is good sized, comfortable and had a great view of the lake.

THE WOODBINE VILLA

(517) 422-5349
COTTAGES

On 300 ft. of sandy beach, these 2 bedroom log cottages are gas heated and include CATV. All are fully furnished with equipped kitchens. Includes use of playground and paddle boats. Modern baths and saunas. Visit our game room.

Weekly $325-$625

LEWISTON

GORTON HOUSE BED & BREAKFAST
LOIS & TOM GORTON

(517) 786-2764
BED & BREAKFAST

Relaxing, peaceful Cape Cod on Little Wolf Lake. Antique "theme" rooms. Canoe, boats, putting green, 1920 pool table, fireplaces. Gazeboed outdoor hot tub. Bountiful breakfast, chocolate chip cookies. Garland Golf package. XC skiing, snowmobiling, antiquing, mushroom hunting, nearby golf courses. Gaylord 20 miles. Six rooms with private baths. Open all year.

Weekly $70-$120

LAKEVIEW HILLS COUNTRY INN RESORT &
NORDIC SKI CENTER

(517) 786-2000
INN/BED & BREAKFAST

* E D I T O R ' S   C H O I C E *

14 rooms furnished in authentic antiques feature different eras in American history. Private baths, CATV and individually controlled heating and A/C. Enjoy the beautifully groomed pro-croquet court, fitness center with whirlpool, sauna and exercise equipment. Full breakfast served with kitchen privileges. Relax in the great room, observatory, library or 165 foot porch. In the winter, enjoy 20 km. of groomed cross-country ski trails.

Daily $89-$135

Editor's Note: Contemporary country styling, beautiful views in a secluded wooded setting. A professional croquet court adds an interesting touch.

PINE RIDGE LODGE   (517) 786-4789 • **EMAIL: pineridg@northland.lib.mi.us**
DOUG & SUZAN STILES   **LODGE**

Grand 7 bedroom log lodge located in the AuSable Forest. Perfect for family holidays, work retreats and couples getaways. Unlimited recreation. Cross-country skiing and mountain biking on-site. Snowshoe rentals, outdoor hot-tub, pool table, fireplace, dart boards and wet bar. Full breakfasts served. Lunch/dinner service upon request. First class amenities with rustic charm. Open year around.

Daily: $54-$89

REGION 3

REGION 3

After crossing the "Big Mac's" five mile span, you will see a place of remote beauty where the interstate highways are nonexistent and fast food restaurants and motel chains are hard to find. In their place are roads "off the beaten path" surrounded by natural beauty, family-run cottages, inns and cafes.

You will walk in the footsteps of our Forefathers and view the marvels of their ingenuity. You are entering a land of a unique combination of dense, unspoiled wilderness, wildlife of all types, streams and waterfalls, yet unnamed mountains and rock formations millions of years old.

You are entering the land of Hiawatha and Gitche Gumee.

ST. IGNACE • SAULT STE. MARIE

COVERS: BARBEAU • CEDARVILLE • DRUMMOND ISLAND • SUGAR ISLAND

St. Ignace is a community established in 1671 by the Ojibwa, Huron, and Ottawa tribes. The French Father, Jacques Marquette, was the first priest at the Mission of St. Ignace and became famous for his travels of the Great Lakes and Mississippi River. He is buried outside a 150 year old church which is now a museum in the Father Marquette State Park, located at the base of the Mackinac Bridge. Native American pow-wows are still held outside the mission church. Some are open to the public with the most popular being held Labor Day Weekend. Be sure to see the Marquette Mission Park and the Museum of Ojibwa Culture where you'll learn about Native Americans at the Straits of Mackinac.

An hour's drive north is **Sault Ste. Marie** (meaning the Rapids of St. Mary), the oldest community in Michigan. The Indians once considered this area their summer gathering and fishing place and the first Jesuit missionaries arrived in 1641. It is often referred to as the Gateway to the North.

Starting at the Sault, you will see the Great Rapids white waters as Lake Superior feeds into Lake Huron. The Soo Locks, an engineering marvel, were built in 1855 to raise or lower vessels up to 1,000 ft. in length through these white waters. Take a boat tour through the Locks, experience the feeling and wonder at the ingenuity of man. Afterwards, walk the path to historic churches and homes and visit the Tower of History. Of course, you must take time to relax and enjoy one of Lake Superior's many sandy beaches. For all those wanting to give Lady Luck a try, this is also the home of The Kewadin Casino, one of the largest casinos in this region. In winter, this region becomes a snowmobilers' heaven. It's also the spot for many winter festivals and outdoor events.

There are several good restaurants in the Sault Ste. Marie area. *Antler's* has been a favorite among vacationers for years. The atmosphere here is fun and laid back and the decor a taxidermist's fantasy with numerous stuffed wildlife found throughout. Expect loud whistles, bells and plenty of good hamburgers (the menu is a fun read, too). If you have a taste for Mexican, try *The Palace Restaurant* or, for an Upper Peninsula flavor, *Abner's Restaurant* is the spot for a traditional "Yooper's" menu which includes, of course, their special pasty. A quieter atmosphere, with good Italian food can be found at *Ang-gio's Restaurant.*

Accessible by ferry, **Drummond Island** is a wilderness paradise. Its natural beauty and wildlife are protected by state and federal laws. The island features over 110 miles of hiking and snowmobile trails and is a wonderful experience for those seeking peace and quiet in natural surroundings. But don't expect total wilderness here. Excellent golfing and refined accommodations are available at the popular Woodmoor. It served as the Domino Pizza's executive retreat for several years and is now opened to the public.

BARBEAU

CHANNEL VIEW RESORT
RICHARD COX

(906) 647-7915
COTTAGES

Located 20 miles southeast of Sault Ste. Marie on the St. Mary's River, the resort offers spectacular views of long ships, and has excellent fishing. Housekeeping units feature 2 bedrooms, double beds, heater, stove with cookware, refrigerator, and color TV.

Weekly $200

RIVERVIEW RESORT & MARINA
AL & ROSIE SCHWARTZ

(906) 647-3033
CABINS

Located 23 miles southeast of the Soo Locks. All units overlook St. Mary's River. Four housekeeping cabins with private bath/shower, complete kitchen, 2 bedrooms (linens included). TV, screened porch, dock and boat ramp. Boat and motor rentals available. Great fishing. Pets allowed on a leash.

Weekly $250*   (assumes 2 people - $5 add'l per person)
Receive a 10% Discount when you mention this listing.

CEDARVILLE

ISLAND VIEW RESORT, INC.
LARRY & JACKIE

(906) 484-2252 • (800) 854-0556
COTTAGES

Two and 3 bedroom cottages with carpeting, showers, gas heat and ranges, refrigerators, dishes and cooking utensils. Linens furnished except towels and wash cloths. Fish cleaning house and freezer. Children's playground. Good swimming area. Great fishing. Boats and pontoon available. Major credit cards.

Weekly $430-$635

DRUMMOND ISLAND

BRETT'S HIDE-A-WAY
BRETT DAVIS

(508) 533-6087 • EMAIL: babybasa@tiac.net
COTTAGE

Log cottage built in 1993 with water view. Located in a quiet wooded lot 300 ft. from the road. Fully equipped and furnished for comfort. CATV, VCR, ceiling fan, 16 ft. boat with 30 HP motor ($175 add'l. weekly), boat dock across the road. New hot tub. *Website: www.tiac.net/users/babybasa*

Weekly $500   Daily $90

CAPTAINS COVE RESORT
TRISH BRUGGER

(906) 493-5344
COTTAGES

Nine remodeled, 1- 2 bedroom cottages in a wooded area on Gold Coast Shores in the heart of Potagnnissing Bay. Some lakefront cabins with fireplaces. All are completely furnished light housekeeping cottages, automatic heat, bathrooms with showers. Boat included. $100 refundable deposit. No pets.

Weekly $300-$350 (4 people)

WA-WEN RESORT
PHIL & MARCIA STITES

(906) 493-5445 • (520) 574-5244 (WINTER)
CABINS

10 acre resort on Maxton Bay near the mouth of the Potagnnissing River. Housekeeping cabins have 1-4 bedrooms. Equipped kitchens, electric stoves, bed linens and towels. Aluminum boat, fish cleaning house, electric scaler and freezer available. Tackle shop. Enjoy shuffleboard, fire-pit, basketball/badminton court, picnic tables, charcoal grills and outdoor pool.

Weekly $330-$530 (prices subject to change, off-season rates available)

WOODMOOR

(800) 999-6343
HOMES/LODGE

❋ E D I T O R ' S   C H O I C E ❋

From family reunions to corporate retreats, Woodmoor offers privacy and comfort on 2,000 acres of beautiful woods and waters. Challenging golf at the "Rock" - considered one of the best courses in the Midwest. Eight homes have stone fireplaces, full kitchens and 1-5 bedrooms. The Lodge offers 40 rooms. Restaurant on premises. Boats, pontoon rentals. Island botanical trips offered throughout the seasons.

Weekly $1,000-$2,750 (cottages)   Daily $69-$550 (lodge or cottages)

Editor's Note: Former Domino Pizza executive retreat. Luxury accommodations with a rustic ambiance. Excellent golf and vacation resort.

ST. IGNACE

BALSAM'S RESORT
BETTY

(906) 643-9121
COTTAGES/MOTEL

At the Straits of Mackinac, 5 miles west of Big Mac, these "real log" cabins have fireplaces and are furnished with equipped kitchens. Linens included. Sorry, no heat. Safe, sandy swimming beach, night bonfires, picnic, playground, shuffleboard, horseshoes, volleyball and badminton/croquet court. Serving guests for over 65 years.

Weekly $455-$490   Daily $65-$90

MICHIGAN COTTAGES • CHALETS • CONDOS • B&B'S

COTTAGE ON THE STRAITS
JIM & DIANNE MASTERS

(612) 646-2915 • (612) 690-0590
COTTAGE

Old world charm, modern amenities, and a spectacular view of the Mackinac Bridge and Island from 100 ft. of private lakeshore. Spacious cottage, newly renovated. Antiques, wicker, quilts, fireplace, screened porch. Sleeps 6. Close to shops, restaurants, ferry. Open year around. No pets/no smoking.

Weekly $700 July/Aug. (Call for other rates/times)

SAULT STE. MARIE

RIVER COVE CONDOMINIUMS - WATERFRONT
AL & LUCY TIPTON

(906) 632-7075
CONDOS/HOUSEBOAT

＊ EDITOR'S CHOICE ＊

Waterfront, two bedroom condos completely furnished in nautical themes. CATV, VCR. Docks available. Handicap access. Also, 34 ft. houseboat, fully furnished. Great view of passing ships. Two miles from Kewadin casinos and Soo Locks. Casino packages available. Open April-December. No pets. *Website: www.rivercove.com*

Weekly $500-$800   Daily $79-$149

Editor's Note: Contemporary, nicely decorated and very comfortable condos. Great spot to watch the big ships pass. Highly recommended.

THE WATER STREET INN
ANNA HENION

(800) 236-1904 • (906) 632-1900
BED & BREAKFAST

1900's Queen Anne home overlooking the St. Mary's River has stained glass windows, Italian marble fireplaces and original woodwork. A wide wraparound porch for watching passing freighters promises a special visit whatever the season. North country breakfast served in an elegant dining room. Only B&B in Sault Ste. Marie. Walk to Locks and fine restaurants. 4 rooms/private baths.

Daily $75-$105

SUGAR ISLAND

BENNETT'S LANDING

(906) 632-2987
CABINS

This fishing resort located on the shores of Big Lake George, has been newly remodeled including a new general store. The cabins offer linens, full kitchen, heat, handicap access and a boat. Rent boats, motors, bait. Propane for RVs. Open April 1-Oct. 15.

Weekly $275   Daily $60

BREVORT • PARADISE • GRAND MARAIS

COVERS: BLANEY PARK • CURTIS • GULLIVER • HULBERT • NEWBERRY • TROUT LAKE

As you travel along M123, stop at **Hulbert** and plan a trip on the Tom Sawyer River Boat and Paul Bunyon Timber Train, or the Toonerville Trolley and River Boat. Both offer 4-1/2 hour round trips to the Tahquamenon Falls with commentary on fauna, flora and various points of interest. Then on to **Paradise**, only 10 miles from the second largest waterfall east of the Mississippi River. It is sometimes called Little Niagara, for here lies Tahquamenon Falls in all its glory. Not far away is Whitefish Point, site of an Audubon Bird Observatory. When you're in the area, be sure to tour the Great Lakes Shipwreck Museum. This is where you will find the "Graveyard of the Great Lakes" and the first Lighthouse of Lake Superior.

Grand Marais is the Eastern Gateway to the Pictured Rocks National Lakeshore. This lovely, unspoiled village offers it all — ladyslippers and trillium, white-tailed deer, black bear, Canadian lynx, moose and — even our own bald eagle resides in this beautiful Upper Peninsula wilderness. As might be expected, boating, fishing, hunting, skiing, and snowmobiling are the thing to do in this area. The Grand Marais Historical Museum, Pictured Rocks Maritime Museum, and the AuSable Lighthouse are some of its attractions. But, of course while you are here, you must be sure to explore their many scenic overlooks including the Log Slide, Munising Falls, Sable Falls and don't forget the unforgettable Tahquamenon Falls and the beautiful Pictured Rocks along Gitche Gumee (Lake Superior). This area is a photographer's dream—bring your camera!

If you're in the **Gulliver** area, enjoy a casual meal at *Fisher's Old Deerfield Inn* which features an informal log cabin atmosphere and quaint dining room.

BLANEY PARK

BLANEY COTTAGES

(906) 283-3163
COTTAGES

11 cottages, 1-3 bedrooms with fireplace, gas heat and color TV (no kitchens). Continental breakfast. Smoking/non-smoking cabins, picnic areas with gas grills and tables. On 40 acres, bike and snowmobile trails at your door. Seney National Wildlife Refuse nearby. Open all year. Pets O.K.

Daily $35-$120

MICHIGAN COTTAGES • CHALETS • CONDOS • B&B'S

CELIBETH HOUSE   **(906) 283-3409**
ELSA R. STROM   **BED & BREAKFAST**
This lovely home on 85 acres overlooks Lake Anne Louise. Rooms are clean, spacious, and comfortably furnished. Guests may enjoy the cozy living room, a quiet reading room, a comfortably furnished front porch, and a spacious deck. Continental breakfast. No smoking. 7 rooms. Mastercard/Visa.
Daily $50-$78

BREVORT

CLEARWATER RESORT HOTEL   **(800) 638-6371 • (906) 292-5506**
AND CONDOMINIUM   **CONDOS/HOTEL**
Just 22 miles west of the Mackinac Bridge. These beautiful, clean and quiet condos face Lake Michigan. Only a few years old, they offer 2-3 bedrooms w/fully equipped kitchens and walkout decks. Most offer dishwasher, microwaves and phone. Towels and sheets provided. Resort includes indoor pool, racquetball, sauna, dining room and lounge.
Daily $45-$75 (hotel); $155-$175 (condos - 4 people)

CURTIS

LOON'S NEST RESORT   **(906) 586-3525**
                                      COTTAGES
Nestled along the south shore of Big Manistique Lake on 8 acres of North Country woods, 3 miles west of Curtis. One and 2 bedroom cottages include private bath with showers, fully equipped kitchens. Also includes 14 ft. aluminum boat. Bring linens. Open all year. No pets.
Weekly $250-$375
Editor's Note: Small to medium size lodgings. Clean with nicely maintained exteriors and interiors.

MANILAK RESORT   **(906) 586-3285 • (800) 587-3285**
                                 CHALETS/HOMES
Two miles north of Curtis, 12 chalets or ranch-style homes (sleep 1-12). Carpeted, fireplaces, full baths, fully equipped kitchens, linens, charcoal grills, picnic tables and decks. Overlooks Manistique Lake. Includes rowboat. Activity area with basketball, volleyball, horseshoes and laundry. Open year around. No pets.
Weekly $500-$1,100
Editor's Note: A mix of old and new accommodations. The new lodgings looked nice.

Sunset Pines Resort
Kay

(906) 586-3199
CABINS

Cozy, romantic cabins in a lovely woodland/lakeside setting. Spacious, well-kept grounds, secluded and quiet. Small playground. Safe swim area. Comfortable, very clean, attractively furnished 1-4 bedroom cabins. Fireplace, TV, laundromat (seasonal), gas grills, posturepedic beds, carpeted. Heated snowmobile repair area. Snowmobile, x-country ski from your door. Guide service for hunting/fishing. Open year around.

Weekly $360-$630 (Off-season rates available)

Sunset Pointe Resort
Mike Soder

(906) 586-9531 (AM) • **(906) 586-9527** (PM)
CABINS

Manistique Lake, 3 miles north of Curtis. 4 spacious cottages on 260' of lake frontage. 2-3 bedroom cottages, fully equipped kitchens, color TV, outdoor cooker. Winter packages include cottages _and_ snowmobile. Outboard motor, pontoon, paddleboat and snowmobile rentals available.

Weekly $450-$550 (June-Aug.); $350-$400 (Fall); $450-$525 (Winter)

Editor's Note: Clean, basic cottages with private baths/showers. Nice sitting/play area for adults and children overlooking the lake.

Trails End Resort
Ron & Judy Borgman

(906) 586-3515
CABINS

Four, 2 bedroom cottages with knotty pine interiors, private showers and TVs. Linens included (bring towels and washcloths). A 14 ft. aluminum boat included with rental (motors available). Campfire site. Open year around. Pets O.K. Great fishing for walleye, pike, perch and smallmouth bass.

Weekly $325

Editor's Note: Traditional cottages with nicely maintained exteriors. We found their location appealing ... at the end of a quiet lane overlooking Cooks Bay on Big Manistique Lake.

GRAND MARAIS

Hilltop Motel & Cabins

(906) 494-2331
CABINS/MOTEL

Five, renovated motel units (2 with kitchenettes). Also 9 furnished housekeeping cabins, 5 are brand new. All include gas heaters, showers and CATV. Outdoor fireplace, grills, picnic and play area.

Weekly $270 (and up)   Daily $40-$70 (Off-season rates available)

MICHIGAN COTTAGES • CHALETS • CONDOS • B&B'S

THE RAINBOW LODGE
RICHARD AND CATHY

(906) 658-3357
CABINS/MOTEL

All new, modern cabins. Full housekeeping services. Each cabin sleeps up to 6 and features a complete kitchen. Linens are furnished — all you need to do is come! 3/4 day minimum stay required. Canoe, fishing, snowmobile. Open year around.

Weekly $235-$375

GULLIVER

FISCHER'S OLD DEERFIELD
MARILYN

(906) 283-3169
COTTAGES

On Gulliver Lake, 21 up-to-date lakeside motel units and housekeeping cottages feature pine paneled walls, bath with shower and automatic heat. Enjoy the private, shallow, sandy beach. Stroll among the well groomed grounds and wooded nature trails. Restaurant, lounge, gift shop, fish cleaning on premises. Open May through November. No pets.

Weekly $294-$470   Daily $30-$36

HULBERT

HULBERT LAKE LODGE & SNO-SHU INN
GREG & MARGE CURTIS

(906) 876-2324
CABINS/APARTMENTS/INN

Hulbert: Five heated log cabins situated 1/4 mile into forest. Furnished but no kitchens. Main lodge offers breakfasts and dinners. Boats, motors, bait available. Enjoy snowmobiling, ice fishing and x-country skiing. *Sno-Shu*: Cabins/apartments, furnished, full kitchens and private bath/shower. Lodge accommodates up to 20. Heated workshops.

Weekly $350-$740   Daily $60-$250

NEWBERRY

NORTHCOUNTRY CAMPGROUND & CABINS
CATHY CLEMENTZ

(906) 293-8562
EMAIL: cclement@up.net
CABINS, LODGE & CAMPGROUNDS

Located on 76 acres, 4.5 miles N. of Newberry on M-123. Close to snowmobile trails. Campgrounds include 2 cozy, 1 room log cabins with rustic charm and modern conveniences (microwave, mini-refrigerator but no kitchen, private bath); plus new Little Lodge. Lodge accommodates a group up to 6 and features kitchen, CATV, VCR and more. Bedding provided for all units. Two are partially barrier free. Open May 1 through snowmobile season.

Weekly $230-$495   Daily $42-$85

Editor's Note: Newly built, 12'x12' white pine log cabins sitting in front of grounds on open land. Very clean, compact with basic comforts. Lodge was under construction when we visited, but it looked nice.

PARADISE

BIRCHWOOD LODGE
STEVE AND CATHY HARMON

(906) 492-3320
CABINS

☀ E D I T O R ' S   C H O I C E ☀

8 modern but rustic log cabins with private baths. Lakefront cabins with fireplaces. Satellite TV/VCR and movie rentals. Fully equipped kitchens with microwaves. Grills. Free use of bikes. Safe, sandy beach, inner tubes, beachhouse, playground. Open year around. Located on Whitefish Point Rd. in a private wooded setting. No pets.

Weekly $325 - $500 (2 people)   Daily $38-$78 (2 people, 3 nights min.)

Editor's Note: Comfortable and very clean accommodation. Steve and Cathy are quite handy at upkeep. Excellent sandy beach. See our review.

MILE CREEK CABINS
DAN & LINDA SMYKOWSKI

(906) 492-3211
CABINS

Authentic log cabins (1-2 bedrooms) are clean, carpeted, comfortable and fully furnished including linens. All cabins overlook Lake Superior and provide a magnificent view in a white birch setting. Each features color TV, fireplace (wood provided). Great swimming on private beach. Centrally located to Tahquamenon Falls and Whitefish Point. X-country ski and snowmobile right from your door. Open year around. Pets allowed but must be kept under control.

Daily $46-$50 (Based on 2 people - $3 ea. add'l. person)

MICHIGAN COTTAGES • CHALETS • CONDOS • B&B'S

WEAVER'S SUNRISE COTTAGES

(888) 244-2545
COTTAGES

Two miles north of Paradise on Whitefish Bay. Traditional, two bedroom cottages with double beds, private bath and shower. Fully equipped kitchens with microwave. Linens/towels provided. TV with VCR. Mini-kayaks, canoes and john-boat available. Pets O.K. Open all year.

Daily: $46-$56 (up to 4 people - $5 ea. add'l person)

Editor's Note: Long, narrow lot with older but clean cottages sitting along a short bluff. Small fence guards against falls. With high water levels at the time of our visit, no beach was visible.

TROUT LAKE

TROUT LAKE RESORT

(906) 569-3810
CABINS

Just 45 minutes from the Mackinac Bridge, these clean, comfortable cabins overlook Trout Lake. Each has a fully equipped kitchenette with microwave, and color TV. Fishing boat is included. Open year around.

Daily $65

TWIN CEDARS RESORT

(906) 569-3209
COTTAGES/MOTEL

The resort provides a private setting. Located in the Upper Peninsula, a 35 minute drive from St. Ignace on beautiful Frenchman's Lake. Cozy, two bedroom cottages and plush motel accommodations. Well established. Extras too numerous to list! For complete information, please phone/write. Modest rates. Address: 95 Trout Lake, Michigan 49793

Call for Rates

Editor's Note: Nice location, friendly owners. Cottages in good condition. The two hotel-type accommodations compare to some of the nicer motel rooms we've seen.

AUTRAIN • GARDEN • MANISTIQUE
MUNISING • WETMORE

J ust north of **Manistique** you will find Palms Books State Park where you will see one of the most unusual water sites in the Upper Peninsula. Take a wooden raft out to the middle of crystal clear Kitch-iti-kipi (Big Spring) and watch as more than 23 million gallons of water daily erupt from the lake's bottom.

Looking for a well-preserved ghost town? Then you'll enjoy Fayette Historic Townsite in Garden. On the north side of Lake Michigan, Fayette was once a

AUTRAIN • GARDEN MANISTIQUE
MUNISING • WETMORE

(continued...)

bustling industrial community from 1867 to 1891. Today there are 19 structures standing with a visitor's center, museum exhibits and walking tours available.

For you fishermen, stop at either Big Bay de Noc or Little Bay de Noc. It was rated in USA Today as one of the top 10 walleye fishing spots in the country. With nearly 200 miles of shoreline, the bay hosts perch, smallmouth bass, northern pike, rainbow trout, salmon and fishing tournaments. You'll also find uncongested and challenging golf courses, and even a Las Vegas style gambling casino called "Chip-in-Casino". In the winter there are pow-wows and sled dog races.

In **Munising**, take a cruise along the shores of the world famous Pictured Rocks — Miner's Castle, Battleship Rock, Indian Head, Lovers' Leap, Colored Caves, Rainbow Cave and Chapel Rock. Most of these can only be seen from the water. Visiting **Au Train,** you will walk in the footsteps of Hiawatha for, according to Longfellow, here lies his home. Es'ca'naw'ba, from the Indian Eshkonabang, means flat rock. Longfellow's Hiawatha tells of the rushing Escanaba River, sometimes referred to as the land of the Red Buck.

While in the Munising/Au Train area, for good family dining at very reasonable prices, check out *Dog Patch Restaurant* or the *Forest Inn.* Another excellent restaurant is the *Camel Riders* restaurant (2 miles east of county highway 450) reservations are recommended. Just west of Manistique at Highway 2 and 13, *Maxie's* provides a simple but homey Yooper's atmosphere with pretty good steaks.

AUTRAIN

COLEMAN'S PARADISE RESORT   **(906) 892-8390**
BILL & MICHELLE COLEMAN   **COTTAGES**
On the west side of AuTrain Lake, this resort offers 1-3 bedroom, furnished cottages. Three bedroom cottages have fireplaces. Large deck overlooks sandy beach. Great swimming. Playground, w/horseshoes, volleyball, badminton, basketball. General store and bait shop. Boats included (motors available).

Weekly $295-$600

MICHIGAN COTTAGES • CHALETS • CONDOS • B&B'S

DANA'S LAKESIDE RESORT (906) 892-8333 • EMAIL: herstad@danasresort.com
AMY & KEVIN HERSTAD   COTTAGES
Located in Hiawatha National Forest on the west shore of AuTrain Lake, 3 miles
south of M-28. Minutes away from Lake Superior sand beaches, Pictured Rocks
National Lakeshore, Grand Island National Recreation Area and Kewadin Casino.
Modern 2 and 3 bedroom housekeeping cottages. Gas heat, sand beach, lighted
boat dock. Screened-in fish cleaning house, boats and motors available.
Shuffleboard, horseshoes. Recreation building with pool table, pinball, video
games, air hockey. Washer and dryer available. Campfires in the evenings. Pets
welcome. *Website: www.danasresort.com*

Call for Rates

NORTHERN NIGHTS   **(906) 892-8225**
HERB & DEBBIE BLACKSTOCK   COTTAGES
In west AuTrain, enjoy excellent fishing in Lake Superior. One to 4 bedroom,
cottages, newly renovated (some with fireplace). Laundry facilities, sauna,
recreation room, large play area. Boat included (motors available). Sandy
beach, nightly campfires, easy access to trails for mountain biking, hiking
and x-country skiing. Snowmobile from your door. No pets.

Call for Rates

NORTHWOODS RESORT   **(906) 892-8114**
ED & PAM KUIVANEN   COTTAGES
Located in Hiawatha National Forest, 2 miles from Lake Superior, with easy
access to all major highways, a paved roadway brings you to the resort. Set
on Au Train Lake, the resort offers good walleye, northern pike and perch
fishing. These 1-4 bedroom cottages, with housekeeping, are fully equipped
and heated. Open year around. Pets allowed.

Weekly $320-$750

PINEWOOD LODGE BED & BREAKFAST   **(906) 892-8300**
JERRY & JENNY KRIEG   BED & BREAKFAST
Massive log home overlooking Lake Superior. Relax on decks, gazebo, atrium,
great room. Enjoy the sauna and stop at our craft store. Walk miles on the sandy
beach. Tour Pictured Rocks, Hiawatha National Forest, Song Bird Trail, water
falls and Seney Wildlife Refuge. Cross country ski. Enjoy year around. 6 rooms.
Private baths.

Daily $95-$125

*Editor's Note: On M-28. Country-styled rooms give a rustic, woodsy feel with
all the modern conveniences. Many of the crafts decorating the rooms are
made with Jenny's skillful hands.*

GARDEN

THE SUMMER HOUSE
JAN McCOTTER
(906) 644-2457
BED & BREAKFAST

Built in 1880, this two-story Colonial Revival home has been restored and decorated in Victorian style. It is located on the picturesque Garden Peninsula, just 7 miles from Fayette State Historical Park. Enjoy swimming, hunting, fishing, hiking and snowmobile trails. Explore area antique shops or just relax! 5 rooms.

Call for Rates

MANISTIQUE

MOUNTAIN ASH RESORT
(906) 341-5658
COTTAGES

On Indian Lake, waterfront housekeeping cabins, screened porches, fully furnished (bring bath towels). Boats included. Picnic tables, BBQ grills. Individual fire pits by all lakefront cabins. Sandy beach. Private dock, enclosed fish cleaning house. Boat motor rentals. Children's play ground. Open all year. Visa accepted.

Weekly $230-$550   Daily $35-$75

WHISPERING PINES RESORT
MIKE HOLM
(906) 573-2480
CABINS

On Thunder Lake, 5 lake front cabins with 1 *plus* or 2 bedrooms, fireplace. Boat included. All kitchens fully equipped. Bed linens included. Sportman's paradise for fishing and hunting. Near to many attractions. Open May-Dec.

Weekly $325-$400

MUNISING

CAMEL RIDERS RESORT
(906) 573-2319
CABINS

Four carpeted, heated, fully furnished housekeeping cabins (2-3 bedrooms) open all year, on the "Chain of Lakes" in a wilderness setting. All bathrooms with modular showers, glass doors and vanities. Knotty pine interiors. Bring towels. Great sandy, swimming beach, 2 docks and 14 ft. aluminum boat. Motors, gas and oil available. Log cabin restaurant overlooks the lake ... rated one of best in the U.P. Full menu.

Weekly $365-$545   Daily $70

MICHIGAN COTTAGES • CHALETS • CONDOS • B&B'S

STURGEON RIVER CABINS   **(906) 249-3821**

CABINS

Year around, new, rustic log cabins in the Hiawatha National Forest. Birdwatcher's paradise, songbird trails, hiking and nature trail. Great snowmobiling and cross-country skiing, fishing and hunting. Full bathroom and kitchen facilities, modern appliances including microwave. 2 bedrooms (sleep up to 8).

Daily $65-$75 (May-Oct.); $75-$95 (Nov.-April)

WHITE FAWN LODGE   **(906) 573-2949**
SANDRA & SCOTT BUTLER   CABINS/LODGE

In the heart of Hiawatha National Forest, lakeside and wooded area cabins. Rooms, suites or apartment units. All have microwaves, refrigerator, coffee makers and color TV's. Community building. Enjoy ATV, hiking and snowmobile trails, hunting, fishing, canoeing and waterfalls. Located 2 hours from Mackinac Bridge/3 hours from Green Bay,

Weekly $375-$450   Daily $50-$125

WETMORE

CABIN FEVER RESORT   **(800) 507-3341 • (906) 573-2372**
RICK & COLLEEN JOHNSON   LOG CABINS

On 30 acres, these log cabins are fully carpeted and completely furnished with log furniture. Each has housekeeping facilities (1 or 2 bedrooms), fully equipped kitchen and private bath w/shower. Use of boat included. Excellent snowshoeing, x-country ski and snowmobile trails nearby.

Daily (summer) *$48; (winter) *$60

*based on 3 night minimum

REGION 4

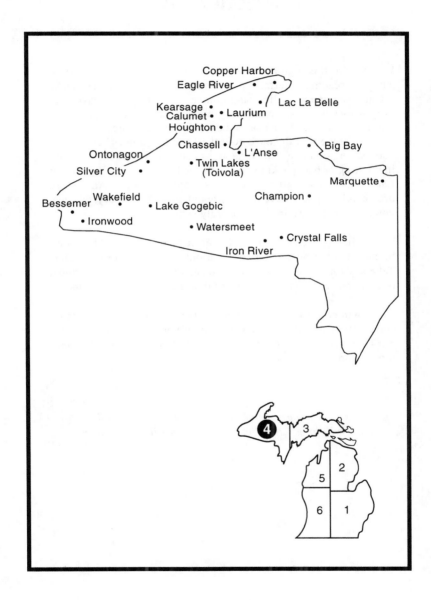

REGION 4

Welcome to this region of deep wilderness. Here is the beauty of nature, cascading waterfalls, panoramas of forest wilderness. A lake set in a sea of red, yellow and orange painted by fall leaves, set deep between and surrounded by mountains. A narrow peninsula that jets into Lake Superior and dares its mighty force and yet so lovely that the wealthy have built their summer homes here. A wilderness so complete that some areas can only be reached by hiking, biking or backpacking. You will see hues of red in the sand as Lake Superior sculptures the dunes along its shores. An area so breathtaking, poets have written about it. Lakes so crystal clear you can see the fish in their leisurely swim.

Take a fishing cruise on Lake Superior and catch that "big one". Salmon fishing here is comparable only to fishing in the ocean. Take any tour by boat or by land to see the mines and the wonder of this area. Stop and eat at one of their many fine restaurants.

In the winter, all you skiers, come to the mountain ranges that receive 250 inches of snow yearly. And, if you dare — go *ski flying*. Ski flying is ski jumping but much higher, much longer and definitely more challenging.

You have now seen Michigan's Upper Peninsula.
You will long remember it — and you will soon return.

MARQUETTE • KEWEENAW PENINSULA • SILVER CITY

COVERS: BIG BAY • CALUMET • CHAMPION • CHASSELL • COPPER HARBOR
EAGLE RIVER • HOUGHTON • KEARSARGE • LAC LA BELLE • L'ANSE •
LAURIUM • ONTONAGON (PORCUPINE MTNS. & LAKE OF THE CLOUDS) •
TOIVOLA (TWIN LAKES)

Marquette, one of the oldest cities in the Upper Peninsula, was initially founded in the 1840's by French settlers to serve the iron-ore mining and lumber industries. Visitors to the area will enjoy the 328-acre Presque Isle Park with its extensive cross country and hiking trails or its International Food Festival in July, hosted by Northern Michigan University. There are plenty of historic sites and outdoor activities to fill your day. As you leave Marquette for Copper Country, you'll want to stop at the *Mt. Shasta Restaurant* in the **Champion/Michigamme** area where several scenes from the 1950's movie, *Anatomy of a Murder,* were filmed. Here you'll find pictures of Jimmy Stewart, Lee Remick and other cast members adorning the walls.

Thrill to a genuine underground adventure—The Arcadian Copper Mines not far from **Houghton/Hancock**. Take a tour and see the geological wonders created eons ago deep inside the earth. Here, too, is a mecca for rock hounds. Then on to the Quincy Mine Hoist (the Nordberg Hoist), the largest steam-powered mine hoist ever manufactured. Not only is the hoist of great interest, but so is the lore of the Quincy Mining Company. You'll have to visit the area to learn more about it.

In **Calumet,** visit Coppertown USA's Visitor Center. It tells the story of mines, communities and the people of the Keweenaw Peninsula. Theater buffs must stop at the Calumet Theatre and walk with the "Greats" — Bernhardt, Fairbanks, and Sousa. While visiting the area, you'll want to stop at *The Old Country House* just two miles north of Calumet known for its fresh Lake Superior fish, prime rib and homemade bread.

Looking to explore a ghost town? Then travel further north, between Delaware and Copper Harbor. In the woods, a block or two south of US-41, you'll find what's left of Mandan, a once bustling community in Michigan's early copper days. A small sign marks the road in.

Then continue on, all the way to **Copper Harbor**, at the tip of the peninsula. Here you'll find a charming little village where everything is less than four blocks away. Stop at the Laughing Loon Gift Shop and from there take a tour into the countryside to view the untouched, towering Estivant Pines. Before the tour, stop for breakfast at the *Pines Restaurant* and taste one of their wonderful cinnamon rolls—a local institution — or *Johnson's Bakery* for great rolls and coffee. The aroma alone from these tasty places will add 10 lbs.

MARQUETTE • KEWEENAW PENINSULA • SILVER CITY

(continued...)

Your trip to Copper Harbor is not complete until you dine at the *Keweenaw Mountain Lodge* which provides well prepared meals in a wilderness setting. Once you've replenished yourself, take a tour of historic Fort Wilkins found along the shoreline of Lake Superior. It was initially built in 1844 to maintain peace in Michigan's Copper Country. Life at the Fort was very difficult with raging waters, frigid winters and heavy snows taking its toll. Much of the Fort's history is retold through museum exhibits, audio-visual programs and costumed interpretation.

Take a boat trip to Isle Royale National Park, a roadless land of wildlife, unspoiled forests, refreshing lakes, and scenic shores. You will find massive waves exploding along rugged coastlines, lighthouses, rolling hills, thimbleberries, vast pines and hardwood forests, a unique culture and accent. Best of all, you can view both the spectacular sunset and sunrise no matter where you are. Here is vacation land at its very best.

For your next adventure head south, back through the Keewenaw and west to **Silver City**. Get ready to experience one of Michigan's biggest and most impressive wilderness retreat, the beautiful Porcupine Mountains. In the Porkies you'll find 80 miles of marked hiking trails in the 58,000 acres of mountainous terrain and more than a dozen rustic trailside cabins. Backpacking the "Porkies" is a challenge reserved only for the strong of heart. For those seeking less challenging experiences but still want to savor the beauty of nature, there are driving tours. You might also enjoy the 1/4 mile hike up to The Lake of the Clouds overlook with a wonderful, panoramic view of the lake's clear waters surrounded by forest (this is a particularly breathtaking view in the fall). Of course, the Porkies also has excellent Alpine and cross-country skiing along with terrific snowmobiling, fishing, and swimming.

Ready for another ghost town? Perhaps one of the UP's biggest and most interesting is Nonesuch which covers a number of acres in the southeast corner of the Porkies. Park interpreters often provide guided tours of the site.

BIG BAY

BIG BAY POINT LIGHTHOUSE B&B
JEFF & LINDA GAMBLE

(906) 345-9957
BED & BREAKFAST

* E D I T O R ' S   C H O I C E *

A secluded retreat from modern life, 7 rooms all with private baths. Living room with fireplace, sauna, 1/2 mile of lakeshore and 50 wooded acres for walking. Ideal area for hiking, mountain biking, snowmobiling, cross-country skiing and more. Open year around. Full breakfasts.

Daily   (May-Oct.) $115-$175; (Nov./Apr.) $85-$145

Editor's Note: This B&B represents one of the few surviving resident lighthouses in the country. Very secluded — a truly unique experience.

THUNDER BAY INN
DARRYL & EILEEN SMALL

(906) 345-9376 • (800) 732-0714
INN

Built in 1911 and renovated by Henry Ford in the 1940's. The Inn was used for filming scenes from "Anatomy of a Murder". 12 guest rooms furnished with antiques. Historic lobby with fireplace. Pub and restaurant on premises. Conference facilities. Gift Shop. Open year around. Private and shared baths. Continental breakfasts.

Daily $55-$105

Editor's Note: This is a classic inn with well maintained rooms which definitely reflect an earlier time.

CALUMET

BOSTROM-JOHNSON HOUSE
CURT & PAT JOHNSON

(906) 337-4651
BED & BREAKFAST

A large Victorian era residence features 4 spacious guest rooms furnished in antiques. Guests will find a friendly, cheerful home within walking distance of Calumet. Cross-country ski and groomed snowmobile trails nearby. Children/pets welcome. 4 rooms/2 baths. Library open for reading or visiting at all times. There is tea and coffee available all day and a full breakfast every morning.

Daily $50

CALUMET HOUSE B&B
GEORGE & ROSE CHIVSES

(906) 337-1936
BED & BREAKFAST

In the Keweenaw Peninsula, built in 1895, B&B features original woodwork, upright piano and antique furniture. Breakfast served in the formal dining room which has an original butler's pantry. Guests can view television in the drawing room by a cozy fire with their evening tea. No smoking/pets. Adults only.

Daily $30-$35

CHAMPION

MICHIGAMME LAKE LODGE COTTAGE
FRANK & LINDA STABILE
(906) 339-4400
COTTAGE

Owners of the former Michigamme Lake Lodge B&B now offer a private cottage on the bluff of Lake Michigamme, fronting 1200 ft. of sandy beach. Canoe with cabin. Sauna by the lake. Cottage features two-bedrooms (sleeps 4), with all the extras including fully equipped kitchen, newly remodeled bathroom, living room with TV, screened porch. Very private. Cottage is furnished with antiques from the Lodge. Swim, bike, fish or canoe. Open May-October. No pets.

Weekly $550 July-August ($500 off-season)

CHASSELL

THE HAMAR HOUSE
(906) 523-4670
BED & BREAKFAST

Built in circa 1903, this turn-of-the-century Victorian, set on spacious grounds, features 2 rooms with adjoining sunroom and 3 rooms with shared bath. Children welcome. Enjoy the 3/5 size playhouse. Parking for snowmobiles and trailers. Close to shops, lakefront, ski/snowmobile trails. Open year around. Check or cash only.

Daily $38 (single) $58-$68 (double)

HELMICK'S LOG CABINS
MARYANN HELMICK
(906) 523-4591
CABINS

3 heated, lakeside cabins. One large room (sleeps 4). Private baths. Equipped kitchen includes refrigerator, stove, pots/pans, dishes, utensils. Porches face the lake. Linens provided (bring towels). Boats available. Open June 1-Oct. 1. No pets.

Weekly $200

MANNINEN'S CABINS
(906) 523-4135 (W) • (906) 334-2518 (S)
CABINS

The 7 housekeeping cabins, located on 60 acres of land, are very accessible. The cabins, on Otter Lake (well known for outstanding fishing), come with boats. Freezer service. Open May 15-Oct. 1.

Call for Rates

NORTHERN LIGHT COTTAGES   **(906) 523-4131 • EMAIL:** mwick@portup.com
GARY & MARGE WICKSTROM
COTTAGES

Three fully furnished cottages on Chassell Bay. Two bedrooms sleep up to 6, bed linens provided. Sandy beach, swimming, fishing, docking space. Boats, sauna and campfire site are available. Rent weekly (Saturday to Saturday).

Weekly $250 (and up)

PALOSAARI'S ROLLING ACRES B&B
CLIFF & EVEY PALOSAARI

(906) 523-4947
BED & BREAKFAST

★ EDITOR'S CHOICE ★

Operating Dairy Farm since the 1920's! Visit the barn and watch the milking or help feed baby calves. Centrally located. Three cozy rooms with shared bath. Enjoy a full country breakfast in this "home away from home". Open year round. Reservations required. No smoking/pets. Access to snowmobile trails, swimming and hiking.

Daily $50

Editor's Note: Operating dairy farm B&B. Rooms are very comfy. A great place to bring the kids. They'll enjoy the farm and so will you.

COPPER HARBOR

BELLA VISTA MOTEL & COTTAGES
DEAN & TODD LAMPPA

(906) 289-4213
COTTAGES/MOTEL

Eight cottages in Copper Harbor. Motel rooms overlook Lake Superior with cottages one block away. Cottages feature kitchens or kitchenettes, color satellite TV, some with fireplaces. Fish off the dock or, if you prefer, boats are available. Open mid-May to mid-October. Pets allowed in cottages.

Weekly $234-$380   Daily $39-$63

BERGH'S WATERFRONT RESORT
HOWARD & PHYLLIS BERGH

(906) 289-4234
COTTAGES

These comfortable housekeeping cottages are fully equipped. They include showers, dishes and linens, also boat with dock available. Resort overlooks harbor near Copper Harbor Marina. Open May 15-Oct. 15. Pets allowed. P.O. Box 37.

Call for Rates

LAKE FANNY HOOE RESORT
ALAN & GRACE CATRON

(906) 289-4451 • (800) 426-4451
COTTAGES/MOTEL

14 units on the lake with 2, 1-2 bedroom cottages and a lakefront motel. Units have private balconies, kitchenettes, private baths, CATV and some gas fireplaces. Sandy swimming beach. Wooded campsites with trout stream. Laundromat, clubhouse, sauna on premises. Boats/canoes available. Major credit cards.

Weekly $410-$455

KEWEENAW MOUNTAIN LODGE **(906) 289-4403**
CABINS/LODGE

✴ E D I T O R ' S   C H O I C E ✴

Charming log cabins and main lodge nestled in the pines south of Copper Harbor. One, 2 or 3 bedroom cabins, most with fireplaces, and motel rooms. Scenic golf course, hiking trails, tennis court, restaurant and lounge. Discover the tradition.

Daily $65-$86

Editor's Note: Picturesque comfort in a wilderness setting. Older cottages are basic but comfortable and clean. The restaurant serves well prepared meals.

EAGLE RIVER

EAGLE RIVER'S SUPERIOR VIEW **(906) 337-5110**
PAUL VACATION HOME

Three bedroom vacation home overlooking Lake Superior and the Sand Dunes. Sleeps 9 comfortably, 1-1/2 baths, fully equipped kitchen, modern decor. Linens provided. Fireplace, washer/dryer. Full screened porch. Excellent snowmobiling, skiing, swimming beach and play area. Pets and smoking allowed. Call for free brochure.

Weekly $525   Daily $75

HOUGHTON

CHARLESTON HISTORIC INN **(800) 482-7404**
JOHN & HELEN SULLIVAN BED & BREAKFAST

Circa 1900 Georgian architecture. Ornate woodwork, library with fireplace, grand interior staircase, antique and reproduction 18th Century furniture. King canopy beds with private baths, TV's, telephones, A/C, sitting areas. Suites, some with fireplace, private verandas. Full breakfast. Major credit cards. Smoking limited. Children 12+ welcome. AAA approved. No pets.

Daily: $89-$165

KEARSARGE

BELKNAP'S GARNET HOUSE **(906) 337-5607**
BED & BREAKFAST

Enjoy the huge porch and 3 acres of this beautiful mining captain's Victorian home. Unchanged throughout the 1900's. Original fireplaces, fur room, leaded/ beveled glass pantries, fixtures, woodwork and servants' quarters. 5 rooms (private/shared baths) are decorated with Victorian theme. Full breakfast. Open mid-June through mid-September. Adults only.

Daily $60-$90

LAC LA BELLE

LAC LA BELLE RESORT   **(888) 809-4273 • (906) 289-4293**
SANDY   CABINS
A quiet place at the end of the road. Basic fishing/snowmobiling camp 35 miles from anywhere! Five cabins (3 on water) 1 and 2 bedrooms. Gas heat, showers, kitchens, linens, dock space. Rental boats. Convenience store with limited groceries, beer and wine. Gas on dock and road. Access to Lake Superior via Mendota Canal. Full service restaurant on-site.

Weekly $250 and up   Daily $50 and up

L'ANSE

FORD BUNGALOW   **(906) 524-7595**
ALVIN BRINKMAN, MGR.   VACATION HOME
Henry Ford's summer home. Spacious retreat (over 5,000 sq. ft.), sitting 30 ft. above the shores of Lake Superior in a densely wooded area. 9 bedrooms/6 full baths (sleeps up to 16). Fireplace, linens provided. Rocky/pebble beach. No pets/restricted smoking.

Weekly $2,100   2 Days $800

LAURIUM

LAURIUM MANOR INN   **(906) 337-2549 • EMAIL: lauriumanr@portup.com**
                                                              BED & BREAKFAST

✸ EDITOR'S CHOICE ✸

Built in 1905, this opulent 13,000 sq ft. antebellum style mansion has 41 rooms (including a ballroom), 5 fireplaces, hand painted murals and gilded leather wall covering. This elegant mansion offers 10 bedrooms (8 private bath, 2 shared bath), king and queen size beds. Take a tour of this mansion and relive the unforgettable wealth that once was Copper Country. No smoking/pets.

	Winter	Summer
Daily	$69-$94 pvt. bath	$79-$119 pvt. bath
	$49 sh. bath	$55 sh. bath

Editor's Note: Elegant and inviting, this is a premiere Victorian styled B&B.

WONDERLAND MOTEL & CABINS   **(906) 337-4511**
                                                              CABINS/MOTEL
These lodgings offer 10 units, 6 housekeeping cabins & 4 motel units. Clean quiet and comfortable.

Call for Rates

MARQUETTE

WHITEFISH LODGE   **(906) 343-6762 • EMAIL: whitefish@aol.com**
KAREN & STEVE PAWIELSKI   **LODGE/COTTAGES**

★ EDITOR'S CHOICE ★

A quiet retreat in the U.P. northwoods on the picturesque Laughing Whitefish River. All new, 2 and 3 bedroom lodgings, each completely furnished throughout including kitchens, bedrooms (queen beds) and baths. Enjoy our outdoor decks, grills, excellent walking and biking trails from door. Great fall colors! Five minutes from Lake Superior and close to Pictured Rocks. Open year around. On snowmobile trail and close to x-country ski trails. Gas available on property. 17 miles east of Marquette and 21 miles west of Munising, off M-28. *Website: http://members.aol.com/whitefishl/*

Weekly $350-$675   Daily $60-$135

Editor's Note: Great secluded/scenic U.P. setting - very clean accommodations.

ONTONAGON & SILVER CITY
(PORCUPINE MTNS. & LAKE OF THE CLOUDS)

LAKE SHORE CABINS   **(906) 885-5318**
                                                        CABINS

Two miles from the Porcupine Mtns. with 500 ft. frontage on beautiful Lake Superior. Experience nature with the calm and comfort of home. Private sandy beach. Fish, hunt, bike, ski, snowmobile and snowshoe right from your door. All cabins offer housekeeping and include sauna bath and screened porch.

Daily $39-$59 (based on 2 people)

Editor's Note: Well maintained traditional cabins highlighted by a large sandy beach. A definite "Up North" feel. Cabins with 1/2 baths. Shower available in sauna cabin. See our review.

LAMBERT'S CHALET COTTAGES &   **(906) 884-4230 • EMAIL: petcot@up.net**
VACATION HOMES (CHUCK/WENDY PETERSON)   **CHALETS/HOMES**

★ EDITOR'S CHOICE ★

On the shore of Lake Superior. 13 chalets with kitchenettes (some with fireplaces) and vacation home (with whirlpool). CATV, phones. Sandy beaches, grills, picnic tables and Porcupine Mountain, gift shop on premises. Major credit cards. Open all year. Some non-smoking units. No pets.

Daily   Cottages: $58-$90   Homes: $225

Editor's Note: Each lodging varies in style and amenities from small to large homes and chalets. All are well maintained and comfy...something for everyone.

TOMLINSON'S RAINBOW MOTEL & CHALET

(906) 885-5348
CHALETS/MOTEL

Overlooking Lake Superior and 5 minutes from the Porcupine Mtns., large, furnished chalets, sleep 10. Includes linens. Equipped kitchens, Jacuzzi, sauna, free in-room phone and coffee. Newer unit with hot tub in room. Restaurant on premises. Credit cards accepted. Open all year. Smoking/pets allowed.

Daily $45-$116 (double occupancy)

Editor's Note: Chalets and motel look very attractive, well maintained and new.

TOIVOLA (TWIN LAKES)

KRUPP'S ALL SEASON RESORT

(906) 288-3404
COTTAGES

Seven units, 1-3 bedroom housekeeping cottages with full kitchens, TV and more. Located on the lake - boating, fishing and swimming. Near golf course, state park, bakery, restaurant, pasties and groceries. Open year round. Gasoline on premises. Major credit cards accepted.

Weekly $150-$400

TWIN LAKES RESORT

(906) 288-3666
COTTAGES

8 units, semi-rustic cabins, 2-3 bedrooms with kitchens, sandy beach, private tub and showers. Safe swimming. Boat included. Located near a golf course and state park. Reservations recommended. Open mid-May thru mid-October. Brochure available.

Call for Rates

IRONWOOD & SURROUNDING AREAS

COVERS: BESSEMER • CRYSTAL FALLS • IRON RIVER • LAKE GOGEBIC • WAKEFIELD • WATERSMEET

Ironwood is known as *"The Big Snow Country"*. But don't let that fool you, it is more than just winter fun. Here among unspoiled forest and mountains are miles of trout streams and hundreds of spring fed lakes. Visitors will enjoy their vacation on the famous Cisco Chain of Lakes, in Bergland/Marenisco. Bring your camera! Here stands "The World's Tallest Indian"—*HIAWATHA.* He towers 150 feet over downtown Ironwood. Also, don't miss the Copper Peak Ski Flying Hill in the Black River Recreation Area, 10 miles northeast of Ironwood.

IRONWOOD & SURROUNDING AREAS

(...continued)

Lake Gogebic is the area's largest lake, with 13,000 acres of prime fishing water. In June, September and throughout the season, fishing tournaments are held. Families will enjoy all sorts of summer fun, sight-seeing, hiking and water sports. Further northeast we come to the Porcupine Mountains Wilderness State Park (15 miles west of Ontonagon).

BESSEMER

BLACKJACK SKI RESORT

(800) 848-1125
CONDOS/CHALETS

Trailside lodging units offer ski-in, ski-out convenience. Cozy fireplaces, new TV systems, complete kitchens and saunas in every building. Longest run over 1 mile. PSIA Ski School, Kinderkamp and nursery. Lodgings range from studio to 1-3 bedroom. Special package rates available.

Daily $60-$100 (per person, per night) Call for special package rates

BIG POWDERHORN LODGING

(800) 222-3131 • (906) 932-3100
CONDOS/CHALETS

Luxury to budget conscious private chalets and condos. Ice rink, horse-driven sleigh rides, x-country skiing, pool, special events, trailside decks, and live entertainment. NASTAR, ski school, ski shop, rentals, Kinderschool and cafeteria. 3 restaurants and lounges, sauna/whirlpool, and fireplace. Credit cards accepted.

Call for Rates

HEDGEROW LODGING
JEFF & SUE SHEPHERD

(800) 421-4995 • (906) 663-6950
CHALETS

Ski and snowmobile right out your door! These cozy, clean, comfortable units (sleeps 6-10) come with furnished kitchenettes and microwaves. CATV, linens and towels provided. Only 5 min. to Indianhead and 10 min. to Big Powderhorn. Special ski packages available. Major credit cards accepted.

Call for Rates

CRYSTAL FALLS

BIRCHWOOD CABINS

(906) 875-3637
CABINS

On Swan Lake in a park-like setting, these 5 (1-2 bedroom) cabins are completely furnished (linens included) and offer equipped kitchens, showers and gas heat. Boat included. Excellent hunting/fishing (walleye and perch), plus easy access to miles of snowmobile, x-country ski trails. Pets allowed.

Call for Rates

WHISPERING PINES RESORT   **(906) 875-6151-(906) 776-0599** (OFF-SEASON)
PAUL & ROSE SCHEIBE
COTTAGES

7, 1-3 bedroom units completely furnished. Nestled in a wooded area and located on 450 ft. of Lake Mary. Sandy swimming beach. Only 6 miles from Crystal Falls. Area noted for fishing, particularly walleye. *Website: www.fishweb.com*

Weekly   (May-Nov. 07) $250-$340 (Off-season rates slightly higher)

IRON RIVER

LAC O'SEASONS RESORT
RANDY & NANCY SCHAUWECKER

(906) 265-4881
COTTAGES

10 min. from downtown Iron River on Stanley Lake, close to x-country ski/ snowmobile trails. Indoor swimming pool, sauna /whirlpool. Newly constructed 2-3 bedroom cottages, some log styled, fully carpeted, electric heat and appliances. Some with fireplaces. Porch w/grills with each unit. Boat, canoe, paddle boats and pontoon rentals.

Call for Rates

IRONWOOD

BEAR TRACK INN

(906) 932-2144
CABINS

Deep within the west end of the Ottawa National Forest, adjacent to a designated national scenic river. Cabins include kitchens, showers, woodburning stoves, all linens. Authentic Finnish wood sauna on premises. Minutes from 5 waterfalls, Lake Superior beach, hiking/mountain biking trails.

Daily $49-$125

MICHIGAN COTTAGES • CHALETS • CONDOS • B&B'S

BLACK RIVER LODGE
(906) 932-3857
TOWNHOUSES/MOTEL/CONDOS

Located 2 miles from Big Powderhorn Mtn., near Copper Peak Ski Flying Hill w/7 waterfalls and Black River Harbor. The lodge offers accommodations to fit all pocketbooks, from motel rooms to spacious townhouses and condominiums. Indoor swimming pool, restaurant, lounge and game room. MC/Visa/Disc.

Call for Rates

RIVER ROCK RETREAT
(906) 932-5638
LOG CABIN

Massive log cabin that sets the highest standard for log cabin construction with many special features including hand-hewn red pine logs. Snowmobile right outside your door and snowshoeing. Fully equipped and furnished, 3 fireplaces, 3 baths, 3 living areas, complete kitchen, jacuzzi, sauna, phone, BBQ. Open year around.

Call for Rates

LAKE GOGEBIC

THE FISHERMAN RESORT
(906) 842-3366
COTTAGES/LODGE

Well maintained cottages on Lake Gogebic. Boats available for rent—or bring your own! Fully furnished with equipped kitchens, private baths. Some fireplaces. Bring towels. Cabins sleep 2-8. Gift shop features handcrafted items. Lodge rooms also available.

Weekly $390 (and up, winter); $375 (and up, summer)

Editor's Note: Well landscaped resort on the shores of Lake Gogebic. Clean and comfortable lodgings — great fishing area.

GOGEBIC LODGE
(906) 842-3321
DON/CHRIS/BRIAN BERQUIST
CHALET/MOTEL/COTTAGES

West side of Lake Gogebic, motel, cottage and chalet accommodations. Cottages feature private bath, CATV, equipped kitchens, and more! The Lodge includes sauna/whirlpool, dining room/lounge. Boat and motor rentals available. Enjoy hunting, fishing, swimming, snowmobiling and skiing. Credit cards accepted. Pets allowed, extra charge.

Weekly $260-$950   Daily $55 (for 2)-$175 (for 6)

Editor's Note: Their resort has established a good reputation on the lake. Book reservations early. The three new chalets built in 1994 looked great.

THE WEST SHORE RESORT

(906) 842-3336
COTTAGES

★ EDITOR'S CHOICE ★

450 ft. on Lake Gogebic. Great fishing for walleye or hunting for bear and deer. All cabins are 2 bedrooms, sleep 6, bath (towels and linens provided). Boat launch on site, docks and boat lifts. Boat and motor rentals. Pets welcome. Open year around.

Weekly $300 (dbl. occ. - $30 each add'l person) Summer Rates
Daily $65 (dbl. occ. - $10 each add'l person) Summer Rates

Editor's Note: Small but very clean, comfortable accommodations — reasonable prices make this a good choice.

MALLARD COVE & TEAL WING
RE/MAX SNOW COUNTRY
TOM & ARLENE SCHNELLER

(800) 876-9751
VACATION HOMES

★ EDITOR'S CHOICE ★

Mallard Cove: Four bedroom, two baths with cedar sauna. Accommodates 8. Features phone, fireplace, Weber grill, fully equipped kitchen with dishwasher, linens, towels. Excellent waterfront view. Lakeside deck and boat dock (boat and motor available). Groomed snowmobile trails and skiing nearby.

Teal Wing: Contemporary, spacious lakeside home on Lake Gogebic. Four bedrooms, two baths (sleeps 8). Fully furnished and equipped including micro-wave, phone, TV/ VCR, stereo. Includes use of boat dock (boat and motor available). Also overlooks Lake Gogebic and is located on snow-mobile route. Available year around. Pets O.K. Private setting on the lake.

Teal Wing

Weekly $895

Editor's Note: The Schneller's have designed and decorated these homes with comfortable elegance. We highly recommend both Mallard Cove & Teal Wing.

NINE PINE RESORT
RON & JOANN MONTIE

(906) 842-3361
COTTAGES

A family resort, centrally located in "Big Snow Country". Snowmobile right to your door. Modern, carpeted housekeeping units (sleep 2-8) with TV. Boats and motors available for rent. 1 cottage with fireplace. Linens provided. Restaurants nearby. Open year around. Major credit cards. Pets allowed.

Weekly $335-$700

SOUTHWINDS COTTAGE
MARLINE & PAT HANSON

(906) 575-3397
COTTAGE

Very cozy, clean 2 bedroom cottage on Lake Gogebic with 220 ft. of sandy beach. Private dock. Sleeps 6. All new carpet and furnishings. Fully equipped kitchen with microwave and grill. Private, very quiet. Lovely wood deck overlooks the lake. Rent year around. Snowmobile/watercraft rentals available. No pets.

Weekly $450

SUNNYSIDE CABINS
SUE GROOMS

(906) 842-3371
CABINS

★ EDITOR'S CHOICE ★

Set along 300 ft. of Lake Gogebic, these 8 well maintained, comfortably furnished lodgings feature fully equipped kitchens including microwaves, knotty pine interiors, satellite TV, private baths, bedrooms with 1 to 2 full size beds. Doorwalls lead to private deck. Linens provided.

Call for Rates

Editor's Note: Spotless cabins with a "luxurious" feel. We were very impressed.

THE TIMBERS RESORT

(906) 575-3542
COTTAGES

New owners completed major renovations in 1995. The resort is on Lake Gogebic midway between Porcupine, Indianhead and Powderhorn Mountains. Featured are 9 cottages fully furnished with equipped kitchens and private baths. Enjoy hunting, fishing, snowmobiling and skiing. Boat rentals available. Pets O.K.

Daily $45-$125

WHITETAIL LODGING
PHIL BERCOT

(906) 842-3589
COTTAGES

★ EDITOR'S CHOICE ★

Two bedroom cottages (2-8 people) on the east shore of Lake Gogebic. Furnished and equipped, knotty pine interiors, tiled bath/shower. Individually controlled electric baseboards. Boats available. Great fishing for walleye, bass, perch. Snowmobile trail to the Porcupine Mountains. Open year around.

Weekly $500-$1,000 (April 16-Nov. 30)   Daily $75-$300 (winter, 3 night min.)

Editor's Note: Newly renovated cottages with fresh, appealing interiors. Clean and comfortable. See our review.

WAKEFIELD

INDIANHEAD BEAR CREEK

(800) 3-INDIAN
CONDOS/CHALETS

Chalets tucked into the woods, condos on or adjacent to the slopes and Main Lodge, an authentic barn converted to a complete and cozy hotel - all are featured at Indianhead. Accommodations include phones, color TV's, VCR's. Lodge rooms with CATV. Some units with dishwashers, washers/dryers, Jacuzzi or sauna. Two restaurants, 2 cafeterias, 5 cocktail lounges, indoor pool and spa, health/racquet club, full service ski shop, child care, Kids 12 and under sleep free with parents. Golfing packages, bicycle tours and races, auto show, kite festival and more — call for special package rates. Pets allowed in some units.

Daily $69-$458 (from basic lodge room to 5 bedroom chalet)

WATERSMEET

THE ARROWS

(906) 358-4390
COTTAGES/HOMES

Modern/ultra-modern cottages and luxury vacation homes with fireplaces, TV, dishwashers, whirlpools, microwaves, washers and dryers. On Thousand Island Lake (Cisco Chain). Sleeps up to 15 per home. Motors and pontoon rentals. Access to snowmobile trails, x-country trails. One hour to downhill skiing.

Weekly $575-$1,280

Editor's Note: The interiors of these cottages are well maintained. The newer homes are very nice. Beautiful, natural setting. Excellent fishing and boating.

CROOKED LAKE RESORT

(906) 358-4421
COTTAGES

On Crooked Lake in Sylvania Perimeter/Wilderness Area. Motors allowed. Six modern (3 newer) 2 and 3 bedroom housekeeping cottages. Everything furnished except personal towels. Each cottage comes with a boat or canoe. Dock space available for rent. Motor rental, bait, gas also available. Open May 15-November. Pets allowed.

Weekly $446-$675

JAY'S RESORT　　　　　　　　　　　　　**(906) 358-4300**
　　　　　　　　　　　　　　　　　　　　　COTTAGES

Lakefront cottages on Thousand Island Lake. Nine, 1-4 bedroom housekeeping cottages, many with fireplaces. Complete kitchen, color TV, sleeps up to 12. Lund boats, deluxe boats and pontoons. Spacious grounds with play area. Seasonal discounts. Call to inquire. Pets with permission, extra charge. Handicap access.

Weekly　　　$400-$950

Editor's Note: Cottage exteriors new — the natural grounds were well groomed. Cute play area for children.

LAC LA BELLE RESORT　　　　　　　　　**(906) 358-4396**
SKIP & CARYL BUCHANAN　　　　　　　　CABINS

★ EDITOR'S CHOICE ★

These well maintained year around cottages are nestled on Thousand Island Lake and each unit has a view of the water. These heated, 1-2 bedroom units have knotty pine interiors, fully equipped kitchens, linens and blankets are provided (bring your own towels). On the grounds they have a fire pit, fish cleaning station and freezer. Boats, guide service, gas and oil are available.

Weekly　　　$445-$495

Editor's Note: Comfortable and affordable lodgings. Much of the woodworking here has been done by Skip.

VACATIONLAND RESORT　　　**(906) 358-4380 • EMAIL: wsmet@portup.com**
BILL & JAN SMET　　　　　　　　　　　　COTTAGES

Housekeeping cottages, 2-3 bedrooms, some with fireplaces, on Thousand Island Lake. Linens furnished (bring towels). Boat included (motors extra). Safe swimming beach. Dock and raft, tennis, volleyball, basketball, fishing and boating. Great x-country skiing, snowmobiling and ice fishing. *Website: www.westernup.com/vacationland*

Weekly　　　$325-$995　　　Daily　　　$65-$200

REGION 5

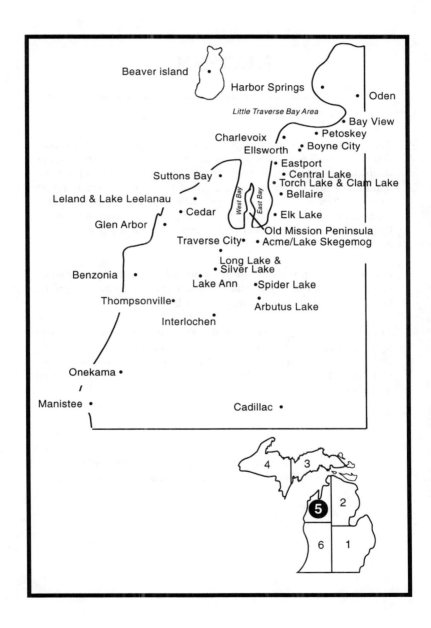

Beaver island •

Harbor Springs •

Oden •

Little Traverse Bay Area

Bay View •

Charlevoix • Petoskey •

Ellsworth • Boyne City •

Eastport •

Suttons Bay • Central Lake •

Torch Lake & Clam Lake •

Leland & Lake Leelanau • Bellaire •

Cedar • Elk Lake •

Glen Arbor • Old Mission Peninsula

Traverse City • Acme/Lake Skegemog •

Long Lake & Silver Lake •

Benzonia • Lake Ann • Spider Lake •

Thompsonville • Arbutus Lake •

Interlochen •

Onekama •

Manistee • Cadillac •

West Bay *East Bay*

4   3

5   2

6   1

REGION 5

There's more to this area than just relaxing on the pure, sandy beaches and watching the sun as it sets on Lake Michigan. It offers miles of scenic drives, wilderness, acres of sand dunes and nature preserves, hundred of lakes, and more varieties of trees than you're likely to find anywhere else. In this area you will also find some of the best salmon, trout and bass fishing in the U.S.A. Within Region 5 lies the Cherry Capital and Summer Golf Capital with many designer golf courses.

If you want things to do, try the festivals, art shows, summer theaters, museums, 19th Century communities and some of the best shopping, gourmet restaurants and winery's around.

The shimmering white snow of winter is broken not only by pine trees, deer and elk, but miles of groomed snowmobile trails, cross-country ski trails and some of the Midwest's finest downhill ski runs. Our lake-effect snow is denser, heavier and more durable than mountain snow.

Nature at its most natural, civilization at its most refined.
The perfect blend in any season.

BOYNE CITY • CHARLEVOIX • PETOSKEY

COVERS: BAY VIEW • BEAVER ISLAND • EASTPORT • ELLSWORTH •
HARBOR SPRINGS • LITTLE TRAVERSE BAY • ODEN

The scenic area of **Boyne, Charlevoix, Harbor Springs, and Petoskey** offers superb sight-seeing, unique shops, fishing, sailing, and some of the best downhill and cross country skiing in Lower Michigan.

Five linear miles of flower-lined streets, a drawbridge, and two lakes have earned "Charlevoix the Beautiful" its name. The village has become the center for the arts complete with galleries and shops. The spring offers Petoskey Stone and other fossil collectors hours of treasure hunting along its many sandy beaches. Don't forget to visit **Petoskey's** unique shops in the historic Gaslight District. **Harbor Springs'** scenic beauty compares to few and includes the very scenic 31 mile route to Cross Village through the Tunnel of Trees. Harbor Springs also features several interesting shops that you'll want to take time and browse. Of course we can't overlook **Boyne's** high peaked hills which provide the scene for some of lower Michigan's finest downhill skiing.

Some outstanding restaurants in the area include *The Rowe Inn* (Ellsworth), *Tapawingo* (on St. Clair Lake) and *Pete and Mickey's at the Edgewater* (Charlevoix). For other good fixin's in Charlevoix, try homestyle cooking at *Darlene's*, dine on the lake at *Round Table Restaurant* or, for a Friday night fishfry, tasty hamburgers, pasties, or Mexican there's the *Lumberjack Saloon*.

BAY VIEW

THE GINGERBREAD HOUSE
MARY GRULER

(616) 347-3538
BED & BREAKFAST

Pastel hues, white wicker and floral gardens provide a romantic setting for this 1881 renovated Victorian cottage situated in the heart of Bay View, a National Historic Landmark. All rooms with view of Little Traverse Bay, private entrances and baths. Deluxe continental breakfast. No smoking/pets. Open May 14-October 25. 4 rooms.

Daily $90-$130

BEAVER ISLAND

THE FISHERMAN'S HOUSE   **(616) 399-4314**
JON & SALLY FOGG   **COTTAGE**
Fully restored, Turn-of-the-Century cottage beautifully decorated with all the modern amenities of a modern 4 bedrooms, fireplace, completely furnished including equipped kitchen. Linens provided. Open June-Sept. No pets/no smoking. Major credit cards accepted.

Weekly: $1,000

BOYNE CITY

ATRIUM CONDOS/DILWORTH INN   **(800) 748-0160 • (616) 582-6220**
MAIN RENTAL OFFICE   **CONDOS/INN**
Built in 1912, the Dilworth Inn has 26 rooms with A/C, private baths, suites (multi-rooms), phone and CATV. Inn offers continental breakfast, excellent dining, and lounge (weekend entertainment). Open year around. Atrium condo units feature 1-3 bedrooms, fully furnished with equipped kitchens (1 bedrooms with limited kitchens), fireplaces, some with Jacuzzis.

Daily (Inn) $49-$99   Daily (Condos) $79-$199

DEER LAKE BED & BREAKFAST   **(616) 582-9039**
SHIRLEY & GLENN PIEPENBURG   **BED & BREAKFAST**
Contemporary waterfront B&B on Deer Lake in quiet country setting. An all season resort area near Boyne Mountain. Features five rooms with private baths, individual heat and A/C. Enjoy full breakfast by candle-light on china and crystal. Personalized classes to make your own 24kt. Gold or Sterling Silver rings are offered by the experts.

Daily $80-$105 (dbl.); $60-$85 (sgl.)

HARBORAGE CONDOMINIUMS   **(800) 456-4313 • (616) 582-3000**
MAIN RENTAL OFFICE   **CONDOS**
Two and 3 bedroom condos, close to Lake Charlevoix and near a full-service marina. Completely equipped and beautifully decorated. Prices exclude holidays.

Weekly $1,325-$1,950   2 Day Pkg. $395-$525

THE LANDINGS   **(800) 968-5115 • (616) 547-1222**
VACATION PROPERTY RENTAL AND MGT. CO.   **CONDO**
Two bedroom/2 bath condos on the shores of Lake Charlevoix in the heart of northwest Michigan's recreational playground. Sandy beach, heated pool, boat slips. Only minutes from Boyne Country Championship Golf. An excellent rental value, located in Boyne City. Call early for best availability.

Weekly $1,600

JOHN C. SCHADE
(734) 675-2452 • (734) 675-2873
CONDO

Spacious, 3-level condo overlooks Lake Charlevoix. Completely furnished (w/linens), sleeps 6. Features king/queen size beds, full kitchen, microwave, dishwasher, Jenn-Aire grill, 4 baths, fireplace, sauna, private beach and dock, balcony, patio, CATV, VCR, washer/dryer. In Boyne City — walking distance to shops. Minimum 1 week rental. $700 non-refundable deposit per week. No pets. References please.

Weekly $ 1,400 ($75 cleaning fee)

NANCY SERRA
(810) 625-8705
CHALET

In prime golf area. Deck overlooks a panoramic view of Lake Charlevoix. Only steps to beach. Conveniently located 2 blocks from marina. Chalet features 3 bedrooms (4 twin, 1 full, 1 queen and queen hide-a-bed). All amenities including CATV and linens. Weekly rentals. $250 deposit. No pets. Rental season May-October.

Weekly $650

WATER STREET INN
MAIN RENTAL OFFICE
(800) 456-4313 • (616) 582-3000
CONDOS

On Lake Charlevoix, these units are set along the sandy beach front near a full-service marina. 27 bedroom suites have Turn-of-the-Century antique decor, Jacuzzi/whirlpool tubs, complete kitchen, gas fireplaces, queen beds. Overnight or weekly packages. Prices exclude holidays.

Weekly $1,000   Daily $70-$175

Editor's Note: Good location and well decorated rooms make this a nice choice.

CHARLEVOIX

AARON'S WINDY HILL GUEST LODGE
(616) 547-6100 • (616) 547-2804
BED AND BREAKFAST

Victorian home with a huge riverstone porch. Enjoy a homemade buffet-style breakfast. Eight spacious rooms have private bathrooms (some with A/C). Two rooms can accommodate up to 5. One block north of drawbridge, one block east of Lake Michigan. Children welcome. Open May - Oct.

Daily $65-$125

MICHIGAN COTTAGES • CHALETS • CONDOS • B&B'S

BOULDER PARK COTTAGES
JOAN CHODAK

(248) 737-1850 • (616) 547-6480
COTTAGES

2 charming stone cottages (1 and 3 bedroom) are located in Earl Young's Boulder Park on 2 acres of land in a park-like setting. Only 800 ft. to Lake Michigan. Includes: bed linens, dishwashers, microwaves, phones, VCR, CATV and fireplaces. Outdoor furnishings, campfire, flowers abound. 50% deposit. Pets allowed.

Weekly $850 (1 bedroom); $1,300 (3 bedroom) Off-season rates available

Editor's Note: Part of Charlevoix's history. These 2 cottages are built in the style of Earl Young's boulder homes and are located on a quiet side street.

THE BRIDGE STREET INN

(616) 547-6606
BED & BREAKFAST

Built in 1895, this Colonial Revival home retains all the charm of yesteryear. Relax on its sweeping porch with view of Lake Michigan or in the bright living room. 8 guest rooms attired with old floral rugs on wooden floors, antique furnishings and plush beds. Breakfast and coffee served in the dining room.

Daily $65-$145 (In-season—May to October)

CHARLEVOIX COUNTRY INN

(616) 547-5134
BED & BREAKFAST

Visitors will feel welcomed as they enter this 1896 country decor inn. Relax and get acquainted in the common room, balcony or porch while watching boats and Lake Michigan sunsets. 8 bedrooms/2 suites, all with private baths. Continental breakfast buffet. Late afternoon beverage, wine and cheese social.

Daily $85-$140

HIDDEN VALLEY RESORT

(616) 547-4580 (Leave Message)
COTTAGES

Quiet, unspoiled resort on 620 ft. of Nowland Lake w/natural shoreline. Though rustic atmosphere, each cottage has been renovated to retain knotty pine charm and modern conveniences. 1-2 bedrooms, private bath, equipped kitchen, TV, screened porch. Sandy beach, excellent fishing lake. Linens not provided. Brochure available.

Weekly $450-$700 (Call for availability of 3 and 4 night rentals /rates)

SUE HUMMEL   **(248) 855-3?**

Lakefront condos sleep 2-8+ with 1-2 baths, A/C, firepl
and CATV. Designer furnished. Includes linens and laundry
distance to Charlevoix, marinas, beach. Heated pool. Lots of
2 hours. Available year around. 50% deposit.

Weekly $400-$1,000   Daily $75-$150   (summer rate

DR. DEBORAH JEAN OR DENISE   **(248) 545-8900** • **EMAIL: dsjean@aol.**
                                                          COTTAG

Log cottage on Lake Michigan, approximately 12 miles from Charlevoix.
Wide sandy beach. Two bedrooms with loft (sleeps 8) includes washer/dryer
and microwave, TV/VCR. Near golf and Michigan's finest gourmet
restaurants. Pets allowed.

Weekly $1,200 (June-Aug.); $450-$900 (Sept.-Oct.)

LARRY KISH   **(517) 349-5474** (HOME) • **(517) 482-7058** (WORK)
                                                   VACATION HOME
Built in 1993, home features 4 bedrooms/2 baths, 128 ft. water frontage, 600
sq. ft. deck, dock, raft, 5 sliding glass doors and lots of windows. Dishwasher,
washer/dryer, TV/VCR and stereo. Vaulted ceiling. Fabulous view. Available
year around.

	Sept.-June	July/Aug.	Xmas/New Years
Weekly	$1,400	$1,900	$1,900

LAKE CHARLEVOIX   **(616) 536-7343**
MARIE YETTAW   **COTTAGES/CONDOS/HOME**
From spacious, 4-bedroom lakefront home or contemporary condominium units
to smaller, traditional 2 bedroom cottages, there's an accommodation available
to fit your needs and budget. Some accommodations include CATV, A/C, boat
wells, washer/dryers, fireplace, private decks/patios. Call for details.

Weekly $450 to $1,980

*Editor's Note: Diverse range of properties. Lakefront home is indeed spa-
cious and the condo units are well decorated and very appealing.*

LAKEFRONT LOG LODGE   **(616) 536-2851**
SHARON & AL FROST   **VACATION HOMES**
These 2 spacious, 7 bedroom vacation homes with serene setting offers a spectacular view of Lake Charlevoix. Features 3 full baths, large modern kitchen,
CATV, fireplace, dock, campfire area and swing set, 3 decks and 200 ft. of sandy
beach. Sleeps up to 25—great for 3 or 4 families. Only 50 ft. from Lake Charlevoix
and 5 minutes from town. Great swimming and fishing. Available year around.
50% deposit. No pets. *Website: www.freeway.net/frosthome*

Weekly $3,500 ea. (off-season rates available)

...ES NORTH INN
...E HAZELTON

(616) 547-0055 • (800) 968-5433
CONDOMINIUMS

...bedroom suites with lofts and full or partial kitchens. Indoor/outdoor pool. ...TV, A/C, VCR and Jacuzzi whirlpools in all units. Located in downtown ...arlevoix. Pets allowed - call for information. Corporate rates available.

...Daily $75-$110 (mid-week); $85-$120 (weekends)

THE BLUFFS
LAURA MCREYNOLDS

(734) 663-8056
LOG CABIN

Charming 1920's log cabin on Lake Michigan with fieldstone fireplace, beamed ceilings, sunroom with gorgeous sunset views, antiques and cozy cabin furniture. Full kitchen, washer-dryer, fenced yard and private beach. 2 bedrooms plus sleeping loft (sleeps 6-8). Open year around.

Weekly $1,300 (June-August — off-season rates avail. Sept.-May)

DUANE TAYLOR

(616) 547-9004 • (616) 499-5246
VACATION HOME

Near downtown and beaches (7 blocks to Lake Charlevoix and 5 blocks to Lake Michigan), this lovely 5 bedroom home is fully furnished (linens included) with large, comfortable deck and warming fireplace. CATV, VCR, stereo. Available June 22-Sept. 2. 50% deposit. No pets.

Weekly $1,200 (assumes 4 adults)

UHRICK'S LINCOLN LOG

(616) 547-4881
COTTAGES/MOTEL/CAMPGROUNDS

25 cottages (1, 2 and 3 bedrooms) include full kitchens, CATV and linens. 2 blocks to beach and 1 mile to town. Open April to November. Pets allowed.

Daily $48-$150 (July/Aug.); $30-80 (off-season)

EASTPORT

EDEN SHORES
MARILYN & CHARLES WILMOT

(616) 264-9604
COTTAGE

Eastport cottage sits in a secluded wooded area. Quiet, clean. Bright sunroom with lots of windows. 5 minute walk to Lake Michigan beach. Recently redone — new carpeting, tile, walls, bathroom. Full kitchen. Linens provided No pets/smoking.

Weekly $450

ELLSWORTH

HOUSE ON THE HILL
CINDY & TOM TOMALKA
(616) 588-6304
BED & BREAKFAST

Elegant farmhouse on 53 acres overlooking St. Clair Lake. Woodlands with walking trails. Walking distance to gourmet restaurants, Tapawingo and Rowe Inn. Featured in Fodor's, Chicago Tribune and other major publications. Evening social hour. Full gourmet breakfast. Centrally located to many attractions. Winter packages available.

Daily $125-$150

HARBOR SPRINGS

HAMLET VILLAGE
c/o LAND MASTERS
(616) 526-2641
HOMES & CONDOS

❋ EDITOR'S CHOICE ❋

Contemporary country styling located in the secluded, rolling hills of Harbor Springs. Slope side condos features ski-in/ski-out access to Nubs Nob. Condos offer 1-3 bedroom + loft. Homes/chalets (between Boyne Highlands and Nubs Nob) vary in size and sleep from 6-12, 1-3 baths. A few miles to beaches/marinas/golf. Prices vary based on season and size of accommodation. Call for special package prices.

	Condos	Homes
Weekly	$798-$1,190	$637-$1,176
Weekend Pkgs.	$260-$1,096	$440-$960

Editor's Note: Scenic locations and very well maintained properties make Hamlet Village accommodations a good choice. You Nubs Nob fans will love the ski-in/out privileges available at their condos.

KIMBERLY COUNTRY ESTATE
RONN & BILLIE KIMBERLY
(616) 526-7646
BED & BREAKFAST

This colonial plantation style B & B welcomes its guests with a lovely veranda and terrace overlooking the swimming pool and Wequetonsing Golf Course. On several secluded acres. Features 6 exquisitely decorated rooms, some with fireplace, sitting area and Jacuzzi. 4 min. to Boyne Highlands or Nubs Nob.

Daily $145-$300

MICHIGAN COTTAGES • CHALETS • CONDOS • B&B'S

THE VERANDA BED & BREAKFAST
DOUG YODER

(616) 526-7782
BED & BREAKFAST

This delightful B&B is as warm and inviting as a Norman Rockwell painting. All guests are treated to a full country breakfast on the wrap around enclosed porch which overlooks the Bay. Conveniently located to shops, restaurants, tennis courts, and beaches. Open year around. 4 rooms.

Daily $95-$195

TROUT CREEK CONDOMINIUM RESORT

(800) 748-0245 • (616) 526-2148
CONDOS

★ EDITOR'S CHOICE ★

Family resort with beautifully furnished units (accommodate 2-12) with full kitchens and fireplaces. 2 outdoor pools, spas, fitness center, indoor pool, tennis courts, trout ponds, nature trails. Nearby skiing with on-site cross-country trails and sleigh rides during winter. Nearby golf, beaches, on-site children's programs during summer. No pets.

Daily $80-$410 (call for special weekly rates)

Editor's Note: Contemporary, comfortable setting with plenty to do for couples or families.

LITTLE TRAVERSE BAY

HOLIDAY ACCOMMODATIONS

(800) 968-4353 • (616) 348-2765
CONDOS/CHALETS/COTTAGES

A variety of cottages, chalets and condos are offers throughout the Little Traverse Bay area. From 1 bedroom log styled chalets to 6 bedroom homes and condos. Prices to fit all budgets.

Weekly $675-$2,500 (June-Aug.); $425-$1,750 (Off-season)

ODEN

WINDJAMMER MARINA & CRAFT VILLAGE

(616) 347-6103
HOUSEBOATS

Stay and cruise in one of our houseboats on Crooked Lake. The 40 ft. Royal Capri sleeps 8 and includes head with hot water, shower, refrigerator with freezer, gas stove/oven, dishes and utensils. The 28 ft. Riviera Cruiser sleeps 4 and has gas stove, ice box, porta potty, hand pump water system, dishes and utensils. Deposit required. Rates do not include gas. No linens. Visa/MasterCard accepted.

Weekly $1,500 (40 ft.); $750 (28 ft.)

(3 Day Weekend or 4 Day Weekday Pkgs. $500-$900)

PETOSKEY

MONTGOMERY PLACE BED & BREAKFAST
RUTH BELLISSIMO & DIANE GILLETTE

(616) 347-1338
BED & BREAKFAST

1878 Victorian, formerly the Ozark Hotel. Located 3 blocks from Petoskey's famed Gaslight Shopping District. Large rooms, private baths; 80 ft. veranda overlooks Little Traverse Bay. Full breakfast — wine and snacks in afternoon. Close to golf, beaches, boating, downhill and x-country skiing. No pets/smoking.

Daily $95-$135

BARBARA MOYERS   **(734) 668-8507 (W) • (616) 347-4043 (S)**
COTTAGE

Spacious, multi-level cottage on Walloon Lake. Four bedrooms (can sleep 10), 2 full baths, 2 kitchens. Bring your own linens. Features lounge deck, fire pit. Aluminum boat. Swimming deck. Prefer 2 week rentals but will except 1 week. No pets/smoking please.

Weekly $1,825 (June-Aug.) Off-season rates available

NORTHERN LIGHTS RETREAT
JAN AND MIKE STAGG

(734) 426-2874
EMAIL: 2staggs@ameritech.net
VACATION HOME

★ EDITOR'S CHOICE ★

Distinctive, family-style 4 bedroom, 2 bath home sleeps 8-10. Large sun/shade deck with grill. 1-1/2 miles to golf, boat launch and swim area; 6 miles to Petoskey/Boyne Highlands/Harbor Springs; 25 miles to Gaylord golf; 35 miles to The Bridge and casinos. Linens included. Sorry, no pets.

Weekly $800 (Memorial Day-Labor Day); $700 (April, May, Sept., Oct.)

Editor's Note: Quality upgrades, appealing decor, spacious outdoor deck and very good price make Northern Lights a dandy. See our review.

MICHIGAN COTTAGES • CHALETS • CONDOS • B&B'S

WILDWOOD ON WALLOON
(800) 632-8903 • (616) 582-9616
MAIN OFFICE - RESERVATIONS
CONDOS

Lovely townhouse community near the borders of Walloon Lake. Enjoy 3 professionally designed holes of golf and two carefully sited tennis courts. Units vary in interior design but maintain a contemporary theme. Units sleep from 6-12 and features up to five bedrooms with 2 baths and fully equipped kitchens. Amenities frequently include fireplace, TV/VCR. No pets.

Weekly (summer) $1,125-$1,425; 2 Night Pkgs. (spring-fall-winter) $350- $600

Editor's Note: On well groomed grounds surrounded by trees, the units we visited varied in decor but maintained a very comfortable, contemporary theme.

TRAVERSE CITY & SURROUNDING AREAS

COVERS:

ACME • ARBUTUS LAKE • BELLAIRE • BENZONIA • CEDAR •
CENTRAL LAKE • CLAM LAKE • EAST BAY • ELK LAKE/ELK RAPDIS •
GLEN ARBOR • GRAND TRAVERSE BAY • INTERLOCHEN • LAKE LEELANAU •
LAKE SKEGEMOG • LELAND • LONG LAKE • OLD MISSION PENINSULA •
PLATTE LAKE • SILVER LAKE • SPIDER LAKE • SUTTONS BAY •
THOMPSONVILLE • TORCH LAKE • WEST BAY

From beautiful sunsets and lazy days on a sandy beach to the rush of downhill skiing—**Traverse City** and the surrounding areas have a variety of fun and excitement in a setting of blue waters, rolling hills, and natural beauty. Dining, shopping, entertainment, and even gambling will fill your days and nights.

One of the City's biggest events is the annual Cherry Festival, held the week of July 4th. Thousands of people come to the area to enjoy parades, concerts, fireworks, air shows, Native American pow-wows and crafts along with other family activities. If you're interested in coming by, we highly recommend you plan well in advance for this very popular event.

Enchanting **Interlochen** is a wonderful place to visit throughout the year. You'll want to stroll along its cool waters, scented pines and natural grounds. Here you'll find the internationally known Interlochen Center for the Arts and the Interlochen Fine Arts Camp where gifted young artists (ages 8-18) develop their creative talents with concentrated studies in their specialized areas of theatre, painting, sculpturing, music and more. In addition to over 750 student performances yearly, the Interlochen Center for the Arts also hosts a variety of nationally known music and recording artists. From classical and folk to jazz, blues and pop, the diversity of music continues to attract area residents and visitors from across the world. For performance and ticket information, call (616) 276-6230.

168   ALL RATES SUBJECT TO CHANGE

TRAVERSE CITY & SURROUNDING AREAS

(continued...)

Want to try something a little *lifting*? Get a really scenic view of the Traverse City area from a hot-air balloon. You'll be awed by views of **Elk and Torch Lakes, East and West Grand Traverse Bay**, Manitou and Fox islands, to name a few. Contact the area Chamber of Commerce (see Chamber section of this book) for further information.

The 70,000 acre Sleeping Bear Sand Dunes National Lakeshore is another must see while visiting the area. Drive south along M-22 through the charming communities of **Leland** and **Glen Arbor**. The Pierce Stocking Scenic Drive (closed in mid-November) is a relaxing and enjoyable car tour. Of course, hiking the dunes in the park has become a fun challenge for youngsters of all ages. And, if you still have energy after getting to the top, take a short walk across the sand to a wonderful overlook of Lake Michigan.

The **Leelanau Peninsula** and **Old Mission Peninsula** are known for their beautiful scenery. They're also known as *wine country*. Winery tours and tasting have become a popular day time diversion for many. Check out our "Michigan Wineries" section for further information.

Feeling like Lady Luck is on your side today? Then put on that *lucky ha*t and head out to one of two area casinos. The Leelanau Sands Casino is 20 miles north of Traverse City near **Suttons Bay**; and the Turtle Creek Casino is four miles east of Acme in Williamsburg. Our Michigan "Casinos" chapter provides phone numbers and addresses of casinos in this area and throughout Michigan.

Take a ride on the Malabar, a two-masted schooner. Then, drop by The Music House north of Traverse on US-31 (Acme) to enjoy a unique museum where history, education and entertainment combine.

Just about time to eat? There are many popular restaurants in the area. Just a few: *Poppycock's* (on Front Street in downtown Traverse City) is known for inventive dinner entrees, fresh pastas and unique salads (we personally recommend their Front Street Salad). Others include *Hattie's Grill* or *Boone's Prime Time Pub* (Suttons Bay); *Trillium* (Grand Traverse Resort); *Boone's Long Lake Inn, Sweitzer's by the Bay* (Traverse City); or *Scott's Harbor Grill* (M-22 on Sleeping Bear Bay Beach), or *LeBea*r (M-22 in Glen Arbor); *Bluebird* (Leland); *or Stubbs* (Northport). *Windows* (on West Bay Shore Drive, north of Traverse City), though pricey, has developed a reputation for preparing some of the area's finest cuisine. *Spencer Creek Fine Dining* in the **Torch Lake/Alden** area (also higher priced) prepares creative and diverse fare with a very distinctive Italian flavor and, being on Torch Lake, the view is wonderful.

TRAVERSE CITY & SURROUNDING AREAS

(continued...)

For tasty and inexpensive "eats" give *Art's Tavern* a try (**Glen Arbor**) for breakfast, lunch or dinner. Their special 1/3 pound ground chuck burger with bacon, blue cheese along with homemade chili (not too spicy) is quite good. For good pizzas and burgers in a country-styled family restaurant, try *Peegeos Restaurant* in the **Spider Lake** area. *Mabel's* (in Traverse City, on Front Street) is known for freshly prepared baked goods and traditional homemade meals. For a fun 50's deco atmosphere and to re-discover the taste of good old-fashioned hamburgers, *Don's Drive-In* is definitely a dandy choice.

We can't forget the *Grand Traverse Dinner Train* for a truly unique dining experience. You'll enjoy a four-course lunch or five-course gourmet dinner while touring the scenic Boardman River Valley area. For additional information on the dinner train, call (616) 933-3768.

ACME

GRAND TRAVERSE RESORT   **(800) 748-0303 • (616) 938-2100**
CONDOS

☀ EDITOR'S CHOICE ☀

Luxury condos — some with wet bars, whirlpool baths and fireplaces. Casual to fine dining in a variety of restaurants. Enjoy shopping galleries, indoor-outdoor tennis, weight room, indoor-outdoor pools and aerobic studio. Children's center. Groomed x-country ski trails and 54 holes of championship golf including *The Bear* and *Northern Knight.*

Call for Rates

Editor's Note: Premier resort. Excellent accommodations with abundant amenities.

ARBUTUS LAKE

GEORGE CZANSTKE   **(248) 373-0005 • (616) 947-0039**
VACATION HOME

Situated on Arbutus Lake with 200 ft. of private sandy beach, this 5 room, 2 bedroom and 1 bath, log cottage is furnished w/fireplace and a fully equipped kitchen. It also offers dock, pontoon boat and raft. Sleeps 5. No pets.

Weekly $900

MAC'S LANDING RESORT

(616) 947-6895
COTTAGES

14 cottages (1-3 bedrooms, sleeps 2-8) on 700 ft. of beautiful lakefront property. Scenic setting and sandy beach. Features docks, great swimming, raft, boats and motors, campfire pits, playground, volleyball and horseshoes. Bring linens. Open June-Sept. Pets allowed.

Weekly $300-$680

PINEVIEW RESORT

(616) 947-6792
COTTAGES

12 cottages on the lake (some fireplaces), 2-3 bedrooms (sleeps 5-8). Fire pit on beach, lounge deck and dock on lake. Enjoy volleyball, shuffleboard, horseshoes and playground area. Boats, motors, pedal boats and pontoons available for rent.

Weekly $570-$660

SHADYCREST RESORT

(616) 947-9855
COTTAGES

Nine cottages, 1-2 bedrooms (sleep 4-8). Provide your own linens and towels. All sports lake and sandy beach. Boats included, motors available for rent. Open year around. Pets allowed.

Weekly $350-$575 (Based on 2 adults w/children. Reduced rates Sept.-May)

BELLAIRE

GRAND VICTORIAN B&B INN
STEVE AND GLENDA SHAFFER

(800) 336-3860
BED & BREAKFAST

1895 Victorian mansion built by lumber barons. On National Register. Inn features antiques, 3 fireplaces, etched glass and wicker-filled porch/balconies overlooking park. Elegant breakfast. Close to golf and skiing. 4 rooms w/ private baths. No smoking.

Daily $100-$130

SHANTY CREEK RESORT

(800) 678-4111
ROOMS/CHALETS/CONDOS

Four season resort on the lake. 3 championship golf courses including *The Legend* by Arnold Palmer. 41 downhill ski slopes, 31 km of x-country trails, ski school. Other amenities include tennis, mountain biking, health club, hiking, beach club and indoor/outdoor pools. Fine dining, live entertainment. 600 rooms, condos and chalets some with full to partial kitchens, fireplaces, Jacuzzis. Great swimming. No pets.

Golf Get-a-way Packages   (starting at) $89 (per person/per night)
Ski Season Packages   (starting at) $45 (per person/per night)

MICHIGAN COTTAGES • CHALETS • CONDOS • B&B'S

RICHARD & JO-ANN SOCHA **(734) 663-3766**
CHALET

This 3 bedroom, 2 bath, year around chalet sleeps 7 and offers a secluded setting. Completely furnished, TV/VCR, fireplace (wood provided), dishes, linen and maid service. It sits at the top of Schuss Mt. and offers ski-in, ski-out. A mecca for golfers, swimming pools in village. No pets/smoking.

Weekly $650*   Daily $200*   (* plus tax)

CLARE TAYLOR (AT SHANTY CREEK RESORT) **(517) 394-4162**
CHALET

On a secluded lot in the wooded, rolling hills area of Schuss Mountain. Lodging features 3 bedrooms/2 baths, fully equipped kitchen with microwave, ski storage area, electric heat, CATV w/remote control, and telephone. Linens provided. Use of hot tub, pool and sauna at Schuss Lodge. Available year around. No pets.

Weekly $500   Daily $125-$225

BENZONIA

HANMER'S RIVERSIDE RESORT   **RES: (800) 252-4286 • (616) 882-7783**
JOHN & BARBARA HANMER   COTTAGES

On the Betsie River, located near the Sleeping Bear Dunes National Lakeshore. 2 bedroom housekeeping units completely furnished with equipped kitchens, A/C, CATV, phone. Decks overlook the river. Enjoy the pool and Jacuzzi. Open year around. Summer fun, winter skiing and snowmobiling, fall/spring steelhead/salmon fishing. No pets.

Weekly $315-$490   Daily $55-$85

CEDAR

SUGAR LOAF RESORT   **RES: (800) 968-0576**
CHALET/TOWNHOUSE

Amenities include golfing, Lake Michigan beach, 3 swimming pools, tennis, casino, biking and hiking. New Palmer golf course. Nursery, kids camp, new water slide, miniature golf. One to 4 bedroom condo and townhouse units. Also motel units. Call for special ski and golf packages.

Chalet/Townhouses: $298 to $1,179 (total, 2 nights package)
Motel: $158-$469 (total, 2 night package)

WINGED FOOT CONDO (AT SUGAR LOAF RESORT) **(616) 846-3978**
JEANNE & JERRY SHERMAN   CONDO

Modern, contemporary, 2 bedroom (sleeps 7) condo on 18th fairway at Sugar Loaf Resort. Fireplace, full kitchen, TV, linens, pools. Overlooks golf course, ski hills (Palmer Course on premises). Lake Michigan beach 1 mile, Leland 6 miles, Traverse City 22 miles. Other nearby activities: Horseback riding, casino, boating. No pets. Open year around.

Daily $200

172   ALL RATES SUBJECT TO CHANGE

CENTRAL LAKE

BOB & BETTY KACZMAREK

(248) 363-8814
EMAIL: kacz@eaglequest.com
COTTAGES

★ EDITOR'S CHOICE ★

Two cottages (Lakeside and River's Edge) on Hanley Lake. Each with two bedrooms (comfortably sleeps 6). Near golf and skiing. Complete kitchens with refrigerators, stoves, microwaves, breadmakers, cooking/eating utensils. TV/VCR, gas grills, fire pit, picnic table, patio furniture, screened porches. Includes pontoon and fishing boats. Pets with security deposit. Short distance to town, beach and park.

Weekly $700   Weekend $300

Editor's Note: ***River's Edge*** *is an Editor's Choice. We enjoyed its quiet setting with relaxing view of the river from the cozy screened porch.*

CLAM LAKE

NORTHAIRE RESORT
MIKE & HELEN LAMBERT

(616) 347-1250
COTTAGES

6 furnished cottages (2-3 bedrooms) on Clam Lake. Great fishing! Docks, boats, paddle boat, grills and picnic tables. Cable-ready for your TV. Serene setting, sandy lake bottom, near nature preserve and marina. Open April 1- Nov. 1. Pets allowed.

Weekly (in-season) $395-$595   Daily (off-season) $50-$60

Editor's Note: Traditional resort with 1950's look. Located in a quiet, lakeside setting. Some newly completed renovations are very nice.

EAST BAY

THE BEACH CONDOMINIUMS

(616) 938-2228
CONDOS

These 30 luxury condos on Grand Traverse Bay feature private sun decks (sleeps 4), whirlpool baths, complete kitchen and 27" stereo CATV. Beautiful sandy beach, outdoor heated pool and hot tub plus daily housekeeping. Adjacent boat launch and close to championship golf. AAA discount, daily rentals, getaway and ski packages.

Daily $99 (and up)

MICHIGAN COTTAGES • CHALETS • CONDOS • B&B'S

NORTH SHORE INN
(800) 968-2365 • (616) 938-2365
CONDOS

Set on 200 ft. of private sandy beach on East Bay, these 26 luxury condos offer 1 and 2 bedrooms. Spectacular views of bay from front decks and balconies. Outdoor pool, sun deck. Full-size kitchens, dishwashers, microwaves, queen-size beds, remote TV w/HBO, VCR. Special fall, winter and spring weekend packages. Open year around.

Daily $189-$229 (prime season); $79-$139 (off-season)

Editor's Note: Well maintained, attractively decorated. All rooms provide waterfront views. Very nice beach area.

STONEWALL INN
(616) 223-7800
COTTAGE

Privately owned log cottage built in 1986 situated on Old Mission Harbor. Has fully equipped kitchen, fireplace, 2 full baths, private beach, washer/dryer, porch overlooking the water. No pets.

Weekly $800   (May-Nov. 1st)

TRAVERSE BAY INN
(616) 938-2646
CONDOS

All units are furnished with equipped kitchens including microwaves, A/C, CATV. Some rooms with whirlpool tub and fireplace. Pool, hot tub, gas grills and complementary bicycles. Swimming beach less than 1 mile away. Pets O.K. Major credit cards accepted.

Weekly $175-$1,175   Daily $35-$165

Editor's Note: Clean, contemporary, well maintained units. Sizes vary significantly.

ELK LAKE/ELK RAPIDS

CEDARS END ON ELK LAKE
(214) 424-2858 • (972) 301-9518
DEAN & SHARON GINTHER
VACATION HOME

Spacious 3 bedroom, 2 bath home on 450 ft. of private east Elk Lake frontage. Furnished, dishwasher, microwave, cookware, 2 fireplaces, dock with boat mooring. 50 acres of woodland attached. Excellent swimming, hiking, biking, boating and fishing. No linens. No pets. Available July-October.

Weekly $1,600 (off-season $1,000)

ELK RAPIDS BEACH RESORT
(800) 748-0049
CONDOS

Luxury condos overlooking Grand Traverse Bay, just minutes from Traverse City. Heated pool (in the summer), in room Jacuzzi and full size kitchen. No pets. Special off-season rates available.

Weekly $1,225 (dbl. occ., summer)   Daily $175 (dbl. occ.)

WATER'S EDGE RESORT

(616) 264-8340
COTTAGES/EFFICIENCIES/MOTEL

Come to the "water's edge" of beautiful Elk Lake ... where your family is treated like ours! For your comfort and enjoyment, we offer cottages, units with full kitchens, motel-type accommodations. Also sandy beach/children's play area, two docks, rowboats, a paddleboat, picnic tables, gas grills. Bring linens. No pets.

Weekly $450-$700

WANDAWOOD RESORT & RETREAT CENTER

(616) 264-8122
COTTAGES/DUPLEXES

On Elk Lake, 17 cottages with lakefront and orchard settings. Each varies in size from small 1 bedroom cottage to duplex and 5 bedroom homes. Full kitchen/bath facilities. 9 beach areas with docks plus 2 swimming rafts. Boats, canoes and paddle boards available. Area for field sports and a paperback book library for those quiet times. Open Memorial Day to mid-November.

Weekly $380-$1,165

WHISPERING PINES
JERRY McKIMMY

(616) 329-1937
LAKEFRONT HOME

3 bedroom ranch, walkout lower level on the west side of Elk Lake (100 ft). Features C/A, washer/dryer, microwave, dishwasher, CATV/VCR. Linens provided. Boat lift. Also, improved back lot with water access. Septic, water and electrical available for separate RV hookup. No smoking/pets.

Weekly $1,600

WHITE BIRCH LODGE

(616) 264-8271 • EMAIL: WBLodge@aol.com
CONDOS/LODGE

Year around resort on Elk Lake. Packages offer 3 meals a day plus water-skiing, wind surfing, sailing, tennis, children's programs and more. Accommodations range from simple lodge rooms to deluxe condominiums. Children 2-12 half price. Call for brochure. *Website: www.whitebirchlodge.org*

Weekly $465-$855 (per person)

GLEN ARBOR

THE HOMESTEAD
MAIN OFFICE RENTALS

(616) 334-5000
CONDOS

★ E D I T O R ' S   C H O I C E ★

1 mile of frontage on Lake Michigan, 3 miles on Crystal River, surrounded by the Sleeping Bear Dunes. Shops, golf academy, tennis, pools, restaurants, x-country and downhill skiing, conference centers, lodge rooms, suites and condos ranging from studio to 4 bedrooms. Closed late Oct.-Christmas; mid-March-May (open winter weekends). Contact the rental office for special package prices.

Weekends $145-$466   Weekly $825-$3,260

Editor's Note: Secluded location in a scenic setting... a favorite of ourstaff for years.

WHITE GULL INN
S. W. THOMPSON

(616) 334-4486
BED & BREAKFAST

Older 2 story home on a lovely wooded lot in Glen Arbor. Nestled between Sleeping Bear Sand Dunes and the lake shore of Sleeping Bear Bay. Walking distance to shops, restaurants, tennis courts, hiking trails. Short drive to golf courses and Glen Lakes. 5 rooms. Major credit cards accepted.

Daily $65-$75

GRAND TRAVERSE BAY

TRAVERSE BAY CASINO RESORT -
THE BEACH

(800) 634-6113 • (616) 946-5262
MOTEL/CONDOS

This all season resort is located on 700 ft. of sugar sand beach on the East Arm of Grand Traverse Bay. Most units face the water and include double or queen size beds and refrigerator. Some include kitchen, microwave, whirlpool tubs, wetbar, and /or patios/balconies, CATV. Sleeps 2-6 people. No pets.

Daily $55-$225

INTERLOCHEN

BROOKSIDE COTTAGES
KEITH & TAMMY ENSMAN

(616) 276-9581
COTTAGES

Located in the Traverse City/Interlochen area, with 250 ft. lake frontage. 13 cottages vary in size (studio - 3 bedrooms) and sleeps 6. Includes fully equipped kitchens. Heated, in-ground swimming pool, game/recreational room. Motors and pontoon rentals. Open year around. No pets.

Weekly $395-$590

Ellis Lake Resort
George & Teresa Hill

Log cabins and rooms on secluded lake surrounded b~
mosphere. Kitchen facilities, some with Franklin fir~
outdoor hot tub, boats, canoes, more. Linens includ~
skiing in winter. Resort featured in *Midwest Living Mag~*

Weekly $435-$550   Daily $54-$114

Judy's Place

(616) 263-7171 • (248) 626-2464
Log Home

★ EDITOR'S CHOICE ★

Log ranch-style home, built in 1992 on 1.12 wooded acres with sandy beach area on small, clean spring-fed lake. 5 miles to Interlochen, 20 miles SW of Traverse City. 4 bedrooms, 3 full baths, can sleep 10. Full kitchen, stacked, full-size washer/dryer. Private outdoor hot tub. Well behaved pets O.K. with an additional $25 charge. Prefer non-

smokers. Photos available. Open year around. Everything provided except food, clothing and guaranteed good weather!

Weekly $1,400   Daily $225   3-Nite Pkg. $600

Editor's Note: Quality home—packed with features and ambiance. Wonderful location. Highly recommended.

Mary Mueller & Mark Payne

(616) 276-6756
Cabin

Cozy cabin on 2-1/2 wooded acres with 125 ft. Green Lake frontage. One bedroom with additional set of bunk beds. Sleeps 2-4. Fully equipped kitchen with microwave. Provide your own linens/towels. Large wood deck. Private dock and 10 ft. rowboat included. Open May-Sept. No smoking. Pets allowed.

Weekly $395

LAKE LEELANAU

OLLI LODGE

(616) 256-9291
Cottages/Apts./Lodge

This homey retreat offers a great view of Lake Michigan from their 5 cottages, 11 apartments and 6 lodge rooms. Apartments (1-3 bedrooms) are newer. Cottages and lodge simply furnished but clean. Several steps down leads to pebbled beach. Tennis, rowboat, kayaking, volleyball and shuffleboard. Open year around. Major credit cards.

Weekly $650-$1,100

MIMI'S RETREAT
MARLENE VANVOORST

(616) 941-1663 • EMAIL: **ac453@tcnet.org**
VACATION HOME

Lakefront home on east shore, 2 bedrooms plus loft (can sleep 6). Screened porch. Furnished except linens. Includes use of rowboat. Safe swimming. No maid service available - guests are requested to leave the cottage in clean condition for the next renters. No pets.

Weekly $540 (and up)

Editor's Note: Simply furnished older cottage. We liked the high, wood beamed ceiling and great view of the lake. Wear aqua shoes to enjoy your swim. See our review.

WEST WIND RESORT

(616) 946-9457
COTTAGES

10 cottages feature 2 to 4 bedrooms (sleeps 4-10) some with fireplaces. Facilities have children's playground, hot tub. Paddle boards, kayaks and canoe rentals. Protected harbor. Open year around. No pets.

Weekly $785-$1,750 (Call for special off-season rates)

LAKE SKEGEMOG

JOHN KING

(248) 349-4716
HOME

Lakefront home on 200 ft. of sandy beach near Traverse City. 4 bedrooms, 2 baths, fully furnished with fireplace. Spacious deck overlooking Lake Skegemog which is part of Elk-Torch chain of 5 lakes. Rowboat. Very clean. One family limit. No smoking/pets.

Weekly $1,400 (June-Aug); $800 (Off-season)

LELAND

MANITOU MANOR   **(616) 256-7712**
BED & BREAKFAST

Beautifully restored 1900 farmhouse surrounded by cherry orchards and woods. Queen size beds, private baths, on the main floor in the wing of the home. Huge parlor with fieldstone fireplace and TV. Breakfast features Leelanau County specialties. Near sand dunes, bike trails, beaches, golf, x-country and downhill skiing. Non-smoking. No pets. Open all years. 5 rooms.

Daily $85-$125

LONG LAKE

RON JONES OR FRED JONES   **(616) 946-5119 • (810) 286-1582**
COTTAGE

Two bedroom log cottage w/knotty pine interior features fireplace (wood provided), color TV and full kitchen with microwave. Private beach, dock, 12 ft. aluminum boat, gas BBQ grill, picnic table, lawn furniture. Bring linens. Located 6 miles from Traverse City. Available year around. Pets allowed.

Weekly $650

LINDEN LEA ON LONG LAKE   **(616) 943-9182**
BED & BREAKFAST

✸ EDITOR'S CHOICE ✸

"Enchanting spot on a crystal-clear lake...reminiscent of on Golden Pond," Fodor's B&B Guide. Lakeside bedrooms with window seats, antiques and treasures. Relax by the fire, listen for the loons. Peaceful sandy beach with row boat, paddle boat. Private baths. Full breakfast. Central A/C. 2 rooms.

Daily $85-$110

Editor's Note: Peaceful, picturesque surroundings and charming hosts make Linden Lea a very nice choice.

OLD MISSION PENINSULA

BOWERS HARBOR BED & BREAKFAST   **(616) 223-7869**
BED & BREAKFAST

1870 fully remodeled country farmhouse with private sandy beach is located in the Old Mission Peninsula. Open year around. Enjoy a gourmet breakfast in the dining room overlooking the Harbor. 3 rooms w/private baths.

Daily $110-$140

MICHIGAN COTTAGES • CHALETS • CONDOS • B&B'S

CHÂTEAU CHANTAL BED & BREAKFAST   **(616) 223-4110**
BED & BREAKFAST

★ E D I T O R ' S   C H O I C E ★

Retreat to the Old World in this *new*, fully operational vineyard, winery and B&B. Set on a beautifully landscaped, scenic hill in the Old Mission Peninsula, this grand estate features an opulent wine tasting room and 3 delightful guest rooms (includes 2 suites) with private baths. Handicap accessible. Full breakfast.

Daily $105-$135   (assumes 2 people - $25 for each additional person)

Editor's Note: Grand estate with a spectacular view of Old Mission Peninsula. You'll enjoy their "Jazz at Sunset" (small charge) program, too.

PLATTE LAKE

PLATTE LAKE RESORT I   **(616) 325-6723**
COTTAGES

On beautiful Big Platte Lake, these 1-3 bedroom cottages are completely furnished and carpeted with kitchenettes. All include dishes, CATV, picnic tables and grills. Fishermen, hunters and golfers welcome. Open April-November. Daily and weekly rentals. No pets.

Daily $50 and up (based on number of people)

RIVERSIDE   **(616) 325-2121**
COTTAGE

All season fun! Fish, swim, canoe, hike, snowmobile, ski, sightsee—be "UP NORTH". Newer two-story home built in 1990, located on the Platte River in Honor, MI, 30 miles from Traverse City; 10 minutes from Lake Michigan. 4 bedrooms, 2 baths, fully equipped kitchen, CATV, VCR. No pets. Available year around.

Weekly $320   Daily $65 - $80

SILVER LAKE

GERALD NIEZGODA   **(616) 943-9630**
COTTAGE

Furnished vacation cottage on Silver Lake offers 80 ft. private frontage, 2 bedrooms (sleeps 4-6), sandy beach, swimming, fishing, sailing, skiing, outstanding view. Only 2 miles from new mall and 4 miles to Traverse City. Includes fireplace, CATV, VCR, microwave, boat and dock. Bring towels. Open all year. No pets/smoking.

Weekly $665   (Based on occupancy of 4)

RAYMOND PADDOCK & JILL HINDS

(616) 943-8506
COTTAGE

Fully furnished 3 bedroom cottage accommodates 8 people and features full kitchen, fireplace, stereo, TV, grill and 2 decks. Also features dock, swim raft, canoe and rowboat. Open June-Sept. Pets allowed.

Weekly $600 (includes tax)

SPIDER LAKE

BEACH HOUSE @ SPIDER LAKE
ROLF & KATHY SCHLIESS

(616) 946-5219
Email: harolds@michcom.com
COTTAGE

✸ EDITOR'S CHOICE ✸

Lots of fun & sun! This private home also includes a bunk house, large family room with a huge brick fireplace, CATV, full kitchen, nice swim area, dock and pontoon boat. A deck across the front offers beautiful lake views. Available all year. No pets. *Website: www.traversecity.com/harolds/*

Weekly (summer) $925 (6-8 people)

Editor's Note: Clean, comfortable and inviting interior. Plenty of windows, great deck with relaxing view of lake. Good swimming area. See our review.

HAROLD'S RESORT
ROLF & KATHY SCHLIESS

(616) 946-5219
Email: harolds@michcom.com
COTTAGES

✸ EDITOR'S CHOICE ✸

7 log cabins sit on a private peninsula overlooking beautiful Spider Lake with a terrific, safe and sandy beach. Open all year. Nightly and Bed & Breakfast package rates available. Most have beautiful lake views from screened porches. Private bath, equipped kitchens, carpet and ceiling fans. No pets. *Website: www.traversecity.com/harolds/*

Weekly (summer) $320 (2 people); $650 (2 bedroom cabins/4-6 people)

Editor's Note: Friendly, cozy, picturesque resort with an excellent beach. Cottages kept in very nice condition. See our review.

L' DA RU LAKESIDE RESORT, INC.
DANNY & JILL RYE

(616) 946-8999
COTTAGES

Built in 1923, this lodge was once the hideout for Al Capone. Come see how the notorious lived. 455' lake frontage. 17 cottages, added in the mid-1950's, have been updated. Each is complete with eating/cooking utensils, coffee maker, toaster and 20" CATV's. Linens and bedding provided. Boats included — motors available. Good swimming beach. Towels $15 per person for a week. Open year around. No pets.

Weekly $550-$1,095 (June-Aug.); $300-$900 (off-season)

Editor's Note: Great beach, private location, nicely maintained, traditional cottages.

MICHIGAN COTTAGES • CHALETS • CONDOS • B&B'S

JACK & ROSEMARY MILLER
(616) 947-6352
COTTAGE

Attractive lakefront log cottage on Spider Lake. Offers knotty pine interior, 2 bedrooms (with linens), fireplace, electric heat, TV and complete kitchen including microwave. This quiet, quaint hide-away is furnished with antiques, oak dining set, china cabinet, brass bed and marble top dresser. 13 miles from Traverse City. No pets.

Weekly $400   (May-Oct.)

MOONLIGHT BAY RESORT
ROGER & NANCY HENDRICKSON
(800) 253-2853 • (616) 946-5967
COTTAGES

8 cottages on wooded setting with direct Spider Lake frontage. 1-3 bedrooms. Fully equipped kitchens. Rowboats, canoes, pedal boat included. Motor and pontoon boat rental available. Open year around. No pets. Call for brochure.

	1 Bedroom	2 Bedroom	3 Bedroom
Weekly (Summer) *	$510-$650	$700-$735	$905

* Off-season rates lower

Editor's Note: Traditional cottages. Nice beach area.

RED RANCH
HAROLD MYERS
(616) 946-3909
COTTAGE

3 bedrooms, ranch-style cottage with kitchen, dining area, living room with fireplace, enclosed porch facing the lake, 2 car attached garage. Located in a quiet, private area. Includes bedding, towels, microwave, washer, dryer, CATV, rowboat and dock. Good fishing/swimming, x-county skiing/snow-mobile trails nearby. $150 non-refundable deposit after May 1st. Pets allowed.

Weekly $600 (Seasonal rates)   Daily $75 (2 day min.)

WILKINS LANDING II
ROLF & KATHY SCHLIESS
(616) 946-5219
Email: harolds@michcom.com
COTTAGE

★ EDITOR'S CHOICE ★

An all glass front overlooks a quiet bay of Spider Lake with a large deck on the front. Fieldstone fireplace, full kitchen, TV/VCP, dock, paddleboat and pontoon boat. Near snowmobile, x-country ski trails and Fall Color Tours. Available all year. Pets with extra security deposit. *Website: www.traversecity.com/harolds/*

Weekly (summer) $850 (4-6 people)

Editor's Note: Airy, spacious home, open windows and great deck to view the lake. Pontoon boat takes you to nice swimming area. See our review.

WILKINS LANDING III
ROLF & KATHY SCHLIESS

(616) 946-5219
Email: harolds@michcom.com
COTTAGE

★ EDITOR'S CHOICE ★

Quiet, private & secluded! Surrounded by private forest. A path through the woods takes you to the waterfront and dock, rowboat and pontoon boat. A screened porch, deck, fireplace, whirlpool tub and queen-size log bed make this a great getaway retreat! TV/VCP. Open year around. No pets. *Website: www.traversecity.com/harolds/*

Weekly $950 (4-6 people)

Editor's Note: Very appealing cedar log home with fresh, open design. Lovely wooded setting. See our review.

WINDJAMMER RESORT

(616) 946-8466
COTTAGES

Clean, comfortable, rustic cottages are completely furnished for housekeeping. Seven cottages, 1-3 bedrooms, bathroom with shower, kitchen, living room, outside deck and grill. Kitchen fully equipped. Pillows/blankets provided (bring your own linens/towels). Sandy beach, hilly wooded, 160 ft. frontage. Boats/canoe available. No pets.

Weekly $500-$650

SUTTONS BAY

THE COUNTRY HOUSE

(616) 271-4478 • (616) 941-1010
VACATION HOME

Fully furnished house in Suttons Bay offers A/C and 2 bedrooms (sleeps up to 6). It is centrally located to Lake Michigan and Lake Leelanau. No pets/ smoking, please.

Weekly $625 (June-Aug.); $375 (off-season)

FIG LEAF BED AND BREAKFAST
JHAKI FREEMAN

(616) 271-3995
BED & BREAKFAST

Bring your camera! One-of-a-kind B&B features charming artistic embellishments throughout, and a 12 ft. natural waterfall. Waterfront park across the street. In Storybook Village of Suttons Bay. Classy and quaint shops, cafes within 2 blocks. Festive breakfasts! Casino, wineries, golf, skiing. Private and shared baths. Visa/MC.

Daily $90-$110

MICHIGAN COTTAGES • CHALETS • CONDOS • B&B'S

OPEN WINDOWS BED AND BREAKFAST　　　　**(800) 520-3722**
DON & NORMA BLUMENSCHINE　　　EMAIL: openwindows@centuryinter.net
　　　　　　　　　　　　　　　　　　　　　　　　BED & BREAKFAST

Charming, century-old home with lovely gardens, decks and old-fashioned front porch for relaxing. This warm, inviting home is decorated with your comfort in mind. Enjoy hearty homemade breakfast and friendly atmosphere. The village with its beaches, shops and restaurants is just a short walk away. 3 rooms (private baths). *Website:www.leelanau.com/openwindows*

Daily　　　$95-$115

STRAWBERRY HILL HOUSE AND CABIN　　　**(314) 726-5266**
CINDY CURLEY　　　　　　　　　EMAIL: cindylagc@aol.com
　　　　　　　　　　　　　　　　　　　　LOG HOUSE/CABIN

Vintage north woods ambiance. Rustic but refined log house on peaceful bluff/shoreline, sleeps 6. Log cabin sleeps 2-3. Panoramic orchard and bay views south of town, sand beach. Spacious, classic decor with stone fireplace and antiques; screened porch has wicker furniture. Beauty, comfort, and privacy. Furnished except linens. Non-smoking. No pets. Open May-November.

Weekly　　　$850-$1,200 (House) ; $475-$600 (Cabin)

THOMPSONVILLE

BETSIE VUE　　　　**(888) 834-0380 • (616) 834-0380**
　　　　　　　　　　　　　　　　　　　　COTTAGE

Year around cottage on Betsie River, 1-1/2 miles from Crystal Mountain Golf/Ski Resort. 2 bedrooms (sleeps 9), 2 baths. Features new furnishings, TV, VCR, CD player. Fully equipped kitchen. Linens provided. Large deck overlooking river. Enjoy skiing, biking, hiking, shopping, canoeing, golf, snowmobiling. No pets.

Weekly　　　$600　　　　Daily　　　$100 (2 night min.)

CRYSTAL MOUNTAIN RESORT　　　**(800) 968-7686 • (616) 378-2000**
MAIN OFFICE RENTALS　　　　　　　　CONDOS/HOMES

Deluxe condos/resort home. Enjoy in-room Jacuzzi, full service dining room, live entertainment, indoor and outdoor pools, fitness center, 36-hole golf course and tennis courts. Ski 34 downhill ski slopes and 35 kms. x-country ski trails, night skiing, rentals, lessons. Summer/winter children's programs. 28 miles from Traverse City. Conference facilities No pets.

Daily　　　from $81 (low season - assumes 2 people)

TORCH LAKE

WAS-WAH-GO-NING
JANE BLIZMAN
(248) 644-7288 • (616) 264-5228
COTTAGES

Two secluded homes on 800 ft. of Torch Lake amid 25 acres of woods and fields. Lodge features antique furnishings, snooker table, swim raft. Each house has fireplace, color TV/VCR, stereo, dishwasher, microwave, washer/dryer, dock with lift, picnic table, grill. No pets.

Weekly $1,350* (2 bedroom); $1,680* (5 bedroom) * Based on 4 people

TORCHLIGHT RESORT
ROBERT & GLENDA KNOTT
(616) 544-8263
COTTAGES

★ EDITOR'S CHOICE ★

Six cottages w/150 ft. frontage on Torch Lake (part of the Chain of Lakes). Features sandy beach, playground, excellent boat harbor, beautiful sunsets. Located between Traverse City and Charlevoix. Near excellent golf courses and fine restaurants. Open May thru October. No pets.

Weekly $500-$700 (Off-season rates available)

Editor's Note: Friendly owners, clean, simple, traditional cottages in a lovely setting make this one an enjoyable retreat.

TRAVERSE CITY

CIDER HOUSE BED & BREAKFAST
LYNN & SHIRLEY BOUTWELL
(616) 947-2833
BED & BREAKFAST

Hilltop colonial overlooking orchards. 5 minutes from Traverse City. Hardwood floors, French doors, bay windows and fireplaces. 4 rooms with twin, queen or king canopy beds, all private baths, CATV. Nearby golfing, swimming, biking and more. Enjoy a sumptuous breakfast on covered front porch - or shaded deck overlooking goldfish pond.

Daily $75

THE GRAINERY
RON & JULIE KUCERA
(616) 946-8325
BED & BREAKFAST

Relax in this 1892 Country Gentleman's farm on 10 lovely, quiet acres. Decorated in the country Victorian tradition. A/C, coffee pot, refrigerator, CATV and outdoor hot tub along with 2 golf greens and a pond. Full country breakfast. 5 rooms/private baths (2 rooms feature Jacuzzi and fireplace).

Daily $75-$139 (in-season); $55-$139 (off-season)

MICHIGAN COTTAGES • CHALETS • CONDOS • B&B'S

JIM & CONNIE LEGATO   **(616) 946-3842** • EMAIL: jthobby1@aol.com
HOME

Well maintained older home, 3 bedrooms, (total 5 beds/sleeps 9). Features CATV, VCR, phone and fully equipped kitchen. Linens provided. Quiet in-town location 2 blocks from swimming beach on Grand Traverse Bay and 4 blocks from town. Available year around. Public lighted tennis court 1 block. No pets.

Weekly $750 (summer); $500 (Winter)

RANCH RUDOLF   **(616) 947-9529**
LODGE/BUNKHOUSE

Entertainment Friday and Saturday nights. Restaurant and lounge with fireplace. Enjoy the hay rides, sleigh rides, river fishing, backpacking, horseshoes, hiking, tennis, swimming pool, badminton, volleyball and a children's playground. Visa and MC accepted.

	Bunkhouse	Lodge
Daily	$160-$210	$72-$89 (dbl.)

(1 day free with full week rental)

TALL SHIP MALABAR   **(616) 941-2000**
BED & BREAKFAST

Unique "floating" B&B! This large traditional sailing vessel offers overnight accommodations along with a 2-1/2 hour sunset sail w/picnic dinner and a hearty breakfast! Come join the crew for a special evening on this 105 ft., two-masted topsail schooner. Reservations 1 month in advance. May-Sept.

Daily $100-$175 (children 8-12 $47.50)

WHISPERING WATERS   **(888) 880-5557** • EMAIL: whisper@gtii.com
BED & BREAKFAST RETREAT   BED & BREAKFAST

Enjoy the tranquility of nature at our retreat surrounded by 42 acres of natural woods and streams. Explore hiking trails, relax in the outdoor hot tub, go tubing in the river. Three rooms/two baths plus 1 cabin. Specially crafted interiors highlight nature. Continental plus or full breakfasts. Personal growth workshops, guided nature walks, therapeutica massage available.

Daily $80-$95 (Rooms); $150 (Cabin)   (2 night min.)

Editor's Note: Lovely setting, creatively and tastefully decorated ... very comfortable for those seeking a quiet, back-to-nature retreat. See our review.

WINTERWOOD ON THE BAY   **(616) 929-1009**
R. SCHERMERHORN   COTTAGE

Recently built beach house on East Bay. Sleeps 4 (2 bedrooms), bath, kitchen, living/dining room, fireplace, hot tub on outside deck. Dishwasher, microwave, VCR and cable TV. Fully furnished kitchen. Linens provided. Private dock. No pets/smoking.

Weekly $775

WEST BAY

La Petite Maison Sur L'eau & Wyndenrock on the Bay

(616) 386-5462
Vacation Homes

2 private lodgings with safe swimming, hiking, bicycling, walking. One mile from Northport. Sorry, no pets.

La Petite: Intimate, charming, attractively furnished, 1 bedroom property features a large window overlooking the lawn to Grand Traverse Bay. Fireplace, fully equipped kitchen. Secluded, ideal for honeymooners or small family.

Weekly: $575-$650

Wyndenrock: 3 bedroom/1 bath, 1920's nostalgia summer home, on quiet, private and wooded lot - 166 ft. bay frontage. Beautiful view from 3 screened porches. French doors lead to outside balcony which overlooks Grand Traverse Bay. Comfortably furnished with piano. A massive stone fireplace adds to ambiance of the home. No smoking.

Weekly $975-$1,150

Editor's Note: Both properties well maintained. Wyndenrock is invitingly decorated with a true 1920's ambiance which is particularly appealing for those who enjoy nostalgia.

Lerew's Cottage
Elizabeth Teyema

(847) 740-7906
Home

Three bedroom home (sleeps 8) on 200 ft. of private sandy beach near Old Mission Light House. It can easily be shared by 2 families. Includes dishwasher, washer/dryer. Shallow water, safe swimming. Tennis and docking nearby. No pets.

Weekly $1,400

Ronald Mallek

(616) 386-5041 • (954) 384-6363
Cottage

This charming, 1 bedroom (sleeps 3), English country cottage features a private patio, many gardens and sandy beach. Fully furnished with fireplace, linens and equipped kitchen. No pets/smoking.

Weekly $500

Private Cottage
Ken

(616) 947-5948
Cottage

★ EDITOR'S CHOICE ★

One bedroom rental, large living room, private sandy beach, Grand Traverse Bay. Three blocks from downtown, 1 block to City tennis courts. Completely furnished, includes TV, microwave, canoe, rowboat. Please provide own linens. $100 deposit. Available June 15-September 10.

Weekly $750   (June - $650)

Editor's Note: Small, private cottage with all the conveniences. Quiet setting, large windows with spectacular sunsets make this one a gem.

MICHIGAN COTTAGES • CHALETS • CONDOS • B&B'S

The Victoriana 1898

(616) 929-1009
Bed & Breakfast

Visitors to this Victorian B&B are greeted with exquisitely crafted tiled fireplaces, oak staircase, gazebo and carriage house. Located in a quiet, historic district, the lodging is close to West Bay, downtown. "Very Special" breakfasts are served each morning. A/C. 3 rooms/private baths.

Daily $65-$90

CADILLAC • MANISTEE • ONEKAMA

The **Cadillac** area is an excellent stop for fishing and water sports enthusiasts with its two lakes (Cadillac and Mitchell) within its city limits, and many other lakes not far away. Wild and tame game are abundant at Johnny's Wild Game and Fish Park which also stocks its waters with plenty of trout. In February, come and enjoy the North American Snowmobile Festival.

On the shores of Portage Lake, with access to Lake Michigan, **Onekama** is a summer resort community with a charter-boat fleet, marina, white sandy beaches and lovely parks.

You'll definitely want to stop by to enjoy the lovely, historic Victorian port city of **Manistee**. The entire central business district of this community is listed in the National Register of Historic Places. You'll be delighted by the district's charming Victorian street lamps, museums, and shops. Stroll along the Riverwalk which winds along the Manistee River for more than a mile. Watch the boat traffic, stop at a restaurant, then take off your shoes and walk in the smooth sand of the beaches along Lake Michigan. The area also offers several challenging golf courses. Of course, you may prefer to take advantage of their charter-boat fishing or river-guide services. In winter, there's plenty of cross-country skiing and snowmobiling trails.

CADILLAC

American Inn Bed & Breakfast

(616) 779-9000
Bed & Breakfast

Built in 1896, this home features stained glass, oak carvings, antiques. Guest rooms include queen/king beds, CATV, A/C. Sauna and hot tub available. Master suite offers private spa, spiral staircase to walkout deck. Hearty, continental breakfast. Corporate rates. 5 rooms with private baths.

Daily $65-$150

MANISTEE

E.E. DOUVILLE HOUSE BED & BREAKFAST
BARBARA & BILL JOHNSON

(616) 723-8654
BED & BREAKFAST

1879 home with ornate handcarved woodwork. Interior shutters, soaring staircase, elaborate archways with pocket doors are original to the house. Charming rooms with antiques and collectibles. Sitting room, continental plus breakfast. Lake Michigan, beaches, Riverwalk, fishing, golf, historical buildings. Victorian shopping village within walking distance. Shared baths. 2 rooms.

Daily $60-$65

LAKE SHORE BED & BREAKFAST
WILLA BERENTSEN

(616) 723-7644
BED & BREAKFAST

Enjoy relaxation on the shore of Lake Michigan. Spectacular sunsets, sunrises, freighters and stars. Delicious full breakfasts served at your leisure in our smoke-free new cedar home. Private decks with a great deck at water's edge. Close to Victorian downtown, Riverwalk, Audubon Center, and year around sports. Shared baths. 2 rooms.

Daily $70-$80

THE MAPLES BED & BREAKFAST
CAROL KRANTZ

(616) 723-2904
BED & BREAKFAST

In the historic district, this spacious 1905 home features open staircase and oak paneling. Parlor suite with fireplace, private bath. Two other rooms (double or twin beds) share a bath. Relax on the wraparound porch and picnic deck. On tourist trolley line. Continental breakfast. Open May 1-September.

Daily $55-$65

ONEKAMA

LAKE MICHIGAN BEACH CHALET
DONNA

(312) 943-7565
CHALET

An elegant, 3,500 sq. ft., 3 bedroom/3 bath home on Lake Michigan. This spacious home features fireplaces, fully equipped kitchen, living room/dining room and family room with pool table, CATV, VCR and CD stereo. Lake and sunset viewing deck in addition to wraparound house deck with BBQ. Private setting. Maid service and linens included. No pets.

Weekly $1,800-$2,100   Monthly $6,000

ALL RATES SUBJECT TO CHANGE

REGION 6

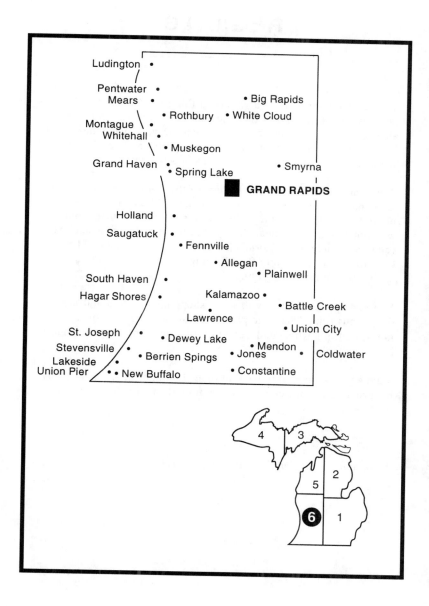

Ludington •

Pentwater •
Mears •   • Big Rapids

• Rothbury   • White Cloud

Montague •
Whitehall •
            • Muskegon

Grand Haven •   • Smyrna
          • Spring Lake

          GRAND RAPIDS

Holland •
Saugatuck •
          • Fennville

          • Allegan
                • Plainwell

South Haven •
Hagar Shores •   Kalamazoo •
                              • Battle Creek
          Lawrence •

St. Joseph •
Stevensville •   • Dewey Lake   • Union City
Lakeside •
Union Pier •   • Berrien Spings   • Mendon
            • • New Buffalo   • Jones   •   Coldwater

                  • Constantine

REGION 6

This unique region offers a variety of things to see and do. Where else would you find a city that can claim to have over 450 lakes. It also boasts over 100,000 acres of nature preserves, sand dunes, great fishing, golf, wonderful beaches, winter sports and one of the most scenic and elaborate bike trail systems in Michigan.

Sometimes referred to as the Riviera of the Midwest because of its land and climate, the area produces some of Michigan's finest premium wines. For something a little different in this orchard country, why not stop at the annual Cherry Pit Spitting Championship. You can relax watching the world's largest Music Fountain or add a new twist to fishing with Party Boat Fishing. If you feel daring, the area is also known for hang gliding.

You can spend the day with great shopping, theaters and double decker bus rides. There are plenty of festivals to enjoy, such as the famous Tulip Festival and Cereal Festival with the world's longest breakfast table.

Maybe you want to skip back in time. Try their museums or many historic districts which incorporate more than 1500 historic houses on 27 square blocks.

If you enjoy traditional vacation fun with a twist, this is the place.

LUDINGTON • GRAND RAPIDS • HOLLAND & SURROUNDING AREAS

COVERS: BIG RAPIDS • GRAND HAVEN • MEARS • MONTAGUE • MUSKEGON • PENTWATER • ROTHBURY • SMYRNA • SPRING LAKE • WHITE CLOUD • WHITEHALL

Nestled between Lake Michigan and the Allegan State Forest is **Fennville.** This community is surrounded by vineyards, such as Fenn Valley Vineyards. Take a tour and sample the premium grape and natural fruit wines.

A boardwalk, stretching for 2-1/2 miles from downtown **Grand Haven** to its pier, is bordered by shops and eateries and many sandy beaches. Be sure to visit Moser's, a unique shop filled with dried-flower arrangements and country style decorations. For a grand tour, hop on board the Harbor Steamer. For a spectacular sight, see the World's Largest Musical Fountain and visit Michigan's second largest zoo which has 150 species of animals, an aquarium, herpetarium, and more.

Grand Rapids, a unique blend of old and new, the city has many activities to keep you busy! Heritage Hill contains almost 100 historical homes. You'll also want to visit the John Ball Zoological Gardens, Roger B. Chaffe Planetarium, and the Voigt House, a Victorian home built in 1895.

People from all over come to **Holland's** special May event, the Tulip Time Festival; but there is much to see here throughout the year. Dutch Village should not be missed — and don't leave without seeing the Wooden Shoe Factory or Windmill Island.

Ludington features one of the largest charter-fishing fleets on Lake Michigan and is well known for its coho and salmon population. A piece of history can be found at the White Pine Village, a 19th century pioneering town. Bike through 22 miles of nature in Michigan's first linear state park, the Hart-Montage Bicycle Trail State Park. Several notable restaurants in the area include *P.M. Steamers* for a good view of marina activities or *Gibbs Country House* to indulge in their truly sticky, sticky buns and well prepared American cuisine in a family atmosphere.

With miles of sandy Lake Michigan beach, **Muskegon** is the place to book a fishing charter boat, Lake Michigan cruise, or rent a canoe or jet boat at one of many area marinas. You'll enjoy a full day of family fun at Michigan's Adventure Amusement Park & Wild Water Adventure (8 miles north of Muskegon, on U.S. 31). It's one of Michigan's largest amusement parks and features thrill rides, games and live shows for all ages.

LUDINGTON • GRAND RAPIDS • HOLLAND & SURROUNDING AREAS

(continued...)

Enjoy the New England charm of **Pentwater**, with its cozy cafes and double-decker bus. Build a sand castle in the Silver Lake State Park which features a huge sandbox with 450 acres of dunes for off-road vehicles and 750 acres for pedestrians only.

Hungry? Try some of Pentwater's unique restaurants: *Historic Nickerson Inn* for a warm and charming atmosphere (reservations requested); the *Village Pub* for casual pizza and fish sandwiches and evening entertainment of comedy or jazz; the *Antler Bar* known for their special burrito; and *Gull Landing* serves up steak and seafood.

With plenty to do in this great lake playground, you will find the atmosphere relaxed, the people friendly, and the scenery beautiful.

BIG RAPIDS

HILLVIEW RESORT   **(616) 796-5928**
GREG/PATTI BEDUHN   CABINS

Seven knotty pine cabins located on Hillview Lake, have 1-3 bedrooms, space heater, shower, picnic table, firepit, and screened porches. Kitchens fully equipped, double beds have pillows and a blanket. Great fishing (blue gill, sunfish, bass, pike), 5 row boats, 2 canoes and 1 paddle boat, included with rental. Sandy beach and swimming area. Boat landing if you would like to bring your own boat.

Call for Rates

GRAND HAVEN

BOYDEN HOUSE INN BED & BREAKFAST   **(616) 846-3538**
CORRIE & BEREND SNOEYER   BED & BREAKFAST

1874 Victorian Home. Its eclectic decor represents our varied interests and welcomes guests. Cozy rooms, delightful breakfasts, books, flowers, walks on beaches and boardwalks. Air conditioned rooms feature TV, some with fireplaces, balconies and whirlpool tubs. 7 rooms/private baths.

Daily $85-$120

GRAND RAPIDS

CHICAGO POINT RESORT **(616) 795-7216 • (517) 321-4562**
MARGUERITE STRAYER COTTAGES
Located between Kalamazoo and Grand Rapids, on the southeast side of Gun
Lake, near Yankee Springs Recreation Area with 5,000 acres of country
wilderness trails. Al Capone was said to have paid a visit here! The resort
features 2-4 bedroom cottages, fully furnished and equipped (provide your
own blankets, sheets and towels), private beach, fishing docks and picnic
area. Rowboats, canoes, paddle boat and motors available. No pets.

Weekly $550-$850

HOLLAND

DUTCH COLONIAL INN B&B **(616) 396-3664**
PAT & BOB ELENBAAS BED & BREAKFAST
1928 Dutch Colonial Inn features elegant decor with 1930 furnishings and
heirlooms. All rooms with tiled private baths, some with whirlpool tub for 2.
Honeymoon suites for that "Special Getaway". Close to shopping, Hope College,
bike paths, x-country ski trails and beaches. Business people welcome/corporate
rates. A/C. 4 rooms. *Website: www.bbonline.com/mi/dutch*

Daily $75-$150

EDGEWOOD BEACH **(734) 692-3941**
GERALYN PLAKMEYER COTTAGE
Located just north of Holland, in Beach Front Association. Home has 2 bedrooms,
1 bath, fully furnished, equipped kitchen, fireplace, central heat and CATV. 150 ft.
back from Lake Michigan, stairway to long sandy beach complete with sunsets
and fire pit. Provide your own linens. Available June to Sept. No pets.

Weekly $500

NORTH SHORE INN **(616) 394-9050**
BEVERLY & KURT VAN GENDEREN BED & BREAKFAST
★ EDITOR'S CHOICE ★
An elegant historical estate overlooking Lake Macatawa. Three guest bedrooms, furnished with antiques and handmade quilts. A three course, home
cooked breakfast is served on the porch or formal dining room. Guests may
choose king, queen or double beds, private or shared bath.

Daily $90-$110
*Editor's Note: Beautiful gardens and landscaped yard with a breathtaking
view of the Lake make this elegant B&B an excellent choice.*

MICHIGAN COTTAGES • CHALETS • CONDOS • B&B'S

THE OLD HOLLAND INN   (616) 396-6601
DAVE PLAGGEMARS   BED & BREAKFAST
Nationally registered B&B features 10 ft. ceiling, brass fixtures, stained glass windows and a lovely brass-inlaid fireplace. Antiques, fresh flowers decorate each air conditioned room. Enjoy special house-blend coffee, fresh muffins, fruit and cheese plates each morning.

Daily $40-$75

THE PARSONAGE 1908   (616) 396-1316
BONNIE VERWYS, HOSTESS   BED & BREAKFAST
Near Hope College and the Convention Center. Elegant European styled lodging, AAA approved. Featured in *Fodor's Guide* and *Detroit Free Press*. Three rooms with A/C (private or shared baths). Full breakfasts. Close to beaches, x-country skiing/bike trails, theater, fine dining and more No pet/smoking.

Daily $75-$110

LUDINGTON

BED & BREAKFAST AT LUDINGTON   (616) 843-9768
GRACE & ROBERT SCHNEIDER   BED & BREAKFAST
Hills, dales, woods, pond and trails, big breakfast, big hot tub, barn loft hideaway. Children invited. Toboggans, snowshoes provided. 3 miles out of Ludington. 3 rooms with private or shared baths.

Daily $40-$60

DOLL HOUSE HISTORICAL INN   (616) 843-2286
JOE & BARBARA GEROVAC   BED & BREAKFAST
Gracious 1900 American Foursquare. 7 rooms including bridal suite with whirlpool tub for two. Smoke and pet free, full Heart Smart breakfast. A/C. Corporate rates, bicycles, x-country skiing. Walk to beach, town, transportation to car ferry and airport. Surrounded by antiques, modern facilities. Murder mystery weekend packages. Closed Jan.-March.

Daily $70-$110

THE INN AT LUDINGTON (616) 845-7055 • (800) 845-9170
DIANE SHIELDS   BED & BREAKFAST
The charm of the past meets the comfort of today in a picture perfect Queen Anne Victorian. Relax and feel at home in casual elegance. Breakfast is an event here, not an afterthought! Bridal suite, fireplaces, CATV, family suite. Walk to shops, restaurants, beach. *Website: www.bbonline.com/mi/ludington*

Daily $70-$90

The Lamplighter B & B
Judy & Heinz Bertram

(616) 843-9792 • Res. (800) 301-9792
Bed & Breakfast

★ E D I T O R ' S   C H O I C E ★

Victorian Style, European Elegance and American Comfort are the hallmarks of "The Lamplighter Bed and Breakfast". Your stay in our individually decorated rooms with queen size beds, private baths, A/C, CATV and phones will be the most relaxing possible. 2 rooms feature a whirlpool for special occasions. All rooms as well as the common areas—parlor, living room and dining room— are decorated with original art and antiques. Full gourmet breakfasts are served either in our dining room or outdoors in the gazebo. We are "protected" by our Cocker Spaniel "Freddie". *Website: www.laketolake.com/lamplighter*

Daily $75-$135

Editor's Note: Charming accommodations and gracious owners. We also <u>*loved*</u> *Freddie.*

Parkview Cottages
Dennis & Jill

(616) 843-4445
Cottages

Nestled in a grove of shade trees only a block from the park on Lake Michigan, these cottages sleep from 2-6. Each features knotty pine interiors, private bath with ceramic tiled shower, fully equipped kitchen, gas heat, CATV (with HBO), fieldstone fireplace (firewood included). Large wood deck with grills and patio furniture. Across the street from public beach. Open year around.

Daily $68 (assumes 7 days or more); $78 (assumes 6 days or less)

Schoenberger House
Marlene Schoenberger

(616) 843-4435
Bed & Breakfast

This singularly beautiful neoclassical mansion, built by a lumber baron in 1903, has been home to the Schoenberger family for half a century. Included in *Historic Homes of America* and *Grand Homes of the Midwest*, this elegantly furnished B&B features exquisite woodwork, magnificent chandeliers, 5 fireplaces,

music room with 2 grand pianos, an intimate library, the master bedroom suite and four other bedrooms, all with private bath. Just minutes from the Lake Michigan beach, city marina, car ferry and the majestic dunes of Ludington State Park. Smoke-free. Visa/MC.

Daily $120-$195

MICHIGAN COTTAGES • CHALETS • CONDOS • B&B'S

TWIN POINTS RESORT   **(616) 843-9434**
JIM & BARB HUSTED   COTTAGES
Ten cottages (1-3 bedrooms) rest on 2 wooded bluffs overlooking lovely Hamlet Lake. Walk down to large and sandy swimming beach. Boaters can back their trailers down with ease. Moor your boat in covered docks. Motors and boats available for rent. Cottages are fully furnished and equipped. Most have knotty pine interiors. Close to Ludington State Park.

Call for Rates

WILLOW BY THE LAKE RESORT   **(616) 843-2904 • RES. (800) 331-2904**
GORDON/DAVID BETCHER & MARTIN LUTZENKIRCHEN   COTTAGES
Attractive, clean, 1-2 bedroom cottages with equipped kitchens. Guests provide linens/towels. Beautiful view of sand dunes and sunsets from east shore of Hamlin Lake. Sandy beach/play areas for children. Dockage/boat rentals available. Open May-October. No pets.
Weekly $355-$450

MEARS

THE LAKE HOUSE   **(313) 886-8996**
                                      COTTAGE
Custom built (1997), very large, 3 bedroom, 2 bath home. One door off of Lake Michigan. 700 ft. of "private" sandy Lake Michigan beach. Large, wrap-a-round and screened porch. 24'x26' great room. 17 ft. vaulted ceiling. Solid oak floors throughout. Six panel doors and wood trim. Antique furniture.
Weekly $600-$1,200

MONTAGUE

LIFE GUARD ROAD HOME   **(847) 441-6075 • (847) 604-2286**
JEFF KINNEY   BEACH HOUSE
Lake Michigan dune beach house adjacent to White Lake with views of both lakes. Near fishing pier and boat dock. 4 bedrooms (10 beds), 2 baths. Moonsets/sunsets. Linens included. Washer/dryer, dishwasher, microwave, fireplace, CATV, telephone, screened porch. Close to *Michigan Adventureland*. No pets.
Weekly $800-$2,000

MUSKEGON

IDLEWILD RETREAT (616) 842-5716
CAROLYN MILLER VACATION HOMES
Beautifully decorated home on Lake Michigan with adjoining efficiency and loft (sleeps 5/efficiency 4). Both have supplied kitchens, baths, linens, TV, phone and heat. Main cottage has dishwasher, washer, dryer and fireplace. Rented together or separately. Private beach. Available May-Dec. No pets.

Call for Rates

PENTWATER

THE CANDLEWYCK HOUSE B&B (616) 869-5967
JOHN & MARY JO NEIDOW BED & BREAKFAST
1868 home offers a unique/comfortable place for families. Six rooms/private baths (2 with fireplaces). A/C and CATV. Individually furnished with Americana and folk art from our gift shop, "The Painted Pony Mercantile". Walk to shops, beaches and pier fishing. Bikes, ski and sports equipment on premise. Full country breakfast.

Daily $75-$95

HISTORIC NICKERSON INN (616) 869-6731
HARRY & GRETCHEN SHIPARSKI BED & BREAKFAST
Serving guests with "Special Hospitality" since 1914. On a bluff overlooking Lake Michigan. Completely renovated, all 11 rooms have private baths and A/C. Three Jacuzzi suites with fireplaces and balconies overlooking Lake Michigan. Two blocks to beach and shopping district. Full breakfasts included. Casual fine dining, cocktails.

Daily $100-$225 (June-Oct.); $90-$200 (Off-season)

PENTWATER INN BED & BREAKFAST (616) 869-5909
BED & BREAKFAST
Beautiful 1869 Victorian home located on a quiet village street just a short walk from Lake Michigan sandy beach, shops and restaurants. 5 antique-filled rooms with private baths. A large parlor with CATV. Full gourmet breakfast. Featured in The Bed & Breakfast Cookbook of Great American Inns.

Daily $75-$125 (weekly discounts)

ROTHBURY

DOUBLE JJ RESORT **(616) 894-4444**
HOTEL/CONDOS

★ EDITOR'S CHOICE ★

Horseback riding, championship golf, archery, rifle range, swimming, boating and a whole lot more at this adult-exclusive ranch/resort. Rooms vary from basic sleeping rooms to luxury condos and hotel rooms. Activities too numerous to mention. Entertainment nightly. Price includes all activities, entertainment, and meals! Call for special package rates.

Weekend $220-$399   Weekly $579-$1,150

Editor's Note: Excellent horseback riding, top-rated golf course, beautiful grounds and friendly ranch hands too...Yee-haw!

SMYRNA

DOUBLE 'R' RANCH RESORT **(616) 794-0520**
CHALETS/BUNK HOUSE MOTEL

Lets go tubing on the Flat River! Great fishing too — pike and small mouth bass. Volleyball, horseback riding, golf, canoeing, hay rides. Each chalet has electric stove, refrigerator and all dishes. Chalets rent by week or day. For overnight stays, try the rustic western atmosphere of the Bunk House Motel.

Call for Rates

SPRING LAKE

SEASCAPE BED & BREAKFAST **(616) 842-8409**
SUSAN MEYER **BED & BREAKFAST**

On a private Lake Michigan beach. Enjoy the hospitality and "country living" ambiance of this nautical lakeshore home. Full breakfast served in gathering room (with fieldstone fireplace) or on sun deck with panoramic view of Grand Haven Harbor. Stroll or x-country ski on dune land nature trails. 3 rooms.

Daily $75-$90 (Special rates Sun-Thur.)

WHITE CLOUD

THE CROW'S NEST
JOYCE & DICK BILLINGSLEY

(616) 689-0088 • (800) 354-0850
BED & BREAKFAST

Experience the warmth and charm at this renovated home on the banks of the White River. Stroll by the river's edge, pick blueberries. Enjoy a full breakfast served in the formal dining room or the glass/screen enclosed porch overlooking the river. 3 rooms with queen beds, 1 with private bath. Open year around.

Daily $45-$65

WHITEHALL

MICHILINDA BEACH RESORT

(616) 893-1895
COTTAGES/LODGE ROOMS

Modified American Plan resort with weekly activities and plenty to do. Well groomed grounds on scenic location. In operation almost 60 years. Cottages and lodge rooms offer private baths and most with sitting areas (no kitchens). Many rooms with lake views. Prices include breakfast and lunch. 49 rooms available. Open May to early October. No pets.

Lodge Rooms	Weekly	$855-$1,325 (dbl.)	Daily	$165-$205 (dbl.)
Cottages	Weekly	$1,095-$1,335	Daily	$215 (and up)

Editor's Note: Well groomed, picturesque resort with plenty to keep families and couples busy. Rooms comfortable and clean.

SCENIC DRIVE HOME
JEFF KINNEY

(847) 604-2286 • (847) 441-6075
BEACH HOUSE

25 yards/35 stairs takes you to 100 ft. of private Lake Michigan sandy, shallow beach. Year around home with 2 fireplaces, 4 bedrooms (10 beds) and 2 baths. Includes A/C, sheltered/screened porch, open deck. Washer/dryer, dishwasher. Linens included. No pets. Close to *Michigan Adventureland.*

Weekly $800-$2,000

WHITE SWAN INN
RON & CATHY RUSSELL

TOLL FREE: (888) 948-7926 • (616) 894-5169
BED & BREAKFAST

1880's Queen Anne home with screened porch. Spacious rooms, mix of antiques and wicker furniture. Walk to shops, restaurants, marinas. One block to White Lake. Enjoy our bicycles on nearby 22 mile paved trail. Features interior design studio and gift shop. Open year around. Delicious breakfasts.

Daily $72-$82

Editor's Note: Cozy B&B with owners taking pride in maintaining a welcoming atmosphere.

SAUGATUCK • KALAMAZOO • UNION PIER & SURROUNDING AREAS

COVERS: ALLEGAN • BATTLE CREEK • BERRIEN SPRINGS •
COLDWATER • CONSTANTINE • DEWEY LAKE • JONES • LAKESIDE •
LAWRENCE • MENDON • ST. JOSEPH • SOUTH HAVEN
STEVENSVILLE • UNION CITY • NEW BUFFALO

Battle Creek, home of the cereal pioneers W. K. Kellogg and C. W. Post, has given this city the name of "Cereal Capital of the World". It is also the site of Fort Custer National Cemetery and the International Hot-Air Balloon Championship which last for 8 days in June.

Kalamazoo — how very diverse. Whatever you wish to do, or see, is here. From Victorian homes and quaint inns, tours, classic cars and aircraft, museums, theaters, sports or historic districts. For galleries and antique shops stop at **Lakeside**. Relax amid historic homes, bed and breakfast inns, fragrant orchards, boat cruises, dune rides, golf courses and antique shops in **Saugatuck**. Take a cruise on the Queen of Saugatuck, a 67 ft. stern wheel riverboat, or ride across the sand dunes. Take a tour of the Tabor Hill Wine Port, and taste Michigan premium wines.

South Haven not only prides itself as the "Blueberry Capital of the World" it is also one of our major yachting and sport fishing ports. Explore the many parks, hike over the sand dunes or, if you dare, go hang gliding in the Warren Dunes State Park just south of **St. Joseph**. In the fall, harvest festivals and color tours are popular. Ice fishing and skiing attract enthusiasts in the winter. May brings The Blossom Time Festival celebrated for over 80 years. In mid-July the Venetian Festival turns the lakefront park and boulevard into a giant midway. You don't want to miss this one.

Getting hungry yet? Try out *Jenny's* on Lakeshore Road (between New Buffalo and Union Pier). Creatively prepared food and homey atmosphere featuring Great Lakes Indian art and high-beamed ceiling with skylights make this a worthwhile stop! Also, *Schu's Grill & Bar* on Lake Boulevard (St. Joseph) prepares excellent meals — their Blackout Cake is a wonderful treat. We understand the *North Beach Inn* serve's up very memorable blueberry pancakes or waffles. For casual dining on the water, give *Three Pelican's* (South Haven) a try.

ALLEGAN

ALVA SPRIENSMA

(616) 538-2575
COTTAGE

Modern lakefront (110 ft. frontage) cottage on Miner Lake near Allegan (Southwestern MI). Miner Lake covers 350 acres, excellent for fishing, swimming, skiing. 2 baths, 2 bedrooms, queen sofa sleeper (sleeps 6). Paddle boat, raft included. Excellent beach. Cooking utensils, dishes provided. Bring linens. No pets. Available spring/summer.

Weekly $400   Weekend $175

BATTLE CREEK

GREENCREST MANOR
TOM & KATHY VAN DAFF

(616) 962-8633
BED & BREAKFAST

This grand French Normandy mansion situated on the highest elevation of St. Mary's Lake is constructed of sandstone, slate and copper. Formal gardens include fountains and cut stone urns. A/C. Private baths. 5 rooms. Featured in "Country Inns Magazine" as "Inn of the Month" and Top 12 Inns of North America of 1992.

Daily $75-$200

BERRIEN SPRINGS

PENNELLWOOD RESORT
JACK & PAT DAVIS

(616) 473-2511
COTTAGES

One price includes everything—meals, lodging, recreation and entertainment. 40 cottages have 2 and 3 bedrooms. Bring beach towels, life jackets and tennis racquets. Enjoy fishing, pontoon rides, volleyball, softball, shuffleboard, square dancing. 2 heated outdoor pools. Reservations require deposit. No pets.

Weekly $395 (per adult - children less)

COLDWATER

CHICAGO PIKE INN
REBECCA SCHULTZ

(517) 279-8744
BED & BREAKFAST

Turn of the Century reformed Colonial Mansion adorned with antiques from the Victorian era. 6 guest rooms in main house, two with whirlpools in Carriage House, all with private baths. Formal dining room, library, and reception room feature sweeping cherry staircase and parquet floors. Full country breakfast and refreshments.

Daily $90-$185

CONSTANTINE

INN AT CONSTANTINE
JAN MARSHALL
(800) 435-5365
EMAIL: Jan@innatconstantine.com
BED & BREAKFAST

Located in Historical Village near antique centers. Inn features antique fireplace mantels, European antiques, in-ground pool. Rooms offers private bath (2 with Jacuzzi) and fireplaces. Full breakfast. Near Amish Shipshewana, Indiana. Canoeing, carriage rides, fishing on St. Joseph River/lakes. 5 rooms/private bath. *Website: www.innatconstantine.com*

Daily $80-$150

DEWEY LAKE

SHADY SHORES RESORT
(616) 424-5251
COTTAGES

On Dewey Lake, 30 miles east of Benton Harbor. Furnished and equipped housekeeping cottages have electric ranges, refrigerators, heat, private bath, blankets and cooking/eating utensils. Includes boats, bicycles, playground, badminton, shuffleboard, croquet and tennis. Safe swimming on sandy beach.

Weekly $355-$480

JONES

SANCTUARY AT WILDWOOD
DICK & DOLLY BUERKLE
(800) 249-5910
EMAIL: wildwoodinns@voyager.net
BED & BREAKFAST & COTTAGES

★ EDITOR'S CHOICE ★

Lodge and cottages rest on more than 90 acres of woods and meadows. The Sanctuary provides security for 2 herds of whitetail deer as well as many waterfowl that visit the pond. Nature is emphasized throughout the lodge. Private decks/balconies. Each room or cottage with private baths, fireplace, Jacuzzi and refrigerator. Heated pool. Special romantic, canoe or golf packages. Deluxe breakfasts served. Conference room available. *Website: www.rivercountry.com/saw*

Daily $139-$179 (2 night minimum)

Editor's Note: Lovely setting, uniquely designed rooms, a true "Sanctuary"...highly recommended. See our review.

KALAMAZOO

HALL HOUSE
JERRY & JOANNE HOFFERTH

(616) 343-2500 • (888) 761-2525
BED & BREAKFAST

"Experience the Difference". Premier lodging in National Historic District. Guests can enjoy the exceptional craftsmanship, polished mahogany, gleaming marble and cozy fireplaces of this 1923 Georgian Revival City Inn. Six large guest rooms offer private bath, CATV, VCR, in-room phone, and A/C. Romantic Jacuzzi suite. Smoke free. *Website: www.hallhouse.com*

Daily $69-$140

LAKESIDE

THE PEBBLE HOUSE
JEAN & ED LAWRENCE

(616) 469-1416
BED & BREAKFAST

1912 Craftsman style buildings connected by wooden walkways and pergolas. Furnished with arts and crafts style antiques. Fireplaces, rocker filled porches, screen house with hammocks, wild flower garden, tennis court. Lake Michigan beach access. Scandinavian style breakfast. Suites available. Outdoor smoking only. 7 rooms/private baths.

Daily $110-$170

LAWRENCE

OAK COVE RESORT

(616) 674-8228 • (630) 983-8025
HISTORIC LODGE/COTTAGES/HOMES

Nestled on 16 wooded acres overlooking beautiful Lake Cora. 7 cottages (no kitchens), 7 lodge rooms plus 4 spacious homes (includes full kitchens and living area). All linens provided. Heated pool, sandy beach, boats, fishing, hiking trails, bicycling, recreation room, FREE golf. Nearby antique shops, flea markets, wine tasting and tours. 3 hearty meals like mother used to make included in price. See our *Website: www.oakcove.com*

Call for Rates

Editor's Note: This traditional cottage resort offers a beautiful lake view, friendly owners, great food and plenty to do.

MENDON

MENDON COUNTRY INN **(616) 496-8132**
DICK & DOLLY BUERKLE **BED & BREAKFAST**
Overlooking the St. Joseph River, this romantic country inn has antique filled guest rooms with private baths. Free canoeing, bicycles built for two, fifteen acres of woods and water. Restaurant and Amish Tour guide. Featured in Country Living and Country Home magazines. 9 Jacuzzi suites w/fireplace. 18 rooms/private bath.

Daily $69-$159

Editor's Note: Charming historic inn. For those seeking contemporary styling, the Creekside Lodge rooms (in the back of the lot) make for one romantic stay.

SAUGATUCK

BAYSIDE INN **(800) 548-0077 • (616) 857-4321**
KATHY & FRANK WILSON **BED & BREAKFAST**
Once a charming boat house now a contemporary B&B. Watch the water activity during the summer or gather around the fireplace in the winter. Located on the water in downtown Saugatuck with 6 guest rooms and two efficiency apartments, all with private bath, private decks. 8 rooms.

Daily $95-$225 (May-Oct.); $60-$175 (Nov.-April)

BEECHWOOD MANOR B&B AND COTTAGES **(616) 857-1587**
JAMES & SHERRON LEMONS **BED & BREAKFAST/COTTAGES**

☆ EDITOR'S CHOICE ☆

The historic inn of Beechwood Manor is a treasure on the hill at the edge of the historic district. Privately owned and fully restored. Built for a diplomat in the 1870's. National Register. Additional features include boat slips, tandum bikes, off-street parking. Walking distance to many fine restaurants, shops and museum. Access to Lake Michigan. Private cottages are also available.
Website: www.yesmichigan.com/beechwood

B&B Daily $125-$150   Cottages Weekly $895 (and up)

Editor's Note: Old -world ambiance with charming and experienced owners. Comfortably located on a residential side street. Several private cottages also available. See our review.

BRIAR-CLIFFE　　　　　　**(616) 857-7041** • EMAIL: witt@iserv.com
DAVID & SHIRLEY WITT　　　　　　　　　　　　GUEST SUITES

★ E D I T O R ' S   C H O I C E ★

Luxury suites on a scenic bluff overlooking the sandy shores of Lake Michigan. Comfortable sitting rooms with woodburning fireplace, TV/VCR. 5 acres of woods provide a relaxing view from the queen sized canopy bed. Ceramic bath with Jacuzzi for two. Refrigerator, microwave and coffeemaker. Private stairway takes you to sandy beach.

Website: www.briarcliffe.faithweb.com

Daily　　　　$95-$150

Editor's Note: Classic stylings combined with antique-filled rooms and a very quiet setting make this a nice place for that special getaway.

GOSHORN LAKE FAMILY RESORT　　　**(800) 541-4210** • **(616) 857-4808**
RIC GILLETTE　　　　　　　　　　　　　　　COTTAGES

20 housekeeping cottages. Some with wood burning fireplaces, A/C. Fully equipped kitchens, picnic tables and BBQ grill. Beautiful sandy, private swimming beach, volleyball, horseshoes, basketball, fire pit area and boat rentals. Near Saugatuck, Lake Michigan beaches and golf. Nearby hiking. Pets allowed. *Website:www.usagetaways.com/saugatuck/goshornlake.*

Weekly　　　$600-$900　　　Daily　　　$85-$125

HIDDEN POND BED & BREAKFAST　　　　　　**(616) 561-2491**
PRISCILLA & LARRY FUERST　　　　　　　　BED & BREAKFAST

★ E D I T O R ' S   C H O I C E ★

Accommodations of quiet traditional elegance. Two bedrooms with private baths, plus five common rooms. 28 acres of private ravined grounds with wildlife and pond. Selected by <u>Frommer B&B North America Guidebook</u> as one of the "50 Best B&B Homes in America".

Daily　　　　$64-$110

Editor's Note: A quiet, picturesque setting and inviting, well decorated guest rooms make this B&B one of our favorites. Contemporary/country styling. See our review.

MICHIGAN COTTAGES • CHALETS • CONDOS • B&B'S

THE KINGSLEY HOUSE
(616) 561-6425
GARY & KARI KING
BED & BREAKFAST

In Fennville, minutes from Saugatuck, 1886 elegant Queen Anne Victorian B&B. Featured in Innsider Magazine, rated as a "Top Fifty Inn" in America by Inn Times. AAA approved. Near Holland/Saugatuck. Private baths, whirlpool/ bath. Special getaway suite. Beautiful surroundings, family antiques. Homemade breakfast. A/C. 8 rooms.

Daily $80-$165

Editor's Note: Well appointed rooms and welcoming proprietors...very nice.

THE KIRBY HOUSE
(616) 857-2904
RAY RIKER & JIM GOWRAN
BED & BREAKFAST

The most popular bed and breakfast in the Saugatuck/Douglas area. Furnished with antiques of the 1890's. Most rooms with private baths, air conditioning and fireplace rooms available. Pool, hot tub and bicycles. Full breakfast buffet. Near shopping and Lake Michigan. Advanced Reservations imperative. Major credit cards accepted.

Daily $95-$135

THE PARK HOUSE B&B & COTTAGES
(800) 321-4535 • (616) 857-4535
LYNDA & JOE PETTY
BED & BREAKFAST & COTTAGES

On National Historic Register. Saugatuck's oldest residence (1857) hosted Susan B. Anthony. Eight rooms, queen beds, private baths. Four cottages with equipped kitchens, TV/VCR. All include A/C. Two luxury suites, two cottages offer jet tubs, fireplaces. Close to town, beach, ski trails. *Website: www.bbonline.com/mi/parkhouse*

Daily $95-$225

WICKWOOD COUNTRY INN
(616) 857-1465
JULEE ROSSO-MILLER & BILL MILLER
BED & BREAKFAST

A charming European-style Inn located in the beautiful Victorian Village of Saugatuck on the Eastern Shores of Lake Michigan. Owner Julee Rosso-Miller, serves up breakfast and hors d'oeuvres daily using recipes from her four best selling cookbooks. "The Silver Palate", "The Silver Palate Good Times", "The New Basics" and "Great Good Foods". 11 rooms with private baths.

Daily $110-$195

ALL RATES SUBJECT TO CHANGE

ST. JOSEPH

THE SILVERBEACH FUNHOUSES

Crystal clear waters and broad sandy beaches are waiting! These quaint, clean cottages are close to the popular silver beach on Lake Michigan. *The Cup* (upstairs) sleeps 4 and *The Saucer* (downstairs) sleeps 10. *The Dollhouse* is a miniature *Funhouse*, right next door, and sleeps 6-8. It is fully furnished including cable,

The Cup & The Saucer

phone and deck. *The Lighthouse* and *Boat House* are 3 family homes that sleep up to 14, have views of the pier and lighthouse. Linens and towels included. Enjoy swimming, fishing, roller-blading, wind surfing, shopping, free concerts. Reserve early.

Weekly $450-$2,050

Editor's Note: Comfortable rooms, __fun__ decor and great location.

THE SAND CASTLES

(800) 972-0080 • EMAIL:info@sandcastlecottages.com
COTTAGES

Located halfway between South Haven and St. Joseph, The Sand Castles offer 11 housekeeping cottages that sleep from 2 to 11. Each has a kitchenette or full kitchen with cooking utensils, coffeemaker, toaster, ceiling fans, A/C, and heat. Larger units have separate bedrooms and living/dining/kitchen areas with microwaves. Bedding is included and Cable w/HBO (bring your own towels & TV). No pets. 4 blocks to Lake Michigan beaches. Restaurants, grocery stores and golf are nearby. *Website: www.sandcastlescottages.com.*

Weekly $275-$650

Editor's Note: Traditional cottages with well maintained interiors and some nice extras like ceiling fans and A.C. Sizes range significantly. Beach access approx. 1/4 mile.

SOUTH CLIFF INN BED & BREAKFAST
BILL SWISHER

(616) 983-4881
BED & BREAKFAST

Overlooking Lake Michigan, traditional brick home has luxurious accommodations and relaxed atmosphere. Tastefully decorated rooms with traditional and antique furnishings. The private beach is just steps away. Continental breakfast. Room with whirlpool tub /fireplace available. A/C. Seven rooms.

Daily (Seasonal) $75-$165

SOUTH HAVEN

ARUNDEL HOUSE—AN ENGLISH B&B
PAT & TOM ZAPAL

(616) 637-4790
BED & BREAKFAST

Turn-of-the-century, fully restored resort home. Registered with the Michigan Historical Society. Rooms decorated with antiques and maintained in English tradition. Continental buffet breakfast and afternoon tea. Walking distance to beach, restaurants, shops, marinas.

Daily $60-$110

Editor's Note: Quaint B&B ... in the English tradition.

A COUNTRY PLACE BED & BREAKFAST & COTTAGES
ART & LEE NIFFENEGGER

(616) 637-5523
BED & BREAKFAST/COTTAGES

※ EDITOR'S CHOICE ※

A restored 1860's Greek Revival furnished with American antiques. 5 charming guest rooms with private baths feature English country themes. A "sin" sational full breakfast served. All 3 cozy cottages feature fresh pine interiors, full kitchens, 1 & 2 bedrooms. 2 have fireplaces, 2 have private beach. Remaining cottage and B&B access Lake Michigan 1/2 block. B&B open all year - Cottages open April-October.

B&B Daily $75-$125   Cottages Weekly $550-$850

Editor's Note: Gracious owners, very inviting accommodations — all of the Niffenegger's lodging are outstanding, P.S. We liked their cuddly cats too!

COTTAGE AT GLEN HAVEN SHORES
ANDREA KULDANEK

(616) 455-5602
COTTAGE

Newly remodeled cottage located in wooded setting on Lake Michigan Bluff. Two bedrooms and sleeping loft (sleeps 8), two baths. Modern kitchen, fireplace, TV/VCR, furnished screened porch and deck. Access to tennis court. Golf courses and bike trail nearby. Provide your own linens and paper products. No smoking/pets.

Weekly $1,200 (July/Aug); $900 (June/Sept.)

GREENE'S VACATION HOMES
MERYL GREENE

(616) 637-6400
COTTAGES

Vacation homes near town and marinas, with public beach access. Linens provided (bring towels). All lodgings have fully equipped kitchens, baths, telephones, CATV, ceiling fans, ome with central air. Sleeps 6 or more. Monthly and off-season rates available.

Weekly $500 (and up, July-Aug.)

LAST RESORT B&B INN

(616) 637-8943
BED & BREAKFAST/COTTAGE

Built in 1883 as South Haven's first resort inn. Watch Lake Michigan sunsets from the deck. Most rooms w/view of the Lake or the harbor. Penthouse suites provide best views and feature Jacuzzi's. A/C. Open April-Oct. 14 rooms/private baths. Also available, cottage for two with view of the harbor.

Daily $75 (and up)

LOKNATH-CHANDERVARMA, HARBOR'S UNIT #32

(616) 344-3012
CONDO

2 bedroom/2 bath condo (sleeps 7). Elegantly furnished, large master bedroom. A/C, CATV, equipped kitchen, microwave, dishwasher. Panoramic view, private beach, pool, laundry, garage. Provide your own towel and linens. Minimum 7 day stay. Available all year. No pets.

Weekly $900 (May-Sept.)

MICHI-MONA-MAC LAKESHORE COTTAGES   **(616) 637-3003 • (847) 332-1443**
COTTAGES

Watch truly spectacular sunsets from the pure, spotless beach. Very clean and well maintained cottages with full kitchens, private baths, ceiling fans. beachside rooms with lovely bay windows and fireplace. Open all year. No pets. Great family vacation or romantic getaway.

Weekly $850 (and up)

Editor's Note: The beach is small but lovely with incline taking you to water's edge. Units are linked together apartment style. Small but well maintained interiors.

MICHIGAN COTTAGES • CHALETS • CONDOS • B&B'S

NORTH BEACH INN & PIGOZZI'S

(616) 637-6738
INN

1890's Victorian styled B&B overlooks Lake Michigan Beach. All rooms offer private baths. Restaurant, Pigozzi, serves full breakfasts, lunch and dinners.

Daily $105-$150

RIVERBEND RETREAT   **(616) 637-3505** • EMAIL: riverbnd@accn.org
COTTAGES

★ EDITOR'S CHOICE ★

Two cozy cedar cottages on beautiful Black River. Come and enjoy the peacefulness. In-ground heated pool, boat dock, canoes, boat, private hot tub, stone fireplace, Kal-Haven pass. Fully equipped for 12 people, including towels and bedding, phone, TV, VCR, dishwasher, laundry. Open year around. Off-season priced for couples or groups. No pets.

Call for Rates

Editors Note: Luxurious vacation homes ... many amenities. Set back from the road on a spacious lot overlooking the Black River. This is another of our favorites. See our review.

THE SEYMOUR HOUSE   **(616) 227-3918** • EMAIL: seymour@cybersol.com
GWEN & TOM PATON   BED & BREAKFAST/LOG CABIN

Enjoy the unsurpassed beauty of this 1862 Victorian mansion on 11 wooded acres. Picturesque 1-acre pond. Trails through the woods. Minutes to Saugatuck, South Haven, beaches, restaurants, galleries, horseback riding, golf and orchards. 5 rooms/ private bath, fireplaces, Jacuzzi. Guest log cabin. A/C, gourmet breakfasts.

Website:www.seymourhouse.com

Daily $80-$145

Editor's Note: Spacious grounds and a well maintained historic home combine for a relaxing stay. See our review.

SLEEPY HOLLOW RESORT

(616) 637-1127
COTTAGES/APARTMENTS/DUPLEX

This 58 years old Art Deco style resort provides the "all in one" family vacation. Theater, restaurant and plenty of activities on the resort promises to keep you busy. Cottages and apartments include partial to full kitchens, private baths.

Weekly $450-$1,040

Editor's Note: Lots of activities at this American Plan resort have made it popular over the years. Lodgings vary significantly.

SOUTH HAVEN VACATION HOMES   (616) 637-5406 • EMAIL: soukup@i2k.com
HOMES

Vacation homes feature 3 bedrooms, 2 baths and large living room, kitchen, dining room and family room. Includes microwave, washer/dryer, CATV. Large yard for family recreation. Walk to Kids' Corner and Lake Michigan

Weekly $850 (off-season rates available)

TANBITHN
MARCIA ROBINSON

(616) 637-4304
COTTAGE

One bedroom (sleeps 5) cottage on North Shore Drive. Features CATV, telephone, ceiling fan and room A/C. Renovated in 1994 including bathroom fixtures, kitchen area. Linens provided (bring towels). Light and airy interior with wicker highlights. Only 1/2 block from beach, 1 block from marina. Fall/winter rates negotiable. No pets.

Weekly $750 (May -Sept.)   Daily $125 (weekends only)

Editor's Note: Small but bright and appealing interior and decor. Sits right off the sidewalk ... fun for people watching. See our review.

THOMPSON HOUSE   (616) 637-6521 • EMAIL: JLT-KKT@cybersol.com
JOYCE THOMPSON
HOME

Charming home, sleeps six. One block to South Beach, Riverfront Park. Great garden, umbrella table, wraparound porch and deck. Enjoy all the modern conveniences including CATV, microwave, dishwasher, laundry, central air, electronic air cleaner, a water purifier and whirlpool bathtub. No pets.

Weekly $850 (June-Aug.); $800 (May, Sept., Oct.)

Editor's Note: Well maintained home on a quiet side street. A nice place to be away from the maddening crowds. Good value.

VICTORIA RESORT B & B
BOB & JAN
(800) 473-7376 • (616) 637-6414
BED & BREAKFAST/COTTAGES

Three acre resort recently renovated. Located 1-1/2 blocks from Lake Michigan. Close to downtown. Some rooms and cottages feature fireplace and whirlpool tub. Outdoor pool, bikes, tennis and basketball courts. Winter packages include two night stay, dinner certificate, video rentals, breakfast in bed, and souvenir mugs. *Website: www.victoriaresort.com*

Rooms Daily (from) $49   Cottages Weekly (from) $875

Editor's Note: Comfortable and very clean accommodations for family fun.

MICHIGAN COTTAGES • CHALETS • CONDOS • B&B'S

YELTON MANOR BED & BREAKFAST
ELAINE HERBERT & ROB KRIPAITIS

(616) 637-5220
EMAIL: elaine@yeltonmanor.com
BED & BREAKFAST

"Top of the crop in luxury B & B's". On the sunset coast of beautiful Lake Michigan. 17 guest rooms with private baths. Some have Jacuzzi, fireplace and private decks. Extravagant honeymoon and anniversary suites. Gourmet hors d'oeuvres, fabulous breakfast and day-long goodies. A true make-yourself-at-home, luxurious getaway. Take a tour at our *website: www.yeltonmanor.com.*

Daily $90-$220

Editor's Note: A premiere resort for executive retreats. No direct view of the Lake, but still a great way to FORGET ABOUT THE...STRESS.

STEVENSVILLE

CHALET ON THE LAKE

(616) 465-6365
CHALETS/CONDOS

51 well equipped, 2-story duplex chalet-styled lodgings, 7 miles south of St. Joseph. 36 acres by Lake Michigan. Lodgings include 2 bedroom condominiums (sleep 8) with full kitchens, dining areas, living rooms, CATV and patios. Resort features nature trails, volleyball, 5 tennis courts, 2 pools and large beach. Bring towels. Open year around. No pets.

Weekly $665-$1,100

UNION CITY

VICTORIAN VILLA INN
RONALD J. GIBSON

(800) 34-VILLA • (517) 741-7383
BED & BREAKFAST

Romantic, 19th Century Intalianate style B&B—perfect for anniversaries or any other special occasion. Tower suites with private parlor, offer an excellent birds-eye view of the town. Restaurant features menus which reflect the tastes and trends of the 19th century and are sure to please. Private baths. 5 rooms and 5 suites (2 with fireplaces and hot tubs). Major credit cards accepted.

Daily $60-$110 (Sun.-Thurs.); $95-$145 (Friday-Sun.)

UNION PIER/NEW BUFFALO

GARDEN GROVE B&B
RIC & MARY ELLEN PASTELWAITE

(616) 469-6346 • (800) 613-2872
BED & BREAKFAST

Pamper yourself with comfort and beauty at a vintage 1925 inn. Whimsically decorated with colorful flair and botanical style; we bring the garden indoors year-round. Deluxe accommodations. Jacuzzi-whirlpools, fireplaces, balconies, private dining. Everything the discriminating inn guest expects: Charm, romance, hospitality, scrumptious breakfast. Outstanding area: wineries, beaches, shopping.

Daily $80-$150

THE INN AT UNION PIER
JOYCE ERICKSON PITTS & MARK PITTS

(616) 469-4700
BED & BREAKFAST

Harbor Country's premier bed & breakfast...just 200 steps from the beach! Choose from 16 spacious guest rooms, most featuring woodburning fireplaces and porches or balconies, 2 Jacuzzi suites. Relax in the outdoor hot tub and sauna. Enjoy bountiful gourmet breakfast and complimentary refreshments. Bicycles. Hosting corporate retreats. *Website: www.innatunionpier.com*

Daily $125-$195

PINE GARTH INN
RUSS & PAULA BULIN

(616) 469-1642 • (888) 390-0909
BED & BREAKFAST/COTTAGES

Summer estate and cottages, located on 200 ft. of sugar sand Lake Michigan beach. B&B rooms have spectacular lake views, queen beds, private baths and TV/VCR. Two-bedroom cottages include full kitchen, fireplace, hot tub, grills, private decks or screened porches and beach chairs. Open year around. 7 rooms, 5 cottages.

	Rooms*	Cottages*
Daily	$125-$170	$220-$250

* In season. Call for off-season rates.

RIVER'S EDGE BED & BREAKFAST
GRETCHEN

(616) 469-6860
EMAIL: zigzag@enteract.com
BED & BREAKFAST

On 30 acres of wooded trails and orchards, bordering the Galient River, you'll find peaceful River's Edge. Four rooms feature double size Jacuzzis (some with fireplace and private deck), TV/VCR and private baths. Furniture styled by artisan Andy Brown. Bike and canoes for guests. Full breakfast.

Daily $89-$200

SANS SOUCI EURO INN & RESORT
ANGELIKA SIEWERT

(616) 756-3141
Email: sans-souci@worldnet.att.net
SUITES/HOMES/COTTAGES

The sophisticated traveler may choose a secluded luxury suite, family home or modern lakeside cottage at Sans Souci, located in a pastoral country-side 70 miles from Chicago. We have 50 acres of spring-fed lakes, whispering pines and abundant wildlife near Lake Michigan beaches. Antique shops, galleries, golf, restaurants nearby. Welcome all.

Website: www.sans-souci.com

	Homes	Cottages	Suites
Weekly:	$1,320-$1,980	$1,170	—
Daily:	$220-$330	$195	$195

ALL RATES SUBJECT TO CHANGE

MICHIGAN FALL COLOR TOURS

What fall time experience is complete without a leisurely stroll or relaxing drive among the vivid colors of Michigan's beautiful landscapes?

BEST COLOR VIEWING TIMES

Mid-September to Early October

Late September to Mid-October

Early to Mid-October

Mid to Late October

Our Favorite Fall Tours

EAST LOWER PENINSULA (Region 1 & 2):

■ *The River Road, National Scenic Byway.* The tour begins three miles south of Oscoda on River Road Scenic Byway. Follow this scenic, 22 mile road which runs along the bluffs above the Au Sable River. This drive offers panoramic views of the river, its forested banks and islands. You'll find outstanding fall colors and the Lumberman's Monument (only 20 minutes west of Oscoda on River Road Scenic Byway) which offers a wonderful overlook. Then, just 1-1/2 miles west of the Monument's Visitors Center, is the *Eagles' Nest Overlook* which has been the home to families of eagles for over 10 years. The overlook also offers a photographer's dream view of Cook Pond and the river valley.

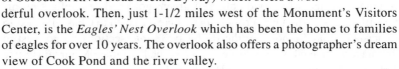

■ *AuSable River Vista.* Listed as a *National Forest Scenic Overlook*, this beautiful vista has breathtaking, vibrant colors in the fall and offers a 20-mile stretch of the AuSable River Valley and Alcona Pond. To begin this tour, go north on M-65 and turn west on F-30 in Glennie. Continue

217

three miles to AuSable Road and turn right. This vista is about four miles north of AuSable Road. Enjoy the view!

■ *Irish Hills Tower*. The lovely hills make this area a choice spot for any driving tour. The variety of trees found here create a beautiful bouquet of fall colors. The Tower (one mile west of US 12 and M-124) offers an excellent, panoramic view of northern Lenawee County.

UPPER PENINSULA (Regions 3 & 4):

The truth is, just about anywhere in the Upper Peninsula is a perfect spot for fall touring. Just taking a quiet side road may bring you to one of the UP's many scenic views or majestic waterfalls highlighted by brilliant fall colors.

If you're not into impromptu exploration, however, here are a few "planned" routes that offer plenty of great scenery with a wonderful blend of autumn colors.

■ *Keweenaw Peninsula* (approx. 125 miles). Take 41 north from Houghton through Calumet and Laurium to Phoenix. Take Highway 26 north through Eagle River and Eagle Harbor to Copper Harbor. Return from Copper Harbor on Highway 41 to Delaware, then turn on the county road to Bete Grise and Lac La Belle. Follow this to Lake Linden and Highway 26. Head south to Hubbell, Dollar Bay and on to Houghton.

■ *Porcupine Mountain National Park & Lake of the Clouds Scenic Overlook* (approx. 170 miles). You can enjoy the colors from your car but will need to do a little hiking if you want to truly experience panoramic views of fall's beauty on this trip. One such view is the Lake of the Clouds Scenic Overlook. It's a 1/4 mile hike up a rather steep hill. However, this is a view you don't want to miss. At the top you'll find yourself perched high above the lake. You'll be awed by the spectacular view of the Porcupine Mountains, filled with vivid colors of green, gold and red, reflecting off the still waters of the lake. From Baraga, take 41 north to Chassell, west to Painesdale. Take 26 north to the Highway 38 intersection and go west to Ontonagon. Take 64 west to Silver City and the Porcupine Mountains State Park. You'll return to Baraga on Highway 38.

■ *Seney National Wildlife Refuse & Tahquamenon Falls* (approx. 88 miles). Again, the beauty here is only enhanced by the vivid colors of autumn. From Grand Marais, go South on 77 to Seney National Refuge where you'll want to explore nature at its finest. Then continue east on 28 to Newberry, north on 123 to Paradise (gateway to the Whitefish Point Lighthouse, Whitefish Point Bird Observatory, and Tahquamenon Falls). To return, follow 123 to 28 and go west, back to 77.

NORTHWEST LOWER PENINSULA (Region 5)

■ *Old Mission Peninsula* (38 miles): Combine stops at roadside fruit stands, charming restaurants and shops with this relaxing fall color tour. This is a delightful trip through the peninsula which divides Grand Traverse Bay into East and West Arms. Take M-37 (Center Road) north from Traverse City's Garfield Road. Stay right where M-37 and Peninsula Drive fork, and continue north to the tip of the peninsula. Backtrack on M-37, and turn right on Peninsula Drive, along the West Bay shore to Traverse City.

■ *Leelanau Peninsula* (approx. 93 miles): Touring through Michigan's "little finger" has been a popular fall experience for generations. It's an easy and beautiful tour which takes you along shorelines, through quaint villages including Suttons Bay, Omena and Northport. You'll enjoy the homey restaurants and shops. If you're feeling lucky, stop by the casino. Then, on to the tip of the little finger. Stop and tour the Grand Traverse Lighthouse. The view from the lighthouse is outstanding. More brilliant colors can be seen as you continue along the western coast through Leland, Glen Arbor and Sleeping Bear Dune where you'll find spectacular colors along the 7-mile Pierce Stocking Scenic Drive. Of course you'll want to checkout the Dune Climb for a little *exercise* before your return trip.

To take this tour, follow M-22, from Traverse City, along the coast to Northport (to get to the "little finger" take M-201 to C-629). M-22 continues south from Northport through Leland into Glen Arbor, then M-109 brings you to the Pierce Stocking Scenic Drive at the Sleeping Bear Dune National Lakeshore. M-109 will meet up with M-22 and M-72 for your return to Traverse City.

■ *Interlochen/Benzie County* (approx. 98 miles): Let the sounds of nature mingle with the sounds of music from the Interlochen Center for the Arts. This premiere music education center is open year around and features well-known professional entertainers as well as student performances. Set in natural grounds, the Center offers inviting pathways through the trees and natural shrubbery which will surround you in the brilliant colors of fall. Then onto your exploration of Benzie County where you'll find fine art and craft galleries and plenty of small town ambiance.

Follow US-31/M-37 south from Traverse City to the M-37 and US-31 intersection. Turn right on US-31, then left on M-137 to C-70, and right in the town of Karlin, then right on County Line Road. This will take you through Thompsonville. Take a right on M-115 and travel to Benzonia and Beulah to loop back onto US-31 south. A left turn at Chum's Corners will return you to Traverse City.

■ *Tunnel of Trees* (50-110 miles, depending on tour route): This is a wonderful drive at any time of the year, but it's really impressive during the fall. We should note this drive is a bit trickier than the others because there are no road shoulders. The driver will have to stay focused on the road.

Leaving from the Harbor Springs area, go north along M-119. If you have time, we recommend exploring the Thorn Swift Nature Preserve on lower Shore Drive. Pass Cross Village and continue a few more miles to the stop sign, turn left following Lake Shore Drive to Lakeview Road. At Sturgeon Bay there's a dune area and beach to explore. Continue on Lakeview which changes to Gill Road.

From here you can take two different routes, depending on your time and interest. The shorter tour will take 1.25 hours with the longer taking 2.5 hours. The shorter one is as follows: Take Gill Road for 3 miles toward Bliss and the Pleasantville Road (C-81) junction. Continue on Pleasantville Road back to M-119 and take a right to return to Harbor Spring.

Here's the long tour: Gill Road to Cecil Bay Road (5 miles). Go left and continue to the road's end, then right on Wilderness Park Drive (if you want to visit the Park, take a left). Continue north passing Colonial Fort Michilimackinaw and pass under I-75 at the base of the Mackinaw Bridge. You'll begin the Cheboygan County Scenic Route on US-23 and continue south along US-23 into Cheboygan. Take a right at the M-27 junction. Continue on M-27 passed Mullett and Burt Lakes which will take you through Indian River to the junction of M-68. Turn right to Alanson and then left on US-31 to Petoskey. Head north on M-119 which will take you back to Harbor Springs.

■ *Jordan River Valley* (50 miles): The Jordan River Valley area is brilliant in the fall. This tour leads you from Boyne Falls into East Jordan. It should be noted that some of the turnoffs are on dirt roads which get pretty bumpy but, if your car can take it, it's well worth the ride.

From Boyne Falls go west to Deer Lake Road (C-48). Stay left and continue past Deer Lake and Boyne Mountain's golf course to the stop sign. Stay left on C-48 which takes you into East Jordan. Pass over the Jordan River bridge and keep right at the blinking yellow light. Turn left onto M-66. Here's an area you may want to take some of the turnoffs. You may even want to explore by canoe which can be rented at the livery there. When you leave, you'll pass Bellaire turn and continue to the top of the next hill. Take a left on Alba Road (there's a scenic turnoff here which you may want to take—but be aware that this is a very narrow 2-track road which is pretty rough). Go left at US-131 (the junction). You'll pass over the 45th Parallel. Continue 5 miles to Dead Man's Hill turnoff and take a left. This is another bumpy dirt road but the view at the end overlooks the Jordan River Valley and is one that should not be missed. The left fork at the overlook gets you closely to the top of the overlook.

SOUTHWEST LOWER PENINSULA (Region 6):

■ *Lakeshore Drive from Grand Haven to Holland* (approx. 22 miles): This beautiful drive on Lakeshore is another photographer's paradise. You'll want to stop at Kirk Park and Tunnel Park to leisurely enjoy the crisp air as you take in the surrounding brilliance of autumn at its best. This drive is a simple one—just start in Grand Haven and go south on Lakeshore Drive.

■ *Grand River Basin* (approx. 40 miles): Scenic bayous and brilliant colors combine to make this tour a fun experience. To begin, start in Grand Haven (Robbins Road) and go east to Mercury Drive (continue east). You'll pass a few Grand River bayous and will want to stop and enjoy the colorful Riverside Park. When you leave, turn south on 104th Avenue and go to Osborn Street. Stay east on Osborn (it turns into Warner Street, so don't be surprised when the name changes). Then turn north on 66th Avenue and cross the bridge at Eastmanville. Travel west on Leonard Road back to Spring Lake.

■ *Circle Spring Lake Tour* (approx. 15 miles): If you don't have a lot of time, this tour is a good one (only about 20 minutes). You'll begin in Grand Haven, starting at US-31 go north across the Grand River draw-bridge. Leave at the Ferrysburg exit and turn east at the end of the ramp. Go north at the flasher located at West Spring Lake Road. Continue on West Spring Lake Road to West Fruitport Road. Turn south at Fruitport Road to M-104 in Spring Lake.

■ *P.J. Hoffmaster State Park to Muskegon* (approx. 20 miles). Here is another nice tour that won't take alot of time. The dunes and nature center along the route make it's a nice choice. Just go west on Pantaluna Road to Lake Harbor Road. P.J. Hoffmaster State is where we highly recommend you explore the dunes area and the Gillette Nature Center. Then head north on Lake Harbor Road to Muskegon.

Have a colorful Michigan Fall Experience!

Michigan Wineries & Casinos—Map

$ = Casinos   🍷= Wineries

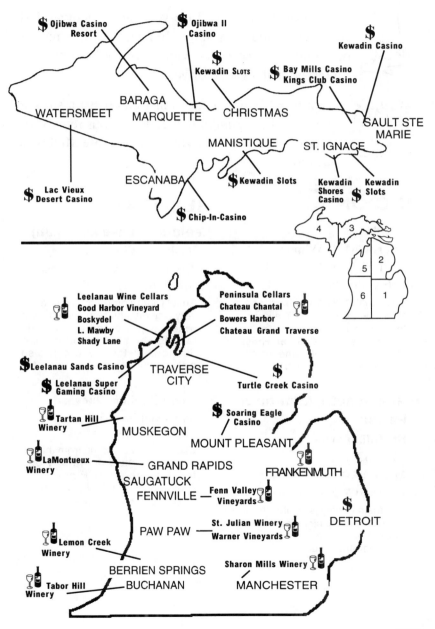

$ Ojibwa Casino Resort

$ Ojibwa II Casino

$ Kewadin Casino

$ Kewadin Slots

$ Bay Mills Casino
Kings Club Casino

BARAGA

WATERSMEET   MARQUETTE   CHRISTMAS

SAULT STE MARIE

MANISTIQUE   ST. IGNACE

Lac Vieux
Desert Casino

ESCANABA

$ Kewadin Slots

Kewadin Shores Casino

Kewadin Slots

$ Chip-In-Casino

4   3

5   2

6   1

Leelanau Wine Cellars
Good Harbor Vineyard
Boskydel
L. Mawby
Shady Lane

Peninsula Cellars
Chateau Chantal
Bowers Harbor
Chateau Grand Traverse

$ Leelanau Sands Casino

TRAVERSE CITY

$ Leelanau Super Gaming Casino

$ Turtle Creek Casino

Tartan Hill Winery

$ Soaring Eagle Casino

MUSKEGON

MOUNT PLEASANT

LaMontueux Winery

GRAND RAPIDS

FRANKENMUTH

SAUGATUCK
FENNVILLE

Fenn Valley Vineyards

$ DETROIT

PAW PAW

St. Julian Winery
Warner Vineyards

Lemon Creek Winery

Sharon Mills Winery

BERRIEN SPRINGS

Tabor Hill Winery

BUCHANAN

MANCHESTER

223

Michigan Wineries

Ahh, fruit of the vine we love ya ... and Michigan has some pretty dandy vines, too. In fact, the wine makers of our fair state have been winning major National and International awards for years.

What true Michigan vacationer can resist a stop or two for a little *sampling*? Enjoy ... but remember moderation ... we want you to have a safe Michigan vacation!

REGION 1

Manchester

Sharon Mills Winery

5701 Sharon Hollow Rd.

616-428-9160

This quaint winery is part of the Henry Ford Heritage Trail and is located in a historic grist mill on the banks of the River Raisin. Grapes used here come from the Old Mission Peninsula.

Frankenmuth, Monroe & Parma

St. Julian Winery

517-652-3281

Monroe: 734-242-9409

Parma: 517-531-3786

The Main Winery is located in Paw-Paw. One of Michigan's oldest and largest wineries. Family-owned and operated since 1921.

REGION 5

Leelanau (Lake Leelanau)

Boskydel Vineyards

7501 E. Otto Road, Lake Leelanau

616-256-7272

Small winery preparing limited but very nice dry and semi-sweet table wines ... presented in a unique tasting room. We understand during Christmas you can also pickup your holiday tree here.

Good Harbor Vineyards

34 S. Manitou Trail

616-256-7165

Excellent wines come from this 50 acre, well-tended vineyard. Known for Chardonnay, Pinot Gris, Riesling, Pinot Noir, Vignoles, Seyval and champagne.

Old Mission Peninsula

Chateau Chantal

15900 Rue de Vin

616-223-4110

An operating Bed & Breakfast, private home and vineyard. Impressive winery ... Old World-styled. Known for Chardonnay, Pinot Gris, Pinot Noir, Merlot, Riesling and Gewurztraminer and champagne.Several award winning specialties. The tasting area offers incredible views of East and West Grand Traverse Bays.

Chateau Grand Traverse

12239 Center Road

616-223-7355

Williamsburg: 616-938-2291

Traverse City: 616-941-4146

Large wine-making facility grows and produces award-winning, premium varietal wines. Estate-grown. Excellent Riesling, Pinot Noir, Merlot, Cabernet Franc and Ice Wine. Also a variety of area specialties like Spiced Cherry Wine, Cranberry Riesling, to name a view. Great location overlooking scenic Grand Traverse Bay.

Peninsula Cellars

18250 Mission Road

616-223-4050 • 616-223-4310

Using the finest grapes in the area, wines are estate bottled with limited production. Specialties include Chardonnay, Dry Riesling, Raftshol Red and a variety of dessert wines.

Omena

Leelanau Wine Cellars

12683 E. Tatch Road

616-386-5201

Very nice selection of dry to semi-sweet wines ... barrel-fermented and aged. Also produces a variety of seasonal and fruit wines.

Suttons Bay

L. Mawby Vineyards

4519 S. Elm Valley

616-271-3522

Limited but pure winemaking production...barrel-fermented made with simple machinery. Specializing in white table wines and methode champenoise sparkling wines.

Shady Lane Cellars

9580 Shady Lane

616-947-8865

Maintains more than 10,000 vines. Relatively new winery production excellent methode champenoise sparkling wines along with Pinot Noir, Riesling and Chardonnay (call for tasting room appt.)

Traverse City

Bowers Harbor Vineyards

2896 Bowers Harbor Road

616-223-7615

Another small but delightful winery offering a beautiful overlook of Bowers Harbor. Chardonnay, Riesling and sparking wines plus specialty fruit wines.

St. Julian Winery

(Main winery in Paw Paw)

Traverse City: 616-933-6120

REGION 6

Berrien Springs

Lemon Creek Winery

533 E. Lemon Creek Road

616-471-1321

Producer of the first commercial, entirely Michigan-grown Cabernet Sauvignon. 11 white/9 red wines. Home winemakers can purchase picked grapes or grape juice.

Buchanan

Tabor Hill Winery

185 Mt. Tabor Road

800-283-3363

Bridgman: 616-857-6566

Saugatuck: 616-857-4859

Knowledgeable wine consultants on hand. Numerous award-winning wines, sparkling wines and non-alcoholic juices. Gift shop. Fine meals served in rustic dining room overlooking the vineyards.

Fennville

Fenn Valley Vineyards

6130 122nd Avenue

616-561-2396

Small winery producing premiums wines. Known for estate-bottled Rieslings, Champagnes, Pinot Gris and barrel-aged red wines. Several speciality wines. Winners of numerous awards and honors.

Grand Rapids

LeMontueux Vineyard

2365 8 Mile Road. N.W.

616-784-4554

Small, family-owned in scenic countryside setting. Variety of wines from French-American hybrid grapes.

New Era

Tartan Hill Winery

4937 S. 52nd Avenue

616-861-4657

Family operated specializing in estate wines from French hybrid grapes. Winner of Gold Medal award for American Wine Society's commercial winery competition. Dry red to sweet white wines.

Paw Paw

St. Julian Winery

716 S. Kalamazoo

616-657-5568 • 800-732-6002

Union Pier: 616-469-3150

Michigan's oldest and largest winery (since 1921). Producer of over 40 wines. Fine dining also available at the Apollo Restaurant.

Warner Vineyards

706 S. Kalamazoo

616-657-3165

Family-operated for over 30 years. Located in a historical structure built in 1898. Produces a variety of sparkling, table and dessert wines.

226

Michigan Ca$inos

Oh Lady Luck you done me wrong ... but I keep coming back for more.

Our fascination and anticipation of winning the big one continues. (NOTE: Detroit is in the process of introducing major casino operations. Since final planning stages were not complete prior to the printing of this book, we suggest you call the Detroit Chamber of Commerce or the Metro Detroit Visitor's Bureau ... see our Chamber listings ... for up-to-date information on Wayne County casinos.)

REGION 3

Brimley
Bay Mills Resort & Casino
11386 W. Lake Shore
906-248-3700

Kings Club Casino
12140 W. Lake Shore
906-248-3241

Christmas
Kewadin Slots
105 Candy Cane Lane
906-387-5475

Hessel
Kewadin Slots
Three Mile Road at M-134
906-484-2767

Manistique
Kewadin Slots
Route 1
906-341-5510

St. Ignace
Kewadin Shores Casinos
3039 Mackinac Trail
906-643-7071

Sault Ste. Marie
Kewadin Casino
2186 Shunk Road
906-632-0530

REGION 4

Baraga
Ojibwa Casino Resort
797 Michigan
906-353-6333

Escanaba
Chip-In-Casino
W399 Highway 2 & 41
906-466-2941
800-682-6040

Marquette
Ojibwa II Casino
105 Acre Trail
906-249-4200

Watersmeet
Lac Vieux Desert Casino
N5384 US 45
906-358-4227

REGION 5

Suttons Bay

Leelanau Sands Casino
2521 NW Bayshore Drive
616-271-4104
800-922-2946

**Leelanau Super Gaming
Palace**
2649 NW Bayshore Drive
616-271-6852
800-922-2946

REGION 5
(continued...)

Williamsburg
Turtle Creek Casino
7741 M-72, E
616-267-9574
888-777-8946

REGION 6

Mount Pleasant
Soaring Eagle Casino
2395 S. Leaton Road
800-992-2306

Main Office:

TRAVEL MICHIGAN

800-5432-YES or 888-78-GREAT

Offices Listed Alphabetically by City

UPPER PENINSULA

Keweenaw Tourism Council
1197 Calumet Avenue
Calumet, MI 49913
906-337-4579
800-338-7982

Delta County Tourism & Convention Bureau
230 Ludington Street
Escanaba, MI 49829
906-786-2192
888-DeltaMI

Keweenaw Tourism Council
326 Shelden Avenue, P.O. Box 336
Houghton, MI 49931
906-482-2388
800-338-7982

Tourism Association of Dickinson County
333 S. Stephenson Ave.
Iron Mountain, MI 49801
906-774-2945

Upper Peninsula Travel & Recreation Bureau
P.O. Box 400
Iron Mountain, MI 49801
906-774-5480

Iron County Tourism Council
50 E. Genesee Street
Iron River, MI 49935
906-265-3822
800-255-3620 (U.S. only)

Western Upper Peninsula CVB
137 E. Cloverland Drive
Ironwood, MI 49938
906-932-4850
800-272-7000 (out of MI)

Baraga County Tourist Association
755 E. Broad Street
L'Anse, MI 49946
906-524-7444

Mackinac Island Chamber of Commerce
P.O. Box 451
Mackinac Island, MI 49757
906-847-6418
1-800-4-LILACS

Manistique Area Tourist Council
P.O. Box 37
Manistique, MI 49854
906-341-5838
800-342-4282

Marquette County CVB
2552 W. US-41, Suite 300
Marquette, MI 49855
906-228-7749
800-544-4321

Munising Chamber & Visitors Bureau
422 E. Munising Avenue
Munising, MI 49862
906-387-2138

Newberry Area Chamber & Tourism Association
P.O. Box 308
Newberry, MI 49868
906-293-5562
800-831-7292

Ontonagon Tourism Council
600 River Road, P.O. Box 266
Ontonagon, MI 49953
906-884-4735

Paradise Area Tourism Council
P.O. Box 64
Paradise, MI 49768
906-492-3927

St. Ignace Area Chamber & Tourist Association
560 N. State Street
St. Ignace, MI 49781
906-643-8717

Sault Ste. Marie Tourist Bureau
2581 I-75 Business Spur
Sault Ste. Marie, MI 49783
906-632-3301
800-647-2858

LOWER PENINSULA

Lenawee County Conference & Visitors Bureau
738 S. Main Street
Adrian, MI 49221
800-248-4491
517-263-7747

CVB of Thunder Bay Region Chamber
235 W. Chisholm Street
Alpena, MI 49707
517-354-4181

Ann Arbor CVB
120 W. Huron Street
Ann Arbor, MI 48104
734-995-7281

Huron Co. Visitors Bureau
250 E. Huron Avenue
Bad Axe, MI 48413
517-269-6431 • 517-269-8463
800-358-4862

Battle Creek Area Visitor & Convention Bureau
34 W. Jackson Street, Suite 5A
Battle Creek, MI 49017
616-962-2240

Bay Area CVB
901 Saginaw Street
Bay City, MI 48708
517-893-1222
800-424-5114

LOWER PENINSULA

Southwestern Michigan Tourist Council
2300 Pipestone Road
Benton Harbor, MI 49022
616-925-6301

Mecosta County CVB
246 N. State Street
Big Rapids, MI 49307
616-796-7640 • 616-796-7649
800-833-6697

Cadillac Area Visitors Bureau
222 Lake Street
Cadillac, MI 49601
616-775-9776
800-22-LAKES (U.S. only)

Charlevoix Area CVB
408 Bridge Street
Charlevoix, MI 49720
800-367-8557 (MI only)
616-547-2101

Cheboygan Area Tourist Bureau
124 N. Main Street, P.O. Box 69
Cheboygan, MI 49721
616-627-7183
800-968-3302

Detroit Chamber of Com.
600 W. Lafayette Blvd.
Detroit, MI 48226
313-964-4000

Metro Detroit Visitors Bureau
100 Renaissance Center, #1900
Detroit, MI 48243
800-DET-ROIT

Elk Rapids Chamber
P.O. Box 854
Elk Rapids, MI 49629
616-264-8202

Frankenmuth CVB
635 S. Main Street
Frankenmuth, MI 48734
517-652-6106
800-FUN-TOWN

Gaylord Area Convention & Tourism Bureau
101 W. Main Street, P.O. Box 3069
Gaylord, MI 49735
517-732-6333

Grand Haven-Spring Lake CVB
One S. Harbor Drive
Grand Haven, MI 49417
616-842-4499

Grand Rapids & Kent County Area CVB
140 Monroe Center, NW, Ste. 300
Grand Rapids, MI 49503
616-459-8287

Grayling Area Chamber & Visitors Council
213 N. James Street
Grayling, MI 49738
517-348-2921
800-937-8837

Oceana County Tourism Council
100 S. State Street
Hart, MI 49420
616-873-3982

Elk County Visitors Bureau
230 N. State Street
Hillman, MI 49746
517-742-3739

Holland Area CVB
76 E. Eighth Street
Holland, MI 49423
616-394-0000
800-506-1299

Houghton Lake Chamber
1625 W. Houghton
Houghton Lake, MI 48629
517-366-5644

Indian River Chamber
3435 Straits Hwy.
Indian River, MI 49749
616-238-9325

Jackson Convention & Tourist Bureau
6007 Ann Arbor Road
Jackson, MI 49201
517-764-4440
800-245-5282

Kalamazoo County CVB
128 N. Kalamazoo Mall
Kalamazoo, MI 49007
616-381-4003

Greater Lansing CVB
119 Pere Marquette Drive
P.O. Box 1506
Lansing, MI 48912
517-487-6800
800-648-6630

Ludington Area CVB
5827 W. US-10, P.O. Box 160
Ludington, MI 49431
616-845-0324
800-542-4600 (U.S. only)

Mackinaw Area Tourist Bureau
708 S. Huron, P.O. Box 160
Mackinaw City, MI 49701
616-436-5664
800-666-0160

Mackinac Island Chamber of Commerce (800-454-5227)

Midland County CVB
200 Rodd Street
Midland, MI 48640
517-839-9901
800-678-1961

Mount Pleasant /Isabella Chamber
144 E. Broadway
Mount Pleasant, MI 48858
517-772-4433
517-772-2396

Niles - Four Flags Area Council on Tourism
321 E. Main Street, P.O. Box 1300
Niles, MI 49120
616-683-3720

Pentwater Chamber
324 S. Hancock
Pentwater, MI 49449
616-869-4150

Petoskey - Harbor Springs - Boyne Country CVB
401 E. Mitchell St., P.O. Box 694
Petoskey, MI 49770
616-348-2755
800-845-2828

Blue Water/St. Claire Chamber/Tourist Bureau

520 Thomas Edison Parkway
Port Huron, MI 48060
810-987-8687
800-852-4242 (MI only)

Rogers City Chamber & Visitors Bureau

292 S. Bradley Hwy.
Rogers City, MI 49779
517-734-2535

Saginaw County CVB

901 S. Washington
Saginaw, MI 48601
517-752-7161
800-444-9979

Saugatuck-Douglas Chamber

303 Culver St.
Saugatuck, MI 49453
616-857-1701

Tawas Bay Tourist & Convention Bureau

402 W. Lake Street
P.O. Box 10
Tawas City, MI 48763
517-362-8643
800-55-TAWAS

Traverse City CVB

101 W. Grandview Pkwy.
Traverse City, MI 49684
616-947-1120
800-872-8377

West Branch-Ogemaw County Travel

422 W. Houghton Avenue
West Branch, MI 48661
517-345-2821
800-755-9091 (MI only)

Ypsilanti CVB

301 W. Michigan Avenue
Suite 101
Ypsilanti, MI 48197
734-483-4444

The sun is setting. It's time to return to daily living. But you'll remember the excitement, the challenge, the peace and serenity ... of green forests, rolling hills, crystal waters and abundant wildlife. And you'll dream of the things yet to come.

For you are the dreamer,
and I am your dream maker ...
the vacation land for all seasons.

Michigan

By C. Rydel

Until We Meet Again...
Your Friends at the Michigan Vacation Guide

Index

MICHIGAN COTTAGES • CHALETS • CONDOS • B&B'S

We're always looking to improve this publication. So, let us know if our book was helpful ... what improvements you'd like to see in our next edition ... and your opinion of the place(s) you've stayed. *We look forward to hearing from you. So write or email us with your comments (see below).*

Send Us Your Comments!

Do you have property you'd like to list in our next publication?

If you have a property in Michigan that you would be interested in listing, please send your name, address, phone number, along with a brief description of your property. We'll have you complete one of our Property Owner's Questionnaires and add you to our contact list. We'll be sure to notify you when we update the next edition!

Need Additional Copies of the Michigan Vacation Guide????

If you'd like to order additional copies of our Guide, please send $12.95 *plus* $2.75 tax and shipping to TR Desktop Publishing c/o The Michigan Vacation Guide at the below address:

THE MICHIGAN VACATION GUIDE

TR Desktop Publishing
P.O. Box 180271
Utica, Michigan 48318-0271
(810) 228-8780
Email: KTedsen@compuserve.com